Democratisation in Myanmar:
Progress and Prospects

Democratisation in Myanmar: Progress and Prospects

Sonu Trivedi

GYAN

The Publication of this thesis was financially upheld by ICSSR and the responsibility of the facts stated, opinions expressed or conclusions reached are entirely that of the author and ICSSR accepts no responsibility for them.

ICSSR Consultant

Professor Achin Vanaik (Retd.), S-314, Panchsheel Park, New Delhi-110017.

First Published, 2018

Published by

GYAN

Gyan Publishing House
5, Ansari Road
Daryaganj, New Delhi-110002
Phone: 9811692060
E-mail: books@gyanbooks.com

Printed at: G. Print Process, Delhi.

Cataloging in Publication Data—DK
Courtesy: D.K. Agencies (P) Ltd. <docinfo@dkagencies.com>

Trivedi, Sonu, author.
Democratisation in Myanmar : progress and prospects / Sonu Trivedi.
pages cm
Includes bibliographical references.
ISBN 9788121213455

1. Democratization—Burma. 2. Burma—Politics and government—21st century. I. Title.

DS530.65.T75 2016 DDC 959.1053 23

Contents

Acknowledgements

I take this opportunity to express my deep regards and profound gratitude to all those who have helped me directly or indirectly in completing this Project. Their blessing, help and guidance from time to time shall go a long way in the journey of life on which I have embarked upon.

As a student of Political Science the concept of 'democracy' has always aroused interest in me because of its contestations and democratic reversals in transitional societies. My further research in the area of Southeast Asian studies brought me closer to the subject of regimes in transition, particularly exploring the transition from authoritarianism to democracy in countries like Indonesia and looking at the reasons for its delay in Myanmar. In this regard, Myanmar has been my primary area of research since the last one decade. Under this background, keeping pace with the internal political developments in the post colonial era and dynamics emerging in the recent times in this nascent democracy, I have tried my best to do justice to the subject.

The charm and allure of this mystic land is based on my personal experiences and inter-connectedness that I have developed during couple of my visits to the country. Apart from the usual official meetings and designated calls, this fascinating land had much to offer which left an everlasting impact on my memory. The overwhelming response from the people of Indian origin (almost the third generation)—was unforgettable. There is much to be treasured in the amazing hospitality which I received from the local Burmese community during each stint of my stay in Myanmar. Besides, the expatriates and the officials from India presently posted in Myanmar gave memories much to be cherished and made it a memorable experience. It was not only an opportunity meant for meeting of minds but rather for meeting of hearts too.

The research for this book was supported by the Indian Council of Social Science Research (ICSSR), New Delhi. I take this opportunity to thank the research and support staff of the Council for providing necessary administrative and financial help for completing the project. Without the generous support of the Council, field visits to Myanmar would not have been possible.

I would like to express my gratitude for the encouragement and support I received during my field trip in Myanmar. For this I am indebted to the Indian Mission in Yangon and the Consulate in Mandalay. I would like to acknowledge the support and cooperation provided by the members of the Indian Diaspora living in Myanmar during my field trip. The hospitality and warmth showed by them was beyond comprehensive. Interaction with the Burmese community and people of Indian origin in Myanmar deepened my insight and existing knowledge of this mystical land.

The help and inputs provided by the refugees from Myanmar staying in Delhi have also been crucial in understanding the process of democratisation and its delay in the country. For this I am deeply indebted to the Burma Centre Delhi and the Euro Burma Office for organizing various workshops and discussions which helped me broadening my understanding of the political problems facing the country and to keep pace with the recent developments and changes taking place in Myanmar. Besides, meetings, interactions and interviews with the experts, particularly the diplomatic circle, think-tanks, civil society organisations and academia both in India and Myanmar have been worthwhile. These interactions and valuable insights have enriched the study and made it a learning experience.

I am also grateful to the Principal and my colleagues in the Department of Political Science at Zakir Husain Delhi College for their encouragement and being a constant source of inspiration during the course of my research. Most of all, I express my appreciation to my family members, especially my husband and my daughters Yati and Yamini whose patient love and tolerance enabled me to complete this work.

Sonu Trivedi

List of Acronyms

ABMA : All Burma Monks Alliance
AFPFL : Anti-Fascist People's Freedom League
AMRDP : All Mon Region Democracy Party
ANFREL : Asia Network for Free and Fair Elections
ASEAN : Association of Southeast Asian Nations
BBC: : British Broadcasting Corporation
BDA : Burma Defence Army
BEWG : Burma Environment Working Group
BGF : Border Guard Force
BIA : Burma Independence Army
BNHR : Burma Network for Human Rights
BNI : Burma News International
BP : Burma Partnership
BSPP : Burma Socialist Programme Party
BWS : Burmese Way to Socialism
CBOs : Community Building Organisations
CNG : Compressed Natural Gas
CNP : Chin Nationalist Party
CPB : Communist Party of Burma
CRPP : Committee Representing the Peoples' Parliament
CSOs : Civil Society Organisations
DSI : Defense Services Institute
DVB : Democratic Voice of Burma
EBO : Euro-Burma Office

FDI	:	Foreign Direct Investment
FPAED	:	Framework for Poverty Alleviation and Economic Development
GONGOs	:	Government Organised Non Governmental Organisations
HRDP	:	Human Rights Defenders and Promoters
HURFOM	:	Human Rights Foundation of Monland
ICG	:	International Crisis Group
ICRC	:	International Committee of the Red Cross
ILO	:	*International Labour Organisation*
IMF	:	International Monetary Fund
KIA	:	*Kachin Independence Army*
KMT	:	Kuomintang
KNDO	:	Karen National Defense Organisation
KNU	:	Karen National Union
MPC	:	Myanmar Press Council
NCCC	:	National Convention Convening Committee
ND-Burma	:	Network for Human Rights Documentation – Burma
NDF	:	National Democratic Force
NGOs	:	Non Governmental Organisations
NLD	:	National League for Democracy
NUP	:	National Unity Party
ODA	:	Official Development Assistance
PBNRDA	:	Progress of Border Areas and National Races and Development Affairs
PSRB	:	Press Scrutiny and Registration Board
PSRD	:	Press Scrutiny and Registration Division
PVO	:	Peoples' Voluntary Organisation
RC	:	Revolutionary Council
RNDP	:	Rakhine Nationalities Development Party

SCME	:	System of Correlation of Man and His Environment
SECC	:	Socialist Economic Construction Committee
SEZs	:	Special Economic Zones
SLORC	:	State Law and Order Restoration Council
SMOs	:	Social Movement Organisations
SNDP	:	Shan Nationalities Democratic Party
SNLD	:	Shan Nationalities League for Democracy
SPDC	:	State Peace and Development Council
UEC	:	Union Election Commission
UMEH	:	Union of Myanmar Economic Holdings
UMP	:	Union Military Police
UNCTAD	:	*United Nations Conference on Trade and Development*
UNDP	:	*United Nations Development Programme*
UNICEF	:	United Nations Children's Fund
USAID	:	*United States Agency for International Development*
USDA	:	Union Solidarity and Development Association
USDP	:	Union Solidarity and Development Party
VOA	:	Voice of America
YMA	:	Young Monk Association

Burmese Terms

Amyotha Hluttaw	House of Nationalities
Bogyoke	General
Hluttaw	Assembly
Loktha Pyithu Nezin	The Working People's Daily
Myanma Alin	The New Light of Burma
Myanmar Naing Ngan	Union of Burma
Pyidaungsu Hluttaw	Union Parliament
Pyidaungsu	Union
Pyithu Hluttaw	Peoples' Assembly
Pyithu Khit	People's Era
Sitwundans	Territorial units
Tatmadaw	Military

List of Figures

List of Tables

Chapter - 1

Introduction

Encyclopaedia of Britannica defines the term 'democratisation' as "a process by which democracy expands, within a state or across the world." The discourse of democracy has infused many struggles against monarchical absolutism, working-class struggles, and the suffragette movement[1]. It may however, be noted that democratisation not only brings about a cosmetic change in the state institutions, but it rather reinforces democratic values and ideals in the daily lives of its citizens. It enables the state to penetrate the society and develop a democratic political culture within which foundations of a durable democratic order could be established. Democratisation does not only mean changes in the political sphere but it also stands for liberal economic changes as well. It is therefore, believed that any effort at economic reforms must be preceded by national reconciliation and political change. In this regard, the reform agenda led by the new regime in Myanmar aims to bring about political restructuring as well as social and economic re-engineering at the same time convincing the military that the process would be gradual and controlled and that the military's role as envisaged in the new Constitution would be respected.

The leadership is trying hard to end its international isolation by promoting the democratic icon Nobel Laureate Aung San Suu Kyi. The regime allowed her party National League of Democracy (NLD) to participate in the April 2012 by-elections and rejoin mainstream politics[2]. ASEAN's decision to allow Myanmar to take up the Chairmanship of the body in 2014 has given the new regime acceptability in the region. Myanmar's leadership which has long counted on China as its main supporter has rolled out a series of reformist measure in the field of health, social security, education and mass media. This has been widely seen as part of its effort to gain domestic and international legitimacy. Furthermore, the new rapprochement marked by the West, particularly the visit by US President Barack Obama and other European Heads of the State after years of estrangement demonstrates that the process of reforms have gained momentum and recognition[3]. However, for any real political change to take place in Myanmar, it has to be preceded by Constitutional reforms and ethnic reconciliation. Nevertheless, the new regime has made significant progress in the field of political and administrative reforms and has now taken up the task of reviewing the 2008 Constitution, which in fact, is the most visible stumbling block in the path of democratisation in Myanmar. In this context, the book studies the process of democratisation, its progress and prospects in Myanmar. It looks as to how the state institutions and authority structures are embedded in their political institutions. Each regime controls its state institutions in accordance with its policies and needs. Therefore, the authority structure that exists in a country is directly related to the political system in that country. The rigid authoritarian authority structures which developed in the post-colonial period in Myanmar have significantly guided the way 'militarised transition' has taken place in the recent times.

This book is a study of the process of democratisation in the 'militarised' state of affairs in Myanmar. With this purpose, attempt has been made to examine the institutional architecture and the authority structure which has developed in Myanmar since independence and to look at the process of democratisation in general and its relevance in the case of Myanmar. The book also explores the emergence of delayed democracy in Myanmar and outlines the role of internal crisis and contradictions in bringing about 'guided transition' towards disciplined democracy in Myanmar. Finally it evaluates the reform agenda of the new regime and challenges of democratisation and political transition in Myanmar.

Trends for democratisation, political transition and change in Myanmar are the core issues which this book seeks to explore. This has been outlined in the hypothesis of the study. Initially, it has been argued that the failure of regime performance in the economic front has delayed democracy in Myanmar. According to the second argument, regime's survival and delayed democracy has rested on the 'military cohesion'. And finally it has been argued that beliefs, actions and strategic choices of political elites are significant variables for democratic transition in Myanmar. None of these elements in isolation could be regarded as a significant variable for the process of democratisation in Myanmar. All these factors, taken together have been a catalyst of political change and transition in the country.

Economic growth, stability and financial security are pre-conditions for regime transition. Economic problems facing the country during 1988 continued to stay till the first decade of this century (Steinberg 2005: Pederson 2005: Than 2007: Maung 1997). Little has changed since that time until the recent political opening and reforms in Myanmar after 2010 general elections. The broad problems facing the country not only include corruption and expanding money supply, but a completely unrealistic exchange rate, hidden subsidies to the public sector enterprises, a public sector deficit, a poor record of privatisation, little foreign investment, an import substitution programme, and a shortage of foreign exchange reserves (Steinberg 2005: 92-93). The social factors of distrust in the stability of the currency due to past demonetisation measures and the lack of timely and accurate information have intensified the rate of inflation. Due to the maintenance of a foreign exchange regime, huge spreads between the official and unofficial black market foreign exchange rates have developed (Maung 1997: 513; 515). Unable to meet government demands or produce enough food for their families, a growing number of small scale farmers are falling into debt and losing their land. As a result of the growing economic plight of the average population, thousands of people have migrated in adjoining areas (Pederson 2005: 164). Furthermore, existence of an 'extra legal economy', larger than the 'formal economy' in the form of narcotics trade, is also causing problems for Myanmar's neighbours, with both Thailand and India expressing public concern over the export of drugs from Myanmar to their territories.

Analysis of much of the recent literatures on democratisation has stressed the importance of regime disunity and splits and schisms in the early stages of the transition. A major split or schism in the military may likely contribute to the break-up of the regime and fragmentation of the rigid authoritarian party cadre that has emerged in recent times. But the 'military cohesion' has been the single most unifying factor and the rationale for the dominance of military in Myanmar for almost five decades. Hlaing (2008: 149-177), asserts that internal factionalism was a major cause for the establishment of caretaker government in 1958 in Myanmar. In late 1990s rumours were rife about possible splits in military (Fink 2001; Alagappa 2001; Taylor 1998; Smith 1999). Although, there were deep differences of opinion between senior commanders, but they made sure they never developed into conflicts of interest (Smith 1999: 424). According to Fink (2001: 94), the differences appeared to be one of tactics rather than goals. Though, there are reports from time to time of splits in top command, these have not been confirmed and despite the pressures the government has faced, it has remained remarkably cohesive over a long period of time (Taylor 1998: 9). The cohesiveness and political reliability of the armed forces are, thus, key to regime's survival in the future. According to Mary Callahan, "in the case of Myanmar, military regime's remarkable survival rests on the Burmese military cohesion" (Callahan 2003).

Beliefs, actions and strategic choices made by the elites within an authoritarian government have been a critical variable for change in most of the countries. The dynamics of the transition process depends upon strategic interactions and tentative arrangements between elites (O' Donnell and Schmitter 1986: 3-5). Given the total domination of the elite class by the ruling minority in decision making and public sphere, there was hardly any significant effort for political dialogue and democratic change in Myanmar until the elections in 2010. The military generals have patronised the ruling elites and perpetuated crony capitalism in the growth and development of the country. In the absence of any clear political vision of reform and change elites have remained a weak force in Myanmar.

Significance of the Study

There is a serious shortage of empirical data and verifiable documentary evidence about current developments. Some foreign journalists and academics have sneaked in crossing the border illegally to observe the conditions first hand[4]. The number of students engaged in the research has grown substantially, but field surveys are still constrained and reliable sources are hard to find. For over more than thirty years, Myanmar has had no census. The last official census took place in 1983. Before that, the last credible census was held in 1931 during British rule. As a result, for years, economists, academics and researchers have relied on unreliable data.

Therefore, it is not easy to carry out independent field survey in Myanmar's closed society. The state maintains strict surveillance over electronic communications, including email, and blocks certain websites. The primary targets for blocking are political opposition or pro-democracy movements, e-mail service providers and free Websites. Myanmar is way down the list in press freedom rankings. Although, military government has relaxed visa controls and now permits foreigners to live in Myanmar for extended period, nevertheless, freedom of speech and association are still severely curtailed. Access to modern means of communication including Internet is restricted.

In the past two years, alongside other reforms, the government had begun visibly to relax its iron grip on the media, allowing coverage of previously taboo topics such as Daw Aung San Suu Kyi and her National League for Democracy. With the abolition of pre-publication censorship, as recently announced, editors are exempt from submitting material to the Press Scrutiny and Registrations Department for approval before printing. But, this does not mean that the Myanmar media is now free to report anything. Among the subjects that remain on the sensitive list are corruption in the Army, and foreign policy. The government also warned against reportage of the communal clashes in bordering areas[5].

Keeping all these limitations in view, the study has attempted to outline the process of democratisation in general and its specific nature in Myanmar. It begins by indentifying various trends for democratisation and mixed varieties of authoritarian and democratic regimes. It further elaborates on the emergence of 'disciplined democracy' in Myanmar. The patrimonial nature of Myanmar's society and the existence of client-patron relationship have guided the way politics has operated in Myanmar since historical periods. Thus, the political culture of authoritarianism has played a significant role in defining the authority structure and its functioning in Myanmar.

The study is significant for the Myanmar watchers since it discusses the post colonial developments in the country with the establishment of parliamentary democracy and its overthrow in a military coup in 1962 by General Ne Win. Internal crisis and contradictions in the regime and the political and national reconciliation process have also been elaborated in detail. The study provides an insight into the institution of political architecture that developed in Myanmar during the military rule since 1962. These institutions have defined the nature of authoritarian rule in Myanmar. In the later part of the book, the study explores the factors responsible for delayed democracy in Myanmar and examines the progress and prospects of democratisation in the country. It further highlights the reform agenda of the new regime since it came to power in March 2011. Various challenges faced by the regime in the political restructuring and social re-engineering have been analysed. A close monitoring of the environmental and health hazards of the various developmental projects have also been critically highlighted. Besides these, the issue of human rights violations and international isolation of the regime have also been studied. It concludes with providing an overview of changing power dynamics in Myanmar, particularly looking into the ideological conflict between the hardliners and the reformist forces; the military and the NLD; the NLD and the other opposition parties and the ethnic nationalities. It further looks into the future roadmap to presidency in Myanmar in 2015.

It is believed that this book would be beneficial to research scholars, academics, area studies analysts, policy makers and journalists as well since it provides an insight into the role of military in the politics of Myanmar and the ongoing phase of democratisation in the country. It would be a significant contribution in the field of area studies programme and those particularly interested in the transition from authoritarianism to democracy in Myanmar.

Methodology

Although, much has been written about the issue of democratisation in Southeast Asia, but this study would be an important contribution to the analysis of the democratisation in an authoritarian regime with a specific case study of Myanmar. The study is based on the field-work undertaken in Myanmar in 2010 and thereafter in 2013 to assess the progress made towards democratisation and national reconciliation. Even though, at the time of my visit in 2010 open discussions and meetings with pro democracy activists were impossible. Besides, all the foreign media and local blogs were either banned or strictly monitored, nevertheless I was able to gather some information in the course of general discussions with the local people.

Mostly people in Myanmar carry out their business on an informal discussion over a cup of tea in the evening when it is the time for the markets to shut down. Most of the business dealings were based on hard cash since the lack of banking facility has been a major hurdle for legitimate transfer of funds and business dealings. Up until the new reformist government took office in March 2011 and the by-elections in April 2012, there was hardly any political space in Myanmar for open discussion and deliberations. Myanmar's reporters had been regarded as among the most restricted in the world. Routine state surveillance which included phone taps, internet access restrictions and other forms of censorship – including restrictions on publication of photographs of Aung San Suu Kyi – were sufficiently intense to render it impossible for independent newspapers to publish on a daily basis. Although, restrictions regarding peaceful assembly of people have been removed by the new regime except for few sensitive regions, but still the crackdown imposed by the previous regime haunts the people.

Amidst all these restrictions and surveillance during the military regime and some openness in the present context, attempt has been made to study the authoritarian authority structure which developed in Myanmar since 1962 and its consolidation in the next five decades. Based on interactions and interviews during the 2013 visit, changes in the regime structure have been observed and identified. As a result of political transformation and change, it was also possible to meet the democratic icon Daw Aung San Suu Kyi at her residence in Nay Pyi Taw. Visit to the Parliament building and interaction with some of the government officials was also made feasible. It was also possible to visit the universities (Yangon and Mandalay) which were till now beyond the reach of the foreigners. These meetings have provided considerable insight into the emerging trends and transformation taking place in the country.

The winds of political change in Myanmar have also provided enough space for the civil society organisations to emerge and flourish. Although, they do not enjoy complete openness, but, still under certain reasonable restrictions, they are providing a ray hope to the severely ostracized society of Myanmar. Interactions with these civil society organisations have provided valuable insights to the study. Some of these organisations are Gender Development Institute, Women's Action Group, Metta Development Foundation, Tampadipa Institute, Myanmar Egress, Yangon School of Political Science. There are a number of International NGOs functioning at the parallel level. Some of these are Action AID Myanmar, USAID Myanmar, *International* Committee of the *Red Cross* (ICRC), CARE Myanmar etc. Establishing contacts and exchange of views with these organisations had a significant role in understanding the political transformation in Myanmar.

For studying the political reforms taking place in the new regime, the study has also made use of the newspapers reports, interviews and opinion surveys conducted on the refugees from Myanmar (such as pro-democracy leaders, trade union activists and journalists) staying in India[6]. The study is also based on lectures and analyses of the experts on Myanmar during the course of various workshops, lectures and Conferences[7]. Interactions at Indian Mission in Yangon and Consulate at Mandalay have also been significant in understanding the political transformation and democratisation process in the country.

The study has also made use of the primary documents such as Constitutional Principles approved by the National Convention; National Convention Procedural Code; SLORC Declarations; Constitution of 'The Socialist Republic of the Union of Burma,' 1974; Constitution of the 'Union of Burma' 1947; System of Correlation of Man and Environment; Burmese Way to Socialism; and Panglong Agreement, 1947. The report of the World Bank, UNCTAD, IMF, International Crisis Group, Human Rights Watch and Freedom House has also been used in the study. A wide range of secondary literatures on regime transition and democratisation, and on military and politics in Myanmar in the form of books, research papers, working papers, monographs and special commentaries have also been used.

Structure of the Book

Book is divided into seven chapters while each of them focusing on a thematic study of the process of democratisation against the backdrop of the post colonial developments in Myanmar. The trends and transformations in the ongoing political dynamics in the country and the trials and tribulations against military and pro-democracy forces have been the primary focus of all the chapters. The first chapter offers an introduction to the study, outlines the main arguments and focuses on the methodology of research. It also provides the context and rationale of the study along with outline of the subsequent chapters.

Second chapter provides a theoretical framework to the study. It elaborates on democratisation and regimes in transition with special reference to the case in Myanmar. The process of regime change along with the trends for democratisation has also been elaborated. The chapter also outlines the critical variables for democratic consolidation and its application in the case of Myanmar.

Chapter three gives a narrative of the political history of Myanmar since independence. Post colonial developments and the emergence of military rule are the main focus areas. It looks into the era of parliamentary democracy and chronologically covers the establishment of military rule which continued in Myanmar for almost five decades under different nomenclatures. The military roadmap to disciplined democracy and the progress made till 2010 elections is the subject matter of the last section in this chapter.

Chapter four looks into the authority structure of military in Myanmar. Main focus of the study is on the autocratic military framework which developed in Myanmar. For understanding the role of military, it is important to highlight the socio-political roots of authoritarianism in Myanmar. The chapter provides a theoretical foundation and justification for continuation of military rule in Myanmar. It also elaborates on the institutions of political architecture that developed during the military rule in Myanmar such as the state apparatus, economy, party machinery and the armed forces.

The fifth chapter focuses on the internal crisis and contradictions in the politics of Myanmar and the forces and events that paved way for democratisation and liberalisation of the political system. Some of these forces include—role of monks and *sanghas*; students and protests movements; 1990 and 2010 general elections and the role of Aung San Suu Kyi and the NLD; generational shift in military; role of the civil society organisations; and beginning of the national reconciliation process. The impact of these forces on regime change has been particularly elaborated. The chapter also analyses the reason for delayed democracy in Myanmar.

Sixth chapter deals with the current phase of transition and emergence of disciplined democracy in Myanmar. The emergence of multi-party elections, political parties, civil society and the reform of the armed forces, particularly show a trend towards cosmetic change and façade of reform in the country. The chapter also covers the challenges of change faced by the new regime.

Finally, the last chapter concludes the study by summarizing the central arguments and validation of the hypothesis. It looks at the emerging political dynamics and the future roadmap to democracy in Myanmar. Role of the reformist vis-à-vis the radicals in the Parliament, Government and the Party; relationship between the military and Daw Suu Kyi; the role of NLD and the other opposition parties; centre-periphery contestations; demilitarizing politics; safeguarding the interest of the minorities; and bridging the 'majority-minority' divide lie at the heart of the political transition in Myanmar.

The huge demonstrations and protests over the past two decades have shown that the regime has outgrown its legitimacy. Cut off from the outside world and denied access from democracy and respect for human rights, it has to fix its society into order. According to Gordon Brown and Nicholas Sarkozy (2007), "a country that has the natural resources to be an economic powerhouse is instead the sick man of Southeast Asia. As the rest of the region advances into the digital age, Burma is in danger of retreating to the dark ages." However, return to constitutional government and 'disciplined democracy' was brought about by the much awaited Constitutional referendum of 2008 and multi-party elections of 2010.

Democratisation process in Myanmar has been risky and fragile. It has a long way ahead for consolidation and deepening of democracy. The militarised government and the military backed Parliament have a wide range of challenges confronting it. The regime has to immediately focus on the issue of state building and national reconciliation. Political institutions necessary for consolidation of democracy needs to be build and the existing ones restored. The issue of ethnic nationalities requires primary attention through a process of national reconciliation and inclusive dialogue. Restructuring of the economy and economic development becomes a necessity for the establishment of political democracy and dialogue. Economic growth, stability and financial security are, thus, pre-conditions for deepening of democracy in Myanmar.

One of the key benchmarks for the future of democratisation process in Myanmar is the role of NLD and Aung San Suu Kyi. As it has been observed, although NLD as a political party was disbanded in the wake of 2010 elections nevertheless it remains the country's best hope for genuine dialogue and national reconciliation. Its performance in the April 2012 by-elections has been overwhelming. Aung San Suu Kyi's intensified meeting and interactions with the new regime, UN officials and members of diplomatic community is a step in that direction. Her appeal to the international community for withdrawal of the sanctions and ending the international isolation has far reaching implications. The whole world is waiting to see her new role in 2015. But for any significant change taking place in this regard must be preceded by the constitutional reform process which is currently in the process of review.

References

1. For details see http://www.britannica.com/topic/democratization
2. The National League for Democracy (NLD), the main opposition party to Myanmar's ruling military junta, was disbanded on 6 May, 2010 because it had refused to register for the upcoming elections in November 2010. The party's Central Executive Committee voted unanimously not to take part in the elections, to protest against elections rules, especially the one that requires it to expel its leader because of prior convictions (particularly Aung San Suu Kyi).
3. Mrs Clinton was the first US Secretary of State to visit Myanmar in December 2011 since John Foster Dulles visited in 1955.
4. Based on personal interaction with journalists like Bertil Linter and Subhir Bhaumik.
5. To change the press scrutiny policies step by step, 38 directives and 20 instructions issued under the 1962 Printers and Publishers Registration Law have been revoked, and only 13 directives and six instructions remain (As reported by Myanmar Times August 27 - September 2, 2012)
6. Interaction with NLD MP (1990 elections) Dr. Tint Swe, Soe Myint, Thin Thin, Dr Aung Zaw Win, Nye Nye, Kim. Htun Htun, Dr Khin Zaw Min, Myo Win, Dr Aung Naing Oo, Aung Marm Oo, Ma Khin Ohmar, have deepened my understanding of Myanmar
7. Insights from policy makers and diplomats like Amb. Shyam Saran, Amb Devere, Amb. Rajiv Bhatia have been really enriching.

Chapter - 2

Democratisation: Theoretical Paradigm

A polarity between authoritarianism at one extreme and democracy at the other has been a dominant theme in various political analyses during the last few decades. Southeast Asia has also been a major domain of some of these studies. With various degrees of explicitness, authoritarianism and democracy are categories representing major regime types in this region. Authoritarianism is considered to be morally repulsive and democracy as essential for good governance and social justice. Within this dominant tradition, the main task of this analysis is to study the dynamics of authoritarian regime and its transition to democracy. Myanmar has been a prime case of arrested development brought about by decades of stubborn, isolationist military rule (Clapp 2007: 1).

In the last quarter of the twentieth century, significant researches have been done and numerous literatures have proliferated on the study of the breakdown of the authoritarian regimes and transition to democracy. These writings have been very influential in shaping our understanding of the process of regime transition (Rustow 1970; Shin 1994; Sorenson 1998; Gill 2000; Carothers 2002; Huntington 1991; Diamond 2000). The transition from authoritarianism to democracy is a complex process involving several phases. One of the earliest and most important work of this type was by Dankwart Rustow. He begins with a 'background condition' which means 'national unity' must be in place before it is possible to conceive of a transition toward democracy (Rustow 1970: 350). According to Rustow, ethnic or other cleavages leading to questioning of 'national unity' must be resolved before a transition to democracy becomes feasible. He has further categorised transition to democracy into three phases: The first phase is the 'preparatory phase' and this is charecterised by a prolonged and inconclusive political struggle between protagonists representing well-entrenched class forces. This often results in polarisation of political sphere; the second, 'decision phase' sees the leaders of these groups accept that a diversity of views exist and thereby seek to institutionalize some crucial aspect of democratic procedure to structure and channel this diversity; and finally, the 'habituation phase' sees political leaders learning from the successful resolution of some issues and thereby placing their trust in the new rules and procedures, which gradually enlarges the degree and range of consensus (Rustow 1970: 352).

Several other transition literatures have further elaborated these stages. According to Huntington (1991: 35), at the simplest level, democratisation involves: (i) the end of the authoritarian regime; (ii) installation of a democratic regime; and (iii) consolidation of a democratic regime. The transition process can be located along a continuum in terms of the relationship between the ruling elites and the opposition. In this context, Huntington has grouped them into three broad types for analytical purposes: Transformation; Replacement and Transplacement. This categorisation is an attempt to distinguish the relative importance of government and opposition (*ibid*: 114).

Carothers (2002), in "The End of Transition Paradigm" observes that democratisation tends to unfold in a set sequence of stages. First, there occurs the *opening,* a period of democratic ferment and political liberalisation in which cracks appear in the ruling dictatorial regime, with the most prominent fault line being that between hardliners and softliners. Then follows the *breakthrough*—the collapse of the regime and the rapid emergence of a new, democratic system, with the coming to power of a new government through national elections and the establishment of a democratic institutional structure, often through the promulgation of a new constitution. After the transition comes *consolidation,* a slow but purposeful process in which democratic forms are transformed into democratic substance through the reform of state institutions, the regularisation of elections, the strengthening of civil society, and the overall habituation of the society to the new democratic "rules of the game" (Carothers 2002: 7).

Democratisation is, thus, a long and divergent process that consists of democratic transition and consolidation. Political liberalisation that brings about a general relaxation of official controls over political rights and civil liberties precedes democratic transition (Lee 2002: 822). Based on the analysis of the various stages of democratic transition as mentioned above in different literatures, four common phases have been particularly identified: (1) decay of authoritarian rule; (2) transition; (3) consolidation; and (4) maturing of democratic political order. As a complex historical process, they are very much empirically overlapping.

Democratisation commonly starts from a condition where, in a non democratic country, there have been growing demands for liberalisation and democracy (Shin, 1994: 143). This preparation stage is followed by a transition period where an authoritarian regime is replaced, whether through mass protests or compromised by a more open and democratic regime. Transition is completed when many democratic institutions replace authoritarian political institutions and a new government emerges from free and fair elections. The third phase is a process of breeding democratic values. Democracy in this phase is consolidated when democratic values are embedded and accepted as the only normal way to organize political life in the country. In a logical sequence, democratisation may run in a smooth path starting from the disintegration of the authoritarian regime and the emergence of the new democratic system, through the consolidation of that regime, to its maturity. However, the process is not that linear or rational in actual application (Sorenson 1998: 39; Shin, 1994: 143). "Some democracies abort as soon as they emerge, while others erode as much as they consolidate" (Larry Diamond 1992). These phases, however, do not represent a pre-determined path that all countries will or must follow. There is no historical law, which says that regimes must move from authoritarianism to democratic system. A more accurate description of typical pattern in the developing world is an uneasy fluctuation between authoritarianism and frail democracy (Carothers 2002: 7; Sorenson 1998: 39). A large majority of the current transition are in the early phases of moving toward democracy. More specifically, they can be described as restricted democracies that are frail and unconsolidated and plagued by acute social and economic problems. The experience of the 'third wave' strongly suggests that liberalised authoritarianism in the name of 'halfway house' or 'hybrid regimes' are widespread in these countries (Huntington 1991: 137; Diamond: 2002: 23).

Stages of Democratisation

On the basis of aforementioned literature the stages of democratisation can be described with the help of the following overlapping phases (Sorenson 1998: 39-40; Gill 2000: 43; Carothers 2002: 7; Huntington 1991: 35, 114; Diamond 2000: 414; Linz and Stepan 1998: 48; Shin 1994: 143-144):

(i) the preparatory phase, or decay of authoritarian rule characterised by a political struggle leading to the breakdown of the non-democratic regime;

(ii) the transition phase, where clear-cut elements of a democratic order are established;

(iii) the consolidation phase, where the new democracy is further developed, and eventually, democratic practices become an established part of the political culture; and

(iv) the maturity phase, where the maturing of a stable political order takes place. This phase also looks at the institutionalisation of democratic practices within state institutions.

The phases, however, do not represent a pre-determined path that all countries will or must follow. There is no historical law which says that regimes must move from authoritarianism to democratic system. However, it must be realised here that the phases outlined are not necessarily negotiated in a smooth or linear manner. There may be crisis or setbacks (Sorenson 1998: 39). The options are all cast in terms of the speed and direction with which countries move on the path (Carothers 2002: 7). The result of the regime change need not necessarily be democracy. It could also lead to replacement of one authoritarian regime by another (Gill 2000: 43). A more accurate description of typical pattern in the developing world is an uneasy fluctuation between authoritarianism and frail democracy. A large majority of the current transition are in the early phases of moving toward democracy. More explicitly, they can be characterised as democracies that are frail and unconsolidated and beleaguered by sharp social, cultural and economic cleavages.

Following the four stages of democratisation mentioned in the literatures on democratic transition which has forward and backward linkages between each successive stage, Myanmar may now be categorised in Stage II (particularly after the 2015 elections). Burmese social and political structure, with its emphasis on hierarchy and status, is not conducive to democracy. Paternalistic authority is inconsistent with democracy's reliance on equality of opportunity, freedom of speech and assembly, and representative institutions (Vatikiotis 1996). Burmese political values and culture is based on paternalistic authority (discussed in Chapter-4). Authoritarian nature of the traditional Burmese state was based on highly personalised concept of power and central authority (Carey 1997: 3). Although, Myanmar was nominally a democracy, authoritarian traditions have guided the way politics operated in post-independence Myanmar (Fink 2001: 26). The Burmese traditional value is based on authoritarianism—a rule pattern which is an expression of their semi-feudal, autocratic government headed by a ruling elite (Gyi 1983). Most of the patrimonial elements and the patron-client relations that dominated the functioning of the Parliamentary governments continued to persist under the two subsequent regimes (Hlaing 2008: 176). It was precisely due to persistence of this patrimonial nature of the state throughout the post-independence period that led to the continuation of the authoritarian rule of military in Myanmar.

For almost all of its history, Myanmar has been ruled by autocratic monarchs and military leaders (Vatikiotis: 1996; Smith 1999: 27; South 2007: 234; Carey 1997: 2; Taylor 1998: 3-4; Thawnghmung 2003: 454). The British occupation which lasted for 62 years established the new Republic of the Union of Burma, but it bore little resemblance to any nation or the state. The institutions of political power bequeathed to the new nation were an 'ill-fitting suit of clothes modeled on the loose pattern of British parliamentary democracy' (Smith 1999: 27). Thus, Myanmar's only experience with democracy was a short period under the 1947 constitution after independence when U Nu supported representative institutions, free elections and civil liberties. The military remained committed to maintaining U Nu's civilian regime until in 1958, the ruling civilian politicians squabbled and the government split. The army was then 'invited' to take over for a six month period until new elections could be held (Taylor 1998: 6). The ineffectiveness of U Nu's rule was used as a rationalisation for the government takeover by the military in both 1958 and 1962. Although, there are many reasons for the failure of democracy in Burma, Silverstein (1977: 30-31) argues that the inability of the party system to become deep and meaningful part of the society was one of its root cause. Second reason for its breakdown was the inability of the national leaders to solve the minority question. As a society, it was divided between the Burman majority and the ethnic minorities of the plains and the hills (ibid: 35). The failure to resolve adequately the ethnic nationalities demands through the constitutional drafting process exacerbated the situation (Fink 2001: 23). According to Thant Myint (2007), the wrong decision to seek a military rather than a political solution to the country's long running civil war lies at the heart of many of Myanmar's problems. Since that time, democratic institutions and behaviour, said to be "foreign to the traditions" of the Burmese and a rejected legacy of the Western imperialism, have been suppressed (Smith 1999: 28). Fourteen years of experimentation with democracy gave way to authoritarian rule while the people looked in 'stoic silence' (Silverstein: 1977: 31).

The military took over political power in Myanmar in 1962 and continues to remain in power to this day, although the November 2010 'free' elections were held to legitimize the military rule. The Revolutionary Council of Burma imposed an authoritarian regime over the political-economic system of the country during the first few years (1962-69), but later on moved towards constitutionalism and economic liberalism. Just like in Indonesia, after the failure of constitutional democracy, Sukarno's Guided democracy prevailed for several years (1958-65) until the military came to power in 1965. The Revolutionary Council of Burma, sought to establish a type of socialism which had many similarities in its ideology, contents and consequences, with Sukarno's Guided Democracy in Indonesia (Islam 1996: 190-191). The political system of Guided Democracy in Indonesia, like that of Revolutionary Council in Burma was designed to impose the paternalistic authority of the government and the state of the people (Sundhaussen 1995: 768-780).

The economic autarchy of the Ne Win era and the one party rule of the BSPP provided a catalyst which resulted in the eruption of widespread public demonstration against the regime from July to September 1988 (Taylor 1998: 3). Although, military resorted to brutal suppression of the crisis, it brought about a fundamental reappraisal of the country's economic orientation and 'Ne Win's *Burmese Way of Socialism* was most certainly dead' (Smith 1999: 23). "Since the popular uprising in 1988, the Burmese military government has toyed with the idea of 'democracy' and a 'multiparty' system manipulating these terms to justify and legitimise its rule" (Thawnghmung 2003: 457).

Myanmar's military government held elections in 1990 which were won convincingly by the opposition National League for Democracy (NLD). The military however, repudiated the results of 1990 elections outright despite international criticism and protest against its violations of human rights (ibid: 446). Although, the Government has paid lip service to implement these concepts, and to the notion of transfer of power to the party with the most popular support, the regime's actual commitment to democracy has been slow and reluctant. Characterised by ethnic conflict, economic stagnation and political oppression, Myanmar has been unable to achieve—the ideal of peaceful, happy and prosperous society. Antagonism to liberalisation still thrives in the country whose ethnic insurgencies and black market activities arise from the military's refusal to share either political or economic powers (Case 1996: 437). Myanmar has been under military rule since 1962 and democratisation continues to be at an impasse, with a military apparatus devoid of all legitimacy hanging on to power through its monopoly of the means of violence (Carey 1997: 3). The effort made by the 'Junta' to democratize the regime by implementing the 'seven-point roadmap' to democracy which *inter alia* includes organizing the National Convention for drafting a new Constitution, adoption of this Constitution in 2008, holding the general elections after a gap of twenty years in November 2010 and convening the new Parliament in January 2011 are all attempts to bring about a façade of electoral change and *disciplined* democracy in the country.[1] The recent 2015 election is considered to the most democratic ending half a century of military rule in Myanmar.

Trends for Democratisation

The spread of democracy throughout Pacific Asia since the mid 1980s has fundamentally altered the 'Asian Values Discourse' because it has rendered the notion that democracy is intrinsically foreign to Asians. The belief that the conduct of the democratic governance in an Asian country should be restrained by a spirit of consensus and deference to rulers has turned out to be obsolete (Barr 2002: 64). According to Huntington (1991: 25) "the pre-existing authoritarian structures lacked sufficient institutional capacity to cope with the high level of societal activation, or to absorb and regulate the diversifying and conflicting demands of society." This led to the reconstruction of the political system, and dismantling of the old party linked institutions (Stepan 1978: 79). Democratic regimes replaced the authoritarian ones in approximately thirty countries in Europe, Asia and Latin America (Huntington 1991: 21). In other countries, considerable liberalisation occurred in authoritarian regimes. In still others, movements promoting democracy gained strength and legitimacy (ibid). Although, there were resistance and setbacks, as in China in 1989 or in Myanmar in 1988 the movement towards democracy seemed to take on the character of an almost 'irresistible global tide moving on from one triumph to the next'.

This democratic tide, described by Huntington as the 'third wave' manifested itself, first in Southern Europe (Portugal and Greece). "In the late 1970s the democratic wave moved on to Latin America (Ecuador, Peru, Bolivia, Uruguay, Brazil, Honduras, Salvadoran and Guatemala). The democratic movement also had its manifestations in Asia (Turkey, Philippines, Korea, Taiwan and Pakistan). At the end of the decade, the democratic wave engulfed the communist world (East Germany, Czechoslovakia, and Romania collapsed; Hungary and Bulgaria began to liberalize). Meanwhile, in the Western hemisphere democratic transition took place in Mexico, Chile, Grenada, Panama Nicaragua and Haiti. The 1970s and early 1980s also witnessed the final phase of European decolonisation (Papua New Guinea, Grenada and Namibia). In Africa and Middle East movement to democracy in the 1980s was limited (Nigeria, South Africa, Senegal, Tunisia, Algeria, Egypt and Jordan). Thus, overall the movement towards democracy was a global one" (Huntington 1991: 21-25).

There are many reasons for this rapid progress of democratic ideals around the globe. Explanations differ from country to country. Viewed under this background, this section identifies critical junctures responsible for 'democratic boom' in 1990s. Some of the common factors of convergence at this juncture are as follows:

Globalisation

Globalisation of world politics has led to widening, deepening and speeding up of worldwide interconnectedness. As globalisation has proceeded so has the recognition of transnational problems requiring global regulations (Mcgrew 2005: 20). In a world where democratic values were widely accepted, the deepening of the legitimacy problems of authoritarian systems and the subsequent growth of democratic values has created a push towards democratic transition (Huntington, 1991: 45). The contemporary wave of democratisation is one of the several consequences of globalisation. In order to understand political and democratic change in Southeast Asia during the last decade, globalisation has been a crucial dimension (Ojendal 2005: 362).

Economic effects of globalisation has been an important factor in the wake of the unprecedented global economic growth which raised living standards, increased education, and greatly expanded the urban middle class in many countries. It has drawn attention to the transformation of a global political economy in which hitherto closed economies dictated by authoritarian regimes were brought into a mutual interdependence through economic and political interconnectedness. This multifaceted interaction between the economic and political reforms has raised demands for further liberalisation and democratisation (Jayasuriya 1995: 131). There exists an extensive trade, finance and production relations amongst societies. These global politico-economic networks have made economic and political liberalisation relatively easier. Thus, the global politico-economic liberalisation has created a free global market that facilitates new form of citizenship, middle class and civil society, which classical democracy theorists considers the main agents of democratisation. Liberalisation led to political changes and reforms in several states and has also affected the capacity and capability of autocratic regime through formal and informal reduction of its financial base and empowering the dissenting groups. The prosperity generated by the global capital produced a well-educated middle class that over time has demanded greater political freedom (Wood 2004: 106).

Democratisation has been advanced not only by globalisation and its subsequent economic factors; rather political developments too play a significant role here. The most momentous political development has been the end of the Cold War and the consequent collapse of the bipolar politics (Giddens 2007: 8). With the proclamation of the New World Order and the break-up of the Soviet empire, liberal democracy was further extended to the new parts of the globe. Following the collapse of the Soviet Union, democracy and human rights became central pre-occupations for the global community (Akkoyunlu 2007: 54). At the end of the cold war, the U.S. and other Western countries embraced the enlargement of democracy as a follow-up to the containment of communism. It involved greater emphasis by the West on policy instruments to promote democratisation. The most common among them included aid conditionality (linking aid to human rights and democracy) and humanitarian intervention (Acharya 1999: 423). Thus in the late 90s under the pressure of IMF conditionalities and inability to deal with the economic decline, the authoritarian regime of Suharto gave way to the establishment of a more fuller form of democracy.

Economic globalisation, including the internationalisation of production and finance, had rendered authoritarian regimes in Southeast Asia more vulnerable to external economic and political pressures. This fact has made democratic breakdowns less likely. In Thailand, a country with a history of democratic breakdowns (largely due to military coups), globalisation provided a crucial support to democracy (Acharya 1999: 424). Economic effects of globalisation have also propelled the push for reform in Indonesia (Akkoyunlu 2007: 53). It has made Southeast Asia more connected with the rest of the contemporary world system (Yamashita 2003: 1). As a result, Indonesia has become more structurally entangled in the global financial market (Hadiz 2004: 66). The proponents of US hegemony after the end of the Cold War consider democracy and free market as closely interlinked. Thus, the economic downturn of the late 1990s has offered democratisation forces a new opportunity in Southeast Asia (Acharya 1999: 432).

The current economic and political turmoil in Southeast Asia shows that the domestic forces that affect democratisation often derive their strength from international ones, including the effects of globalisation and the spread of democratic values. Moreover, in the early 1990s, amid much talk about the Asian economic "miracle," scholars had focused on the relationship between economic growth and political change. The Asian economic crisis, on the other hand necessitated further investigation into the impact of economic downturns in facilitating or inhibiting the democratisation process.

International anxiety has also pressurised Myanmar to call for democratic reforms and improvement of human rights. The primary impetus came from the United States and European Union. China, India, and Japan are also important as regional players hoping for the restoration of democratic government in its neighbour (For details see Katanyuu 2006: 841-845; International IDEA 2001: 69-85, 108, 131-181; Levesque 2007: 31-33).

Democratic Values and Human Security

Growth of democratic values and realisation of a more humane and just world order has created demand for a reformed and more democratic system of global governance (Mc Grew 2005: 36-37). Furthermore, institutionalisation of some of the core values of social democracy—the rule of law, political equality, democratic governance, social justice and social solidarity and human rights—has created conditions benefiting the realisation of a more humane and democratic global politics. There has been a shift from 'state-security' to 'human security' (Lawson 2003: 90-91). This has encouraged a more sustained focus on the fact that human rights abuses not only constitute a serious security issue, but often occurs as a direct or indirect result of state sponsored activities. Political repression has, often, been justified by reference to 'national security' in most authoritarian states. In fact, the growth of human security paradigm since sixties has encompassed a range of concern that has taken the concept of security into almost every area of human life.

The globalisation of democratic values also made its mark on authoritarian societies, especially among the better educated younger generations (Akkoyunlu 2007:54). This has put the authoritarian regimes under substantial social pressure during the era of reforms during 1990s. Furthermore, the notion of "Asian values," once credited with the region's economic success, and for some time a powerful conceptual justification for authoritarian rule, has also been challenged (Acharya 1999: 418). Global push towards democratisation has also been initiated by the Western powers especially following the end of the Cold War towards a multi-party electoral system, rule of law and protection of human rights (Wah 2005: 19-20). There has been an unprecedented emphasis on democracy promotion as a strategic imperative (Diamond 2000: 87). Thus, Myanmar military's continued disregard for human rights and good governance has put it at odds with the changing global values. The globalised discourse of 'good governance' and 'responsible government' has challenged the autocratic regime—which has failed to couple economic liberalisation with political liberties. To cope with such changes, military needed to re-define its socio-political role.

In countries where diverse societies have been held together by autocratic rule, which purposely exacerbates internal animosities and impedes the development of complex civil society, transition has often been plagued by internal conflict and tension, making democratic outcomes all the more difficult. In fact, lack of political and civil institutions and a reliable economic structure impede and prolong transition to pluralistic governance (Clapp 2007: 3-4). This is the problem that confronts us in the newly established disciplined democracy in Myanmar especially in the wake of ethnic conflict and sectarian violence in recent times.

Trans-national Actor

Another source of pressure for change emanating from the international environment is non-state actors. The rise of the transnational actors has also been a significant variable for democratisation (Smith and Baylis 2005: 3). There are a number of non-state actors that have greatly influenced developing and promoting issues on the international agenda (Holtsi 1995: 60). Although, there are a great variety of non-state actors functioning today, but those having most impact on international politics are—multinational organisations and inter-governmental organisations. Transnational actors such as the international NGOs (INGOs) and their linkages with the new social movements based on ethnicity, gender, religion and concern for the local community and the environment has intensified the push for more autonomy and democracy (Wah 2005: 7, 21). In general, the non-state actors can play several roles in international politics, such as introducing an issue onto the international diplomatic agenda; publicise and raise citizen conciousness regarding certain global or regional problems; lobby national governments and international organisations to make favourable decisions; and seek an outcome through direct action, sometimes through use of threat or force. There are several instances of these actors playing a significant role in exercising political pressure for regime transition.

In some specific cases of regime change, such influences have been significant (Gill 2000: 20). Transnational government organisations too are offering material support to reward democracies and applying sanctions to punish non-democracies. They have encouraged democratic reforms with material and moral support for the expansion of autonomous organisations (Shin 1995: 153).[2] As the effects of globalisation are increasingly being felt in the third world regions, with increasing attention on issues such as transparency, accountability and good governance by multilateral institutions, donors, international media, NGOs and corporate entities, the pressure for democratic transition and change has increased.

Mass-media

The role of the media and information technology cannot be under estimated (Giddens 2007: 3). Journalists and media have played an important role in the democratisation process in Southeast Asia (Luwarso 2000). Technology has helped free the media in nations under the stranglehold of authoritarianism. The transition period from authoritarianism to democracy is a period of struggle between power and freedom. Once democratic governments have formed, it is the media which safeguards this new freedom by aggressive reporting on corruption and misuse of authority (Luwarso 2000). The "snowballing" or demonstration effects, enhanced by new means of international communications has stimulated and provided models for subsequent efforts at regime change in other countries (Huntington, 1991: 45). In the post-authoritarian phase, media facilitates the process of reification (extent to which the party's existence is established in the public imagination) and thus, serves as an effective means of interaction with the public (Tomsa 2007: 81). Media is of utmost importance here, not only because it magnifies the impact effectuated by the other factors, but also because it provides the parties with the only means to communicate with their members and supporters, but also with the general public.

In the 1980s and 90s, South-East Asian journalists felt the need to involve the society they wrote for, rather than to just report on what other people did and said. The economic crisis that hit the region has made its citizens aware of the need for transparency, and the urgency of access to information. They began to set the political agenda and to play a significant role in freeing several South-East Asian nations from the stranglehold of authoritarianism: first in the Philippines, after the fall of Marcos in 1986; then in Thailand, following the 1992 coup; and subsequently in Indonesia, after Soeharto was forced to resign in 1998 (Luwarso 2000). Media on a regular basis has offered significant advantage for the institutionalisation of political parties in Indonesia. While many of the smaller parties that were formed after the fall of Suharto are still struggling to make their existence known, the two parties with the highest levels of media coverage—Golkar and PDI-P—have become household names (Tomsa 2007: 81).

Externally driven pressures are also being mounted by the rapid development of new communications technology, such as the internet, satellite telephones, and satellite TV and radio. It is now increasingly difficult for the regime, in Myanmar, to insulate its urban population from the outside world (Clapp 2001). According to Tint Swe, "although there is no independent media in Myanmar, but, the wide coverage of the brutality of the regime during crackdown of 'saffron revolution' has significantly molded the public opinion worldwide. Response from international community also came-up as a result of awareness created by the media."[3] For decades, Myanmar imposed total control on its media, with even the ownership of computers, facsimiles and modems contingent upon permission from the regime. Myanmar is still one of the most closed countries in the world: it does not possess an independent media and foreign journalists have very little chance of being allowed to enter the country. According to Kingston (2008: 3) "a major surprise from their government came in 2008—annual satellite TV fees had jumped from $5 to nearly $800, equivalent to a university lecturer's yearly salary. This media-muzzling initiative, implemented without warning, reflects official displeasure with foreign coverage of political events in Burma." A few seconds of footage has undone all the goodwill and public relations generated over the years by generals pretending to be devout Buddhists in highly publicized prayers and alms offerings involving compliant abbots. According to Kingston (2008: 3), "erecting a 'bamboo curtain' to keep the people uninformed about the world and their own nation is the junta's futile hedge against what remains an explosive situation." However, the present regime is talking about the media freedom and loosening of the censorship as a part of its current reform initiative.

Regional Influence

Democracy has become an increasingly important factor affecting the relationship between Southeast Asian states and the wider international community (Acharya 1999: 426). "Since the 'people's power' revolution in the Philippines in 1986, Southeast Asia has experienced an incremental process of democratisation. The Philippines was followed by Thailand, then Cambodia, and more recently Indonesia" (Acharya 2003: 376). Once discredited modernisation theory—which claimed that economic development leads to social and then political mobilisation that ultimately results in democratisation—was revived in the region (Thompson 2004: 1079).

Democratisation is also a condition necessary for membership in a regional association as well as international foras (Shin 1995: 152). It may secure better support for regional integration and co-operative projects for development assistance from outside powers (Acharya 2003: 378). In the changing international order, democracy and human rights have become more globalised and influential. Thus, authoritarian states defying international norms are not likely to find sympathy and support from international benefactors.

The issue of democratisation is also shaping intra-regional relations, including regional multilateral cooperation, within Southeast Asia. Political change in Thailand, the Philippines and Indonesia has engendered efforts at democratising regionalism (Acharya 2003: 376). The retreat of the doctrine of non-interference in the Association of Southeast Asian Nations (ASEAN) has created space for a more open form of regionalism in Southeast Asia, which could aid the cause of human rights and democracy (Acharya 1999: 420).

In the name of good governance, reformist movements have turned against democratically elected Leaders such as in the Philippines (Joseph E Estrada), Indonesia (Abdurrahman Wahid) and Thailand (Thaksin Shinawatra) (Thompson 2004: 1099). According to William Case (2005: 235), when economies declined in Singapore and Malaysia, governments responded with artful manipulations. Most crucially, they maintained tight limits on civil liberties, and deftly reorganised electoral districts. In the Philippines, where the military lost unity, politics advanced to fuller democracy. According to Hadiz, South Korea can provide an important example for Indonesia to follow (quoted in Akkoyunlu 2007: 55). Belated promises of greater electoral competitiveness, thus, led to Suharto's withdrawal, and democratic change (Case 2005: 236). The downfall of the Suharto regime may not be a classic case of democracy's snowballing effect. But the Indonesian military was unnerved by democratisation elsewhere in the region. As a senior adviser to President Habibie noted, "The Indonesian military saw the coming of democracy to Asia and Indonesia, and are preparing for that" (quoted in Acharya 1999: 427).

The international community has a vital role to play in helping Myanmar escape its history, but it is greatly circumscribed by current priorities and approaches. Since the military crackdown on monks and pro-democracy protestors in August September 2007, foreign governments and intergovernmental bodies have responded in varying ways (Human Rights Watch 2008 a). It has sought to threaten the credibility of ASEAN, for which Myanmar has become an ever present reminder of the grouping's unfulfilled promise of community building and political integration. Members of the international community have condemned the junta for its brutal response to September 2007 protest, calling upon it to exercise restraint, to free NLD leader Aung San Suu Kyi and to recognize the basic democratic rights of freedom of expression and assembly (Polk 2008: 69). However, the U-turn policy of the United States and other European powers after regime transformation in Myanmar is a case in point. The recent policy of pragmatic engagement of the United States and the easing of sanctions by other European powers displays the eagerness of the Western powers to engage with the new regime for economic dividends.

Mixed Cases of Authoritarian and Democratic Regimes

There have been ambiguous political regimes which can neither be described as fully democratic nor clear-cut authoritarian. These political systems remain in a continuum moving toward either democracy or authoritarianism. They live in a state of fluidity and their political structures tend to be volatile. Thesw different trajectories of political change may be described with the help of a 'polity authority continuum' developed by Monty G. Marshall. According to this model, 'coherent autocracy' and 'coherent democracy' lie at either end of the polity scale with incoherent (mixed trait) polities in between (see the figure below—based on an analysis by Monty G. Marshall). "While autocracies and democracies make use of distinct authority patterns, instruments, and strategies to control and manage societal conflict processes, governing authority in 'incoherent polities' is weakened by confused, contradictory, inconsistent, and conflicting norms, roles, and institutional procedures. Incoherent regimes have difficulty responding coherently, consistently, and decisively to petitions and provocations and are, thus, much less effective in managing societal conflicts and averting a concerted and sustained resort to force by challengers. As such, autocracies and democracies are relatively stable forms of regime authority, while incoherent polities are unstable" (stability as measured by persistence of particular patterns of authority over time).

Autocracy

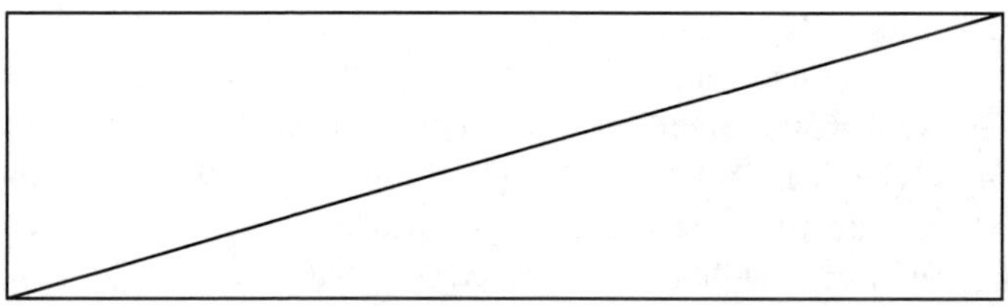

Democracy

Source: Marshal, Monty G. *Authority, Opportunity, and Outbreaks of Violent Societal Conflicts 1955-1999.*

Figure 1: Polity authority continuum

Various nomenclatures have been used for the non-democratic or mixed cases of authoritarianism and democracy. These may include "hybrid regime," "semi-democracy," "virtual democracy," "electoral democracy," "pseudo-democracy," "illiberal democracy," "semi-authoritarianism," "soft authoritarianism," "electoral authoritarianism" etc. According to Huntington (1991: 137), they are presented as "half-way houses," straddling uncomfortably the democratic and authoritarian categories that tug them in contrary directions. All these types of mixed regimes are under a period of delayed transition. Broadly each of these cases could be categorised as "hybrid," "semi-democratic," or "partly free," and such labels obscure crucial differences—differences that may have important causal implications (Levitsky and Way, 2002: 51). According to Juan Linz and Alfred Stepan there are five modern ideal types of political regime, one of which is democratic, and the rest are nondemocratic (totalitarian, post-totalitarian, authoritarian, and sultanistic) (Linz and Stepan, 1996: 54).

These regimes fall into the 'gray zone'. The concept of the gray zone was introduced as a solution to the problem of identifying the growing quantity of hybrid political systems. The problem of defining the gray zone regimes remains one of the central themes in contemporary transition and democracy studies. In recent years, many political scientists have tried to solve this problem. However, there is still no consensus on how to name the hybrid regimes.[4] This is precisely because of its non-democratic or more, ambiguous nature. As Steven Levitsky and Lucan A. Way rightly wrote, "whereas an extensive literature has emerged concerning the causes and consequences of democratisation, emerging types of democracy, and issues of democratic consolidation, remarkably little research has been undertaken on the emergence and persistence of non-democratic regimes" (Levitsky & Way, 2002: 52). Similarly, Ottaway has pointed out that, "despite their growing importance, however, semi-authoritarian regimes have not received systematic attention" (Ottaway, 2003: 5).

Guillermo O'Donnell and Philippe C. Schmitter two of the most prominent scholars of transition and consolidation studies, argue that there might emerge two kinds of gray zone regimes: *democraduras* (democrahard) and *dictablandas* (dicta-soft). *Democradura* connotes a "restrictive, illiberal democracy," and *dictablanda*, a "liberalised authoritarian regime" (O'Donnell and Schmitter, 1986: 9, 14). Schmitter (1994:58) argues that although these regimes have some pluralist aspect, they remain dominated by a single ruler or a ruling group. O'Donnell continues the discussion of the gray zone in his 1996 article, "Illusions about Consolidation," in which he claims that there is a category of countries that "reverted to new brands of authoritarianism;" these are the countries that "seem to inhabit a gray area; they bear a family resemblance to the old established democracies, but either lack or only precariously possess some of their key attributes" (O'Donnell 1996: 34). Accordingly based on the overview of literature, the following section discusses these mixed regime types as categorised by various thinkers.

Hybrid regimes

There are cases in which authoritarian regimes are compelled to amend the constitution and hold elections under democratic conditions, but the old government remains in power because the opposition gets split up. Such type of regimes is in the transition process and has come to be charecterised as a type of '*hybrid*' regime. This is located in between dictatorship and democracy and oscillates between the two ends of the pendulum with crucial human rights violations. Hybrid regimes resemble democracy due to the fact that its access to power and its legitimation is ensured by free elections. Larry Diamond's "Thinking about Hybrid Regimes" is an excellent account of hybrid regimes. The author explains his view on hybrids by stating that "one of the most striking features of the 'late period' of the third wave has been the unprecedented growth in the number of regimes that are neither clearly democratic nor conventionally authoritarian" (Diamond 2002: 25).

Southeast Asia offers a testing ground for the erstwhile and existing hybrid regimes. According to William Case, "through varied manipulations, the competitiveness of elections has been curbed, with politics cumulating less readily in full democracy than in stunted hybrid regimes. Indeed, these regimes constitute the modal type in Southeast Asia, having been introduced in Singapore during the late 1960s; in Malaysia, the Philippines, and Indonesia during the 1970s; in Thailand during the early 1980s; in Burma, at least briefly, in 1990: and in Cambodia shortly thereafter. However, while hybrid regimes may form frequently in Southeast Asia, their persistence varies, turning contingently on the artfulness with which governments carry out their manipulations. We find that in Southeast Asia some hybrid regimes have persisted for long periods, others have come under strain then re-equilibrated, and still others have finally unraveled, tipping back into hard authoritarianism or lurching ahead into democracy" (Case, 2005: 216). A brief analysis of the Indonesian case shows clearly that hybrid regimes can be democratized by the bottom-up replacement approach and the participation of voters.

Electoral Authoritarianism

Andreas Schedler discusses the concept of electoral authoritarianism and how political regimes couple formal democratic institutions such as multiparty elections with authoritarian practices (2002; 2006; 2010). He delineates a broad range of "menus of manipulation" in diverse institutional arenas. The new electoral authoritarian regimes of the post–Cold War have set up the full panoply of liberal-democratic institutions—from constitutions to constitutional courts, from legislatures to agencies of accountability, from judicial systems to federal arrangements, from independent media to civic associations. Most important of all, they hold regular multiparty elections at all levels of state power. In their institutional forms, these regimes are virtually indistinguishable from liberal democracies. Yet authoritarian rulers invariably compensate for these formal concessions with substantive controls. While renouncing the suppression of representative institutions, electoral authoritarian regimes specialize in their manipulation. Authoritarian rulers may deploy a wide range of strategies to keep control over their agents, as well as their adversaries, in various institutional arenas. In electoral authoritarian regimes, election constitutes the central arena of struggle (Schedler 2010: 71). They have at their disposal a broad array of manipulative tools for reducing the uncertainty that elections can bring such as disempowerment, market restrictions, preference alteration and vote distortions (ibid:73).

According to Andreas Schedler (2006), "under electoral authoritarian rule, elections are broadly inclusive (they are held under universal suffrage) as well as minimally pluralistic (opposition parties are allowed to run), minimally competitive (opposition parties, while denied victory, are allowed to win votes and seats), and minimally open (opposition parties are not subject to massive repression, although they may experience repressive treatment in selective and intermittent ways)" (p. 3). The electoral contests are severely manipulated by the state and there is hardly any scope for electoral democracy. This when studied in the wake of the 2010 elections in Myanmar could be easily validated.

Although, the elections held in Myanmar in 2010 was supposed to be inclusive but, yet it debarred a large section of people from voting.

Elections were cancelled in several violence hit regions inhabited by ethnic nationalities. This had disenfranchised a large section of the population from participation in the country's largest democratic exercise in the last 20 years (TNI 2010). Opposition has claimed of widespread electoral irregularities, including intimidation of voters by the government. There were serious allegations with regard to the actual vote count, particularly in relation to the advance vote (Turnell 2011; TNI 2010; ICG 2011a). Advance votes were collected with allegations of serious irregularities. Election Laws were in itself discriminatory. Out of 37 parties which were registered only, 23 parties participated in the election. The largest opposition party, NLD was forced to disband, but however one of its splinter group NDF participated. In the absence of any major opposition, the government backed USDP was able to back around 80 per cent of the seats in the Parliament. Heavy restrictions were also imposed on the media coverage and no foreign observers were allowed inside the country. Several restrictions were imposed on campaign speech and media airtime. Thus, the manner in which the elections were conducted depicts Myanmar's transition not to a full fledged civilian democracy, rather a move towards electoral authoritarianism. According to Schedler (2006), "Authoritarian manipulation may come under many guises, all serving the purpose of containing the troubling uncertainty of electoral outcomes. Rulers may devise discriminatory electoral rules, exclude opposition parties and candidates from entering the electoral arena, infringe upon their political rights and civil liberties, restrict their access to mass media and campaign finance, impose formal or informal suffrage restrictions on their supporters, coerce or corrupt them into deserting the opposition camp, or simply redistribute votes and seats through electoral fraud."

Delegative Democracies

The emergence and workings of delegative democracy are seen as closely interwoven with the deep social and economic crisis that some newly democratized countries are undergoing. Guillermo O'Donnell calls it as a "new species," a subtype of existing democracies, which has yet to be, theorised (O'Donnell 1994: 55-56). "Delegative democracies are characterised by low levels of horizontal accountability (checks and balances) and therefore, exhibit powerful, plebiscitarian, and occasionally abusive executives." Delegative democracy is not alien to the democratic tradition. Actually, it is more democratic, but less liberal, than representative democracy. Deligative democracy is strongly majoritarian. It stands for free and fair elections, and empowerment of the common masses.

Often delegative democracies use devices such as the ballot if elections do not directly generate a clear-cut majority, than majority must be created for supporting the myth of legitimate delegation. "Furthermore, delegative democracy is strongly individualistic, but more of a Hobbesian than a Lockean variety. Voters are supposed to choose, irrespective of their identities and affiliations, the individual who is fit for taking care of the destinies of the country. Elections in delegative democracies are a very emotional and high-stakes process. Various candidates compete to be the absolutely zero-sum winner of the delegation to rule the country with no other constraints than those imposed by non-institutionalised—power relations. After the election, voters and delegators are expected to return to the condition of passive, but hopefully cheering, spectators of what the President does" (ibid: 60). Yet such regimes meet minimum standards for democracy. Delegative democracy thus, applies to such cases as Argentina, Brazil, Peru, Ecuador, and Bolivia, in addition, the Philippines and Korea, some Central and Eastern European countries, and many of the countries that emerged out of the dissolution of the Soviet Union in 1990s.

Electoral Democracies

In determining whether a country is an electoral democracy, Freedom House examines several key factors concerning how its national leadership is chosen. To qualify as an electoral democracy, a state must have:

1. A competitive multi-party political system;
2. Universal adult suffrage for all citizens;
3. Regularly contested elections conducted in conditions of ballot secrecy, reasonable ballot security, and in the absence of massive voter fraud that yields results that are unrepresentative of the public;
4. Significant public access of major political parties to the electorate through the media and through generally open political campaigning.

In short, elections take place, but democracy has not developed in most other respects. Examples of 'electoral democracies' are Brazil, Burkina Faso, Congo, El Salvador, Indonesia (under Suharto), Kenya, Malaysia, Russia, Tanzania, Turkey, Ukraine, and Zambia (Sorensen, 1998).

Illiberal Democracies

In 'illiberal' notion of democracy liberties such as freedom of speech, assembly, and competition for political office are sharply limited and government intervention in private interests may occur. However, the term is almost always used to denote a particularly authoritarian kind of representative democracy, in which the leaders and lawmakers are elected by the people, but do not permit basic individual rights.

"Today the two strands of liberal democracy, interwoven in the Western political fabric, are coming apart in the rest of the world. Democracy is flourishing; constitutional liberalism is not." Such a phenomenon according to Fareed Zakaria has given rise to a disturbing phenomenon in international life – 'illiberal' democracy. Far from being a temporary or transitional stage, it appears that many countries are settling into a form of government that mixes a substantial degree of democracy with a substantial degree of illiberalism (Zakaria, 1997:22).

Semi-Democracies

In a semi-democratic regime elections are regularly held, but they provide limited civil liberties beforehand. This hinders opposition parties in contesting effectively. More specifically, opposition parties are permitted to organize, operate headquarters, solicit contributions, select their own leaders and candidates, then recruit cadres and core constituencies. On the other hand, they are prevented from reaching wider audiences by the government's owning most media outlets, they are restricted in circulating their own party publications, and they are barred from organising mass rallies, even during campaign periods. In Southeast Asia, today, the best examples of semi-democratic regimes are Malaysia and Singapore. In both settings, opposition parties encounter all of the restrictions on civil liberties enumerated above (Case, 2002:6-7). Indonesia's "guided democracy" under Sukarno during the early 1960s provides a good example (Case 1996: 439).

Semi-democracy cannot equally be called "semi-authoritarianism." Semi-authoritarianism can be described as liberal participation without electoral contestation. Interest groups and opposition parties are permitted by the government to form but are ignored or suspended in dense webs of patrimonialism or corporatism. Direct opposition to the government's tenure is even more tightly barred, mainly through the closure of electoral routes to state power.

Competitive Authoritarianism

Competitive authoritarianism describes countries in which elections are competitive and the primary means of gaining power but in which civil and political liberties are regularly abused by incumbents seeking to preserve power. Such regimes need to be treated as a separate regime type rather than as in transition to democracy. They have existed for long periods of time, do not necessarily democratize, and raise a set of questions ignored in studies of either fully democratic or fully authoritarian regimes (Levitsky and Way 2002: 53).

"Formal democratic rules are viewed as the principal means to obtain power but the incumbents tend to violate these rules, which is why these regimes fail to meet the procedural minimum for democracy" (ibid: 52). Although elections take place, the incumbents abuse state resources, violate opposition's rights to oppose, manipulate election results. But, such regimes cannot be referred to as complete authoritarianisms because incumbents are unable to completely eliminate the democratic rules of the game or reduce them to a mere facade. The existence of democratic institutions creates special arenas (electoral, legislative, judicial, the media), through which opposition forces may pose significant challenges. The coexistence of democratic rules and autocratic methods aimed at keeping incumbents in power creates an inherent source of instability.

Semi-authoritarianism

Semi-authoritarian states refers generally to those states where authoritarianism is a determining factor in the political dynamic but where there is limited space for political activities that are independent from and even in opposition to the regime. Often such states are characterised also by corruption and clientalist, patronage systems. Semi-authoritarian regimes are political hybrids that combine features of both democracy and authoritarianism (Ottaway 2003:3). Democracy has a certain façade character, because there are no checks for strong personal power in such a political system, because there are no strong formal institutions. Ottaway's explanation for choosing the term semi-authoritarianism is more advantageous as compared with other terminological speculations:

> "The term semi-authoritarian is used to denote these hybrid regimes because labels including the word democracy are not adequate to capture their defining features, namely, their deliberate nature. Semi-authoritarian regimes are not failed democracies or democracies in transition; rather, they are carefully constructed and maintained alternative systems. If semi-authoritarian governments had their way, the system would never change."

According to Marina Ottaway, all semi-authoritarian regimes share the following fundamental characteristics: limits on the transfer of power; weak institutionalisation; disconnect between political and economic reform; and limits on civil society. Semi-authoritarian regimes are not simply interim political constellations that will necessarily end up as consolidated democracies with the completion of transformations. They are distinct political systems that are consciously and purposefully maintained by political elites who are highly interested in their longevity. One important thing about semi-authoritarian regimes is that they are not necessarily transitional. To make their systems live longer, political elites play games: they manipulate the election process, manage media flows, and impede the strengthening of political institutions, and so on. However, there are also structural conditions that are not as conducive to democratisation in these countries, including state building, socio-economic conditions, ethnic or religious polarisation, and the lack of embeddedness of the elites.

Semi-authoritarianism can be described as liberal participation without electoral contestation. Interest groups and opposition parties are permitted by the government to form but are ignored or suspended in dense webs of patrimonialism or corporatism. Direct opposition to the government's tenure is even more tightly barred, mainly through the closure of electoral routes to state power. Indonesia's "guided democracy" under Sukarno during the early 1960s provides a good example (Case 1996: 439; Ottaway 2003: 20-21). Moreover, to the extent that liberalizing concessions are made, O'Donnell and Schmitter (1986: 10) argue, they emit from cracks in the governing coalition of elites. Semi-authoritarianism is also intrinsically unstable; each liberalizing concession unleashes social pressures on elites for still greater liberalisation. It may easily tip back into a deeper authoritarianism that stamps out both participation and contestation, as in Indonesia under Suharto, especially after opposition parties were fused through pseudo- democracy in 1973 (Case 1996: 439).

Pseudo-Democracies

Pseudo-democratic regime refers to countries where authoritarianism is less pronounced, where formal elements of liberal democracy exist (such as diverse political parties, a parliament with some ability to question government, a degree of press freedom and some level of civil society activity) and where there is even some alternation of governance – but where corruption, clientalism and other factors negate the democratic substance of politics. It is a category in which elections are also held regularly. However, these elections are rigid, while civil liberties are nearly extinguished, with rights of expression, information, and assembly all rigidly controlled. Opposition parties are permitted no autonomy, with governments interfering deeply in their formation, organisational structure, selection of officers and candidates, fund raising and campaigning. In addition, the elections through which they gain entry to the legislature are rendered less competitive and they are also less meaningful. Most notably, these legislatures seldom possess any serious role in policy making. Policy is instead a prerogative of unelected chief executive then to be shared with top bureaucrats, generals, and favoured business elites.

In Southeast Asia, record of Indonesia and Myanmar offers good examples of pseudo-democracy. (Case, 2002: 8-9). Further during 1974-78, General Ne Win operated the Burma Socialist Programme Party, reliably winning elections and stacking the Parliamentary *Hluttaw.* However, while Ne Win was chair of this party he remained outside the Parliament, basing his state leadership more secularly in military. However, it was Indonesia during the Presidency of Suharto that best institutionalised a pseudo-democracy. The press was restrained through arbitrary licensing requirement, while opposition parties, NGOs, and trade unions were tightly constrained. Here, differences between semi and pseudo democracies must be understood. The most striking qualitative difference between semi-and pseudo-democracies appears in the respective approaches taken towards opposition parties. Opposition parties are permitted no autonomy. One clear difference lies in the amount of legitimacy that legislative governments are able to claim. Semi-democratic regimes charecterised by limited competitiveness may stabilize more readily than pseudo–democracies. Pseudo-democracies, in contrast, charecterised by greater coercion, may mask a fragility of inter-elite and elite-mass relations, through so long as growth continues.

The above-mentioned analysis of different mixes of authoritarian and democratic regime types offers an explanation to diverse socio-economic and political systems. Their unique features have different implications for economic performance, human rights, and the prospects for democracy in their respective regimes. It provides a theoretical basis for understanding mixed-type of regime structure that has come into existence in Southeast Asia over the years. In addition, this chapter also provides an understanding of the stages, processes and trends responsible for regime transition. These nuances help us to comprehend with the dynamics of democratisation process. Under this background, the following section analyses regime transformation in Myanmar on the basis of certain critical variables of change and how authoritarian rulers devise strategies to exert control over their agents.

Disciplined Democracy in Myanmar

Given this background of mixed regime types as studied through the lenses of the available literatures on transition regime, this section would look into the nascent democratic structure emerging in Myanmar under the nomenclature of 'disciplined democracy'. For studying this emerging dynamics in Myanmar, various 'areas of contestations' and 'menu of manipulations' as mentioned by Levitsky and Way (2002) and Andreas Shedler (2010) respectively, have been used for the analyses. These are means by which "authoritarian rulers domesticate formal representative institutions." Some of these instruments have been summarised below.

Legislature

In competitive authoritarian regimes, legislatures tend to be relatively weak (Levitsky and Way 2002: 55). In authoritarian regimes, according to Schedler, in order to ensure legislative subordination, rulers may pursue tactics like exerting formal constraints and restrictions on the legislature's power; controlling selection of legislators-either by directly appointing deputies or by choosing who runs for elective office; and fragmentation by keeping the Assembly divided and encouraging factionalism (Schedler 2010: 71). In this regard, the 2008 Constitution in Myanmar has relatively circumscribed the power of the Parliament. After USDP engineering the 2010 elections in the absence of the opposition party NLD due to its boycott, Parliament in Myanmar has just remained as a figurehead of democracy. Thus, majority of members who took up seats in the *Hluttaw* were either former military Generals or a quarter of whom were directly appointed from the armed forces unless NLD joined after the by-elections in April 2012. There were only few non-military MPs, mainly from minority ethnic parties who struggled to be heard in the Parliament.

The National Assembly established in accordance with the 2008 Constitution is not representative of the multi-ethnic identities of the residents of Myanmar. While legislative and executive power for the first time has been partly decentralised in Myanmar, it lacks trust, mutual cooperation and understanding between the Union Government and Region/State Government and between *Pyidaungsu Hluttaw* and Region/ State *Hluttaw*. All these structures are dominated by the USDP or the military appointees. All the Speakers of the State Legislatures are USDP representatives and all the chief Ministers, except the Kayin State who is a military legislator, are dominated by the USDP (TNI 2011: 2-3). This ensures that the USDP or the military will control decision-making on issues of national concern.

The lack of experience and knowledge of most legislators, inefficient procedural rules, the very ambitious legislative agenda that is being pursued and the speed with which legislative decisions are being taken all raise profound questions about the effectiveness of law-making going forward (ICG 2012: 4). Working methods will need to be reformed because of the lack of knowledge and capacity on legislative functioning, including on the part of the Speakers of both houses. Democratic nations should step forward to provide expertise and training to help these nascent institutions develop in the right direction (ICG 2011 b: 12).

One of the most important preconditions for legislative reforms is the amendment of the 2008 Constitution which gives military officers control over twenty five percent seats in the Parliament. Even after the elections in 2010, the democratic character of the legislature is far from the reality. Another irony facing the constitutional reform is the fact that support from more than 75 percent of legislators is required for any amendment to become a reality. Given the fact that USDP along with the military representatives control more than 80 per cent seats in the Parliament, constitutional reforms seems to be a daunting task in Myanmar. However, the Union Parliament has unanimously approved a proposal on March 20, 2013 allowing for the formation of a committee to review the military-backed 2008 constitution.

Judiciary

The weakest form of reform is in the judiciary. Unless the judiciary is reformed, democracy does not have much meaning and rule of law is impossible to achieve. The judicial system is practically in doldrums in the country, where most judges are controlled by army personnel. Governments in authoritarian regimes attempt to subordinate the judiciary through various mechanism and patronage (Levitsky and Way 2002: 56). According to Schedler (2010: 72) authoritarian rulers can place formal constraints on the power of courts, limiting their jurisdiction to specific issue areas. They can also limit the range of discretion of the courts by bureaucratizing judicial deliberations. The authoritarian rulers may also control the judges through appointment procedures and contain judicial activism by engineering fragmented judicial systems.

From 1948 to early 1962, the judiciary in Burma was independent. The concept and practice of judicial independence faded with the military takeover in 1962 (Zan 2000: 35). The 1974 Constitution further subordinated it to the one party system of the BSPP and the Burmese Way of Socialism. However, a professional judiciary was restored by the SLORC after 1988, but "judges were accustomed by then to act as administrators rather than arbiters, basing decisions on state policy, instead of legal reasoning and the application of precedent" (IBAHRI 2012: 56). This policy, nevertheless, continued over the next two decades.

Around five decades of military rule in Myanmar has subjected the judicial system to a mere hostage. A special apparatus of military run criminal tribunals were established (Cheesman 2009/10: 602). Administrative bodies were entrusted with judicial powers which finally cast a shadow on the existing judicial bodies. In reality, Courts in Myanmar have remained an appendage to the executive authority. Rule of law have been truncated and narrowly defined in Myanmar.[5] It remained subjected to the ruling party elites during the BSPP era (Zan 2000: 36). "In Myanmar successive military rulers have made the courts into a reliable instrument for authoritarian control. The army is comfortable in using rather than circumventing the judiciary" (Cheesman 2009/10: 611). Rule of law and judiciary has been controlled in Myanmar to ensure durability and sustainability of the authoritarian regime.

Accordingly, Myanmar needs to reform its judiciary and constitution in order to embed the major changes launched by President Thein Sein in transition from authoritarianism to democracy. Corruption is a serious issue in the judiciary and major efforts are needed to control it. Debureaucratizing and reforming the Criminal Justice system is necessary for democratic functioning of the judiciary. According to the Myanmar Rule of Law Assessment Report, reforming the judiciary by developing a system for appointing judges through independent selection panels, and establishing comprehensive programmes for training and for addressing corruption is imperative. Legal aid for criminal cases and legal education are also needed. After the new government took office, an action committee against corruption is formed to fight the corruption and bribery in governmental organisations. The lack of proper culture and training of judicial personnel in a climate of genuine constitutionalism and judicial independence makes the implementation of the idea of judicial independence a gigantic task. Establishing rule of law beginning with judicial reform, has been a top priority for Daw Aung San Suu Kyi and other members of the National League of Democracy.

Elections

Authoritarian rulers may deploy a wide range of strategies to keep control over their agents, as well as their adversaries, in various institutional arenas. Elections constitute an important arena of contestation, according to Levitsky and Way (2002: 54). In authoritarian states, electoral competition is eliminated and elections either do not exist or are not seriously contested. However, in electoral authoritarian regimes, election constitutes the central arena of struggle (Schedler 2010: 71). They have at their disposal a broad array of manipulative tools for reducing the uncertainty that elections can bring such as disempowerment, market restrictions, preference alteration and vote distortions (ibid:73). In competitive authoritarianism, the electoral process is characterised by large-scale abuses of state power, biased media coverage, harassment of opposition candidates and activists, and an overall lack of transparency (Levitsky and Way 2002: 55). "Although, elections are regularly held and are generally free of massive fraud, incumbents routinely abuse state resources, deny the opposition adequate media coverage, harass opposition candidates and their supporters, and in some cases manipulate electoral results. Journalists, opposition politicians, and other government critics may be spied on, threatened, harassed, or arrested. Members of the opposition may be jailed, exiled, or even assaulted and murdered" (Levitsky and Way 2002: 53).

The electoral contest in Myanmar held in 1990 exhibits the features of a hard authoritarian regime, but the 2010 general elections to a large extent replicates the model of electoral and competitive authoritarianism as mentioned above. The 2010 elections in Myanmar, were the fifth step of the "Roadmap to Democracy" as announced by the military junta in 2003. The electoral administration was appointed unilaterally by the regime on March 11, 2010, and soon showed itself to heavily favour the regime and its allies. The Union Election Commission (UEC) lacked independence. It was appointed directly by the SPDC with no public input. Political parties had to register with the Union Election Commission and request permission to run. The election laws were developed by the military government and effectively prohibited longstanding opponents of the regime from contesting the elections. One of the laws, on political party registration, resulted in the silencing of many of the most prominent opposition voices.

The Election law required all political parties to reregister in order to remain in existence and compete in the elections. But parties could do so only if none of their members were currently imprisoned based on a court conviction. This requirement presented parties with a choice of either expelling prominent imprisoned members, or declining to reregister. Many countries demanded the release of Myanmar's democratic icon, and Nobel Laureate, Daw Aung San Suu Kyi, and her full participation in the election. However, the National League for Democracy soon announced it would boycott the election rather than expel its leader.

Eventually, 47 political parties attempted to register. The UEC initially approved 42 to contest the elections. However, the commission then dissolved five of the parties, leaving 37 approved parties and over 80 individual candidates. By Election Day, 23 parties remained to participate in the elections. Many ethnic politicians saw this election as a rare opportunity to campaign for ethnic rights and democracy. Therefore, they formed new parties to run in the elections. Some ethnic armed groups agreed to be transformed into members of the junta-controlled Border Guard Force (BGF).

The Censorship Board (The Press Scrutiny and Registration Board, or PSRB) issued a directive prohibiting all weekly publications in the country from publishing any commentary or analysis on the electoral laws. Also, the approved political parties needed to apply for permission from the PSRB within 90 days after registering with the UEC for permission to print their own campaign materials. Each party had also to deposit 500,000 Kyats (USD 500) with the PSRB.

The UEC announced nine restrictions for campaign speeches, while also limiting each party to 15 minutes of media airtime each. Media organisations and political parties faced numerous obstacles, such as only having 15 minutes of airtime for the entire campaign, restrictions, communications and internet slowdowns, threats of punishment, and cyber attacks. The SPDC's Union Election Commission held the elections on November 7, 2010. During the election period, it became increasingly clear that the use of advance votes obtained through coerced voting or outright fraud was a major problem. These advance votes were often taken before the official advance voting period of November 5–6. This advance voting seems to be part of a systematic operation to give the USDP an insurmountable lead before Election Day. These ballots were generally collected in every manner possible, often relying on proxy voting, ghost voting, or coerced voting using threats and intimidation. Allegations of fraud and counting/advance voting irregularities were common. The voter turnout was 76.48 percent, in which a vast majority of the seats in Parliament were won by the USDP.

On 16 September 2010, the UEC issued notification No. 99, No. 100, No. 101, No. 102, and No. 103. In these notifications, the Union Election Commission announced that, according to Article 8 (f) of the Union Election Commission Law, voting will not be held in some areas in Kachin, Shan, Karenni, Karen and Mon states because they are in no position to host free and fair elections in the Multiparty Democracy General Elections to be held on 7 November 2010. This affected about 300 village-tracts in 32 townships in 5 States. Therefore, hundreds of thousands of people could not vote in this election, thus depriving the ethnic political parties of several thousand votes in these areas.

Except the USDP and NUP, most political parties have complained about the short campaign period and a lack of funds. According to the regime's party registration laws, parties must submit a list of party members to the UEC within 90 days of being approved as political party. If a party intends to contest nationwide, it must submit a list of 1000 party members, but if the party is going to contest only in a State or Region, it must submit a list of 500 party members. Some political parties faced problems while campaigning. The USDP had organised the Rohingya community in Maungdaw, Arakan State, to gain their support by issuing a National Identity Card (White card). It is the only way for Rohingya residents to obtain the card. As well, the USDP has been discretely collecting new member signatures from residents of Mudon and Thanphyuzayart townships, Mon State, during September. Adding their signatures to the party's membership list serves as a commitment the signers will vote for the party in the upcoming elections. Some government officials have been canvassing for votes along with candidates of the USDP in their respective area. But, according to the election laws, government staff shall not get involved in political campaigning. More interestingly, the regime had collected over 70,000 names of voters in four areas near the China-Myanmar border, in northeast Shan State, and ordered them to vote for the government backed USDP. The USDP party had recruited Burmese business tycoons as party candidates. Therefore, the USDP party had enough funds and human resources to pay for their campaign. On the other hand, some opposition parties attempted to raise funds by collecting donations at markets, but the local municipal committee tried to stop these activities.

The Media

Media in an authoritarian state is charecterised by 'misinformation and disinformation', according to Schedler (2010: 74). The media, in words of Levitsky and Way (2002: 57) are 'entirely state-owned, heavily censored, or systematically repressed' in autocracies. Non-democratic rulers can place restrictions on means of communication, media content and media consumption (Schedler 2010: 74). In competitive authoritarian regimes, independent media outlets often play a critical watchdog role by investigating and exposing government malfeasance. Rulers in competitive authoritarian regimes often seek to suppress the independent media, using more subtle mechanisms of repression such as bribery, state advertising, the manipulation of debts and taxes owed by media outlets, and restrictive press laws that facilitate the prosecution of independent and opposition journalists (Levitsky and Way 2002: 58).

Myanmar is one of the countries in the world that had no media freedom until very recently. There are many laws restricting the press in Myanmar. Censorship was a fact of life. The Censorship Board is very important and pervasive. All private journals are required to submit every one of their articles for approval before publication. If journalists do not follow the laws, their journalist licenses are taken away. Restricting of media content through various restrictive Press laws and self censorship in the wake of recent media reforms is an important arena of contestation in the disciplined democracy in Myanmar.

The absence of media freedom is one of the major challenges for democratisation process in Myanmar. In Myanmar, military regime has used the propaganda and censorship as a very effective weapon in governing the country. Military junta uses propaganda as an effective weapon for stability of their power and to persuade ignorant public to be their force (Myay 2011). After General Ne Win seized the state power in 1962 Press Scrutiny Board was established to exert strict control on print media. The regime exercised state monopolies of print, broadcast and electronic media (as described by Schedler under Electoral Authoritarianism). In general, the whole media had been monopolised, overwhelmed by military junta since 1962.

Levitsky and Way (2002: 57) regards that in an authoritarian regime, journalists who provoke the ire of the government risk arrest, deportation, and even assassination. Arrests and intimidation of journalists has been a common feature of authoritarian media regime in Myanmar. According to various reports (unofficial) a reporter, Hla Hla Win, was sentenced on December 31, 2009 to 20 years' imprisonment for violating the Electronics Act, and an additional seven years for violation of the Import-Export Act, 5(1). Another (undercover) reporter from the Democratic Voice of Burma (DVB) was sentenced to a total of 13 years in 2010. Reporter Ngwe Soe Lin was given a 10-year jail sentence for violating Section 33(a) of the Electronics Act, and an additional three years for violating Section 13 (1) of the Immigration Emergency Provisions Act. A journalist, Maung Zeya, and his son were arrested by the police on April 17, 2010, after Maung Zeya's son took pictures of the sites of three bomb explosions in Rangoon. Aung Thu Nyein, 28, an intern for "Weekly Eleven Journal", was arrested on September 13, 2010, for taking photos of the flooding that hit Magwe in central Myanmar.

The military rulers have used their propaganda on all state owned media as the most effective tool to create a socio-political environment where the citizens were ignorant of politics. Knowledge of citizen rights and democratisation process has been belied. After the military junta announced its plans to hold elections in Myanmar, the PSRB issued a directive on March 8, 2010, prohibiting all weekly publications in the country from publishing any comments or analysis on the electoral laws being announced daily through the state-owned media. The Censorship Board took another step on July 20 when it issued a directive prohibiting journals from publishing discussion or analysis of the 2008 constitution or the 2010 election laws with the threat that failure to comply would result in the journals losing their publishing license.

On March 17, 2010, the military junta announced that political parties would have to register for permission to print any election-related materials with the government following the 1962 Printers and Publishers Registration Act. According to this act, each political party would need to seek permission from the Censorship Board within 90 days after registering with the Election Commission. If the political parties would like to publish, the parties would have to deposit 500,000 Kyats (US$ 500) for permission to print. The government's UEC issued a notice on September 14 granting "legal" parties the right to campaign on state-run radio and television, with 15 minutes allotted for each campaign speech by their chairmen or secretaries before October 25, 2010. The draft copy of their speeches, as expected, had to be approved in advance by the Censorship Board. Though the opposition parties were denied access to the state's broadcasting facilities, candidates were still able to spread their campaign messages through private publications.[6]

According to Schedler, consumption of information is legally prohibited and mass access to information is disabled in an electoral authoritarian regime (Shedler 2010: 74). Looking into the case of Myanmar, the military junta intentionally launched 'cyber attacks' in the lead up to the 2010 elections against the websites of Burmese exiled media, including The Irrawaddy, Mizzima, and DVB. These media organisations suffered from attacks that temporarily shut down their websites. A week before the election, Internet speed in Yangon was severely slowed down. Internet cafés had to close due to the abnormally slow connections that frustrated many customers. Connection speeds in other parts of Myanmar, including Arakan, Kachin, and Karen States, and Tenasserim, Mandalay and Sagaing Divisions, were also reported to be very slow. The military junta always attempts to control the media by imposing laws and regulations. However, inside and exiled media made attempts to cover the election news as much as possible. Apart from media, CBOs and NGOs monitored the elections and documented information related to the election. These CBOs and NGOs included ANFREL (Asia Network for Free and Fair Elections), HRDP (Human Rights Defenders and Promoters), BNI (Burma News International), BP (Burma Partnership), ND-Burma (Network for Human Rights Documentation – Burma), BNHR (Burma Network for Human Rights), and HURFOM (Human Rights Foundation of Monland). These organisations issued statements, published reports, news, and interviews about the elections, as well as human rights abuses committed during the election period.

Those laws, in place since a military coup in 1962, include edicts prohibiting journalists from writing articles that could threaten peace and stability, oppose the constitution or insult ethnic groups. Critics say some laws are open to interpretation and give the government enormous power to silence dissent. They have been used repeatedly in recent years to jail members of the press. Myanmar's reporters had long been regarded as among the most restricted in the world. But President Thein Sein's reformist government has significantly relaxed media controls since 2011, allowing reporters to print material that would have been unthinkable during the era of absolute military rule – such as photographs of Aung San Suu Kyi when she was under house arrest in Rangoon.

However, the remnants of old regime was still seen when, in June 2012, the government's Press Scrutiny and Registration Department ordered the suspension of a magazine called Snapshot. It was reported that Snapshot had published a photo of a woman who was raped and murdered in Arakan State, igniting a wave of violence in the remote region of western Myanmar. In July, the censor board again showed its strength by ordering the suspension of two weekly magazines, the Voice Weekly and Envoy, for speculating on a still-anticipated cabinet reshuffle. Those punishments have since been lifted, and the two magazines are due to begin publishing again on 18 August 2012.

On August 20, a Ministry of Information official announced that editors of news publications would no longer have to submit stories to the censorship board ahead of publication. This unprecedented reform eliminates a draconian provision that has been in place since the PSRD was established in 1964 by Myanmar's then military regime. The new rules will impact a range of news and religious journals that have been heavily censored up to this point. However, editors will still be held accountable for the content and required to adhere to sixteen guidelines. Some of these are loosely worded and prohibit reporting on issues deemed "sensitive" and would ban stories that "harm national security" or the "dignity of the state." Recently a provisional Myanmar Press Council (MPC) has been formed to consider media affairs before a new media law is formally enacted by the Burmese Parliament. The reformation of the provisional press council comes after protests from domestic journalists who called for more say in the national press council.

References

1. The seven steps in the Roadmap to Democracy are –
   (1) Reconvening of the National Convention that has been adjourned since 1996.
   (2) After the successful holding of the National Convention, step by step implementation of the process necessary for the emergence of a genuine and disciplined democratic system.
   (3) Drafting of a new constitution in accordance with basic principles and detailed basic principles laid down by the National Convention.
   (4) Adoption of the constitution through national referendum.
   (5) Holding of free and fair elections for Pyithu Hluttaws (Legislative bodies) according to the new constitution.
   (6) Convening of Hluttaws attended by Hluttaw members in accordance with the new constitution.
   (7) Building a modern, developed and democratic nation by the state leaders elected by the Hluttaw; and the government and other central organs formed by the Hluttaw.
2. Some of the examples of these organizations are: National Endowment for Democracy, United States; Konrad Adenauer Foundation, Friedrich Ebert Foundation in Germany; Henrich Bol Foundation in Netherlands.
3. Interview with Dr. Tint Swe, NLD MP (1990 Elections) living in exile in New Delhi.
4. For the discussion of the gray zone refer William Case, "Can the 'Halfway House' Stand? Semi-democracy and Elite Theory in Three Southeast Asian Countries," *Comparative Politics* 28 (July 1996): 437–64; Steven Levitsky and Lucan A. Way, "The Rise of Competitive Authoritarianism," *Journal of Democracy* 13, no. 2 (April 2002): 51-65. Larry Diamond, "Thinking about Hybrid Regimes," *Journal of* Democracy Vol.13, no. 2 (April 2002):21-35; Fareed Zakaria, "The Rise of Illiberal Democracy." *Foreign Affairs* 76 (November-December 1997): 22–41; Thomas Carothers, *Aiding Democracy Abroad: The Learning Curve* (Washington: Carnegie Endowment for International Peace, 1999); Gordon P. Means, "Soft Authoritarianism in Malaysia and Singapore," *Journal of Democracy* 7 (October 1996): 103–17; Andreas Schedler ed. *Electoral Authoritarianism: The Dynamics of Unfree Competition,* Lynne Reinner (2006).

5. Based on interview.
6. Restrictions were imposed on campaign speeches which were broadcast on state-run media. Some of these restrictions included the following:
    1. Must not include any speech that can lead to disintegration of the Union or national solidarity, or be detrimental to national sovereignty.
    2. Must not include any speech that can harm security, the rule of law, or community peace.
    3. Must not disobey the Constitution (2008) of the Union of Myanmar (Burma) or any existing laws.
    4. Must not stimulate sedition or include any speech that can tarnish the image of the state.
    5. Must not include any speech that can lead to the collapse of the Tatmadaw (armed forces) or tarnish the image of the Tatmadaw.
    6. Must not include any speech or undertake organizing measures that can lead to conflicts or harm the dignity or moral conduct in connection with racism or religion or affairs of an individual or community.
    7. Must not abuse religion for political ends.
    8. Must not include any speech that can harm the peaceful pursuit of education.
    9. Must not include any speech that can discourage service personnel from performing their duties or to abet them to stage protests against the government.

Chapter - 3

Political History of Myanmar Since Independence

Post Colonial Developments

The key to a contemporary understanding of the prospects for democratisation lies in the understanding of the role of the military in politics at various junctures of institutional changes in Myanmar (i.e. in 1948, 1958, 1962, 1988 and 2010) (Steinberg 1981; 1982; Silverstein 1977; 2004; Smith 1999; Fink 2001; Taylor 1998; Carey 1997; Callahan 2001). The modern military in Myanmar began as part of the independence struggle in the 1930s. On the eve of World War II, the Myanmar army was more an embodiment of British colonial attitudes than of Burmese reality. Until the 1930s British policy excluded Burmans from the armed forces (Steinberg 1981: 12). By keeping the ethnic minorities in the hills and the people in the plains divided, it was easier for the Britishers to maintain control (Fink 2001: 18). In 1940 the Thakins, the political movement of the students and young intelligentsia, secretly sent one of their leaders, Aung San, to China to seek aid for their revolt (Silverstein 2004). Picked up by the Japanese in Amoy, he was taken to Tokyo. There he met leaders of the Japanese Army command who were aware of the independence aspirations of the Thakins. Aung San entered into an agreement with them. It was agreed that Japan would help Myanmar to gain her independence by supplying her with necessary arms. At the same time, an underground revolutionary movement began to form inside Myanmar in preparation for the anticipated uprising against the British.

Aung San returned in 1941 and recruited twenty-nine Burmans to go secretly with him to Hainan Island where they would be given military training by the Japanese. These 'Thirty Heroes' formed the nucleus of the Burma Independence Army (BIA) (Fink 2001: 21). The army, thus, organised was a "political force first and a military force, second—the officer corps seeing themselves as freedom fighters, not professional soldiers" (Taylor 1998: 6). When the Pacific War broke out, they returned to Thailand, recruited the first members of the Burma Independence Army and followed the Japanese into Myanmar. Some of their units fought the British and the experience gave them pride and confidence.

During the four years of occupation, the Japanese did not succeed either in bringing the whole of Myanmar under their control or in winning the universal support of the people. Faced with harassing tactics by the Allies and the threat of invasion, the Japanese tried to gain support from the Burmese only by promises of freedom (Silverstein 1977: 16). During the war the army's name was changed, first to the Burma Defence Army (BDA) in 1942, then the Burma National Army (BNA) and at the end of the War in 1943, to the Patriotic Burmese Forces. On 27 March 1945 it revolted against the Japanese and joined with the Allies in their final phase of the war against the Japanese (Steinberg 1981: 13).

During the Japanese occupation many Burmese acquired administrative experience by filling important positions in the government. When Japan allowed Myanmar to proclaim independence on August 1, 1943, a government headed by Ba Maw was permitted to take charge of most of the administrative apparatus under the supervision of the colonial masters (Silverstein 1977: 17). In this period of nominal independence an anti-Japanese resistance movement arose under the direction of the Anti-Fascist People's Freedom League—AFPFL—whose leadership included a number of Burmese who had been cooperating with the Japanese. The AFPFL opened its ranks to all the people of Myanmar regardless of ethnic group, religion or political belief and after the war it emerged as the most important voice in Burmese politics. It was an anti-fascist organisation which included the Communist Party, the Socialist Party and independent nationalists (Gravers 1999: 51). Aung San was the leader of the AFPFL and was not aligned to the parties which established the league. The Communists were however, excluded from the AFPFL in 1946 on account of their unwillingness to promote a negotiated settlement with the British (*ibid*).

The negotiation of independence was hurried and carried out against the background of sudden collapse of British power in India and the beginning of the Cold War (Horton 2005: 112). A meeting between British Prime Minister Clement Atlee and Aung San took place in London in January 1947. Although, no exact timetable was laid down, the agreement set out the course of events leading up to Myanmar's independence. In April elections were to be held to a Constituent Assembly to determine the future of the Constitution. Until the transfer of power, the Governor's Executive Council was to act as the interim government in Myanmar (Smith 1999: 78).

In order to solve the problems of the frontier areas, in between the 'January Agreement' and April elections, Panglong Conference took place in February 1947 (Smith 1999; Diller 1993; Fink 2001; Gravers 1999; Silverstein 1977). On the basis of this agreement the principle for the formation of new Myanmar was agreed. Under the Agreement, the Shans, Kachins, and Chins were to cooperate with the interim Burmese government in framing the Constitution on the condition that they receive full autonomy in internal administration and enjoy all the rights and privileges regarded as fundamental in democratic countries (Diller 1993: 395). The Kachins agreed to have the question of an autonomous Kachin State considered further by the Constituent Assembly to be elected. The concept of a federal union was agreed upon, and ethnic states were to be created with full autonomy over their internal affairs (Fink 2001: 22).

Although, the conference agreed to cooperate on the political freedom of internal administration amongst the minorities, and Aung San promised to secure cultural and democratic rights for the ethnic groups, there were, however, several shortcomings (Gravers 1999: 49). Only four representatives of the Karens attended the Conference as an observer and did not took part in the proceedings. The Mon and Arakanese from ministerial Burma and Pao and Wa from Frontier Areas were also not represented (Smith 1999: 79). The inadequacies of the agreement reached at Panglong became apparent with independence. The general terms of the Agreement resurfaced in the Constituent Assembly debates and ultimately in the Constitution adopted on

24 September 1947. However, the Conference also confirmed the ethnic difference, and when independence came in 1948 the inconsistencies in the different conceptions of national identity and political union were brought sharply and implacably into focus (Gravers 1999: 49). A final settlement between Nu and British Prime Minister Clement Atlee was signed on October 17, 1947. This agreement provided that Myanmar would become a fully sovereign and independent state outside the Commonwealth. The agreement was ratified by the Brirish Parliament in December and Myanmar became independent on January 4, 1948 (Silverstein 1977: 21).

However, with the assassination of Aung San, the stage was set for Myanmar's tragedy. Myanmar lost the politician who most clearly understood the dangers of making ethnicity and religion the cornerstone of nationalism and of incorporating this mixture in the state apparatus (Gravers 1999: 49). The Panglong agreement was never fully honoured: the crucial clause five, guaranteeing full autonomy in internal administration, was omitted from the text (Horton 2005: 112). In the Constitution there was no mention of the term 'federal' or 'federalism', however, this was its main intention. Discussions leading to promises made by the Burman leaders to the minorities resulted in the creation of a unique federal union, which was more unitary than federal, and led to most Karens and Karennis rejecting it (Silverstein 2004). The 1947 Constitution formed a multi-party bicameral parliamentary democracy. Although, the new Constitution recognised the rights of the ethnic minorities it, nevertheless, emphasized on a single centralised government (Diller 1993: 395).

The Shan State was to be reconstituted as one, with the extraordinary right of secession after a ten year trial period. Karrenni states were similarly to be reconstituted as one with the same right of secession. Kachin, however, abandoned this right in return for the inclusion in the new Kachin State of the two major towns of Myitkyino and Bhamo. The Chins, who were politically quiescent ended up without even a state, instead they were formed into a special division (Smith 1999: 80; Diller 1993: 395; Fink 2001: 22-23). The final designation and status of a Karen territory and political rights were left to be decided after independence, while the Mon and Arakanese of the Ministerial Burma received no distinctive recognition at all. Thus, as the Constitution drafting took place, groups of Karens, Karennis,

Mons, Buddhist Arakanese and Muslims in Arakan territory began preparing for armed struggle. In fact, the failure to resolve adequately the demands of the ethnic nationalities during the constitutional drafting process set the conditions for the outbreak of the violence later (For details see Article 201-206, Constitution of Burma, 1947) (Fink 2001: 23). The document also contained guarantees for the democratic rights of all citizens, irrespective of race, birth, religion and sex. Heavily influenced by Socialism, the constitution also established a welfare state providing for individual rights to education, employment, health care, and support for the aged (Diller 1993: 395)

Myanmar at the cusp of independence had an uncertain future and was caught in the chaos as political rivals took up arms to advance their claim to power (Taylor 2005: 15). During the first decade (1948-1958) an enduring insurrection kept the country in a state of semi-war. There were particularly, three groups which could be identified—the Communists, Peoples' Voluntary Organisation (PVO), Karen National Defense Organisation (KNDO) (Silverstein 1977: 26).

Peoples Volunteer Organisation (PVO) was formed by Aung San from the Burman soldiers who were not taken into the new army, as a home guard to help maintain law and order in the countryside (Fink 2001: 23). But its real mission was political: to give the AFPFL a vehicle by which to intimidate the colonial rulers in the growing struggle for independence (Silverstein 2004). Such forces existed in the 1930s and were nothing new for Myanmar. Since, the PVO members shared the ideas and values of and had close personal ties to the leaders and men in the new army and the rival political parties in and out of the AFPFL – the socialists and communists – doubts were raised in many minds as to whether there was a real separation between the professional army, the political army and the parties. So long as Aung San lived, the PVO remained united and loyal to him and the AFPFL. Aung San's assassination in 1947 left the PVO leaderless and subject to the persuasions of rival political groups seeking to lead the nation (Gravers 1999: 51-52).

The Communists initiated revolt on 28 March 1948 to institute a 'Communist State' through an armed revolution. During this time the PVO split and the dissent group joined the Communists in revolt (Fink 2001: 24; Silverstein 1977: 26; Gravers 1999: 52). The army also began to come apart. Thus, when the Communist Party went into revolt, less than three months after independence, divisive forces began operative. The 1st and 3rd Burma Rifles – two Burman battalions – deserted with their weapons and joined forces with the revolutionaries. Significantly, the fourth Burma Rifle, commanded by Brigadier Ne Win remained loyal to the government (Gravers 1999: 52). Following, independence and the failure of the Constituent Assembly to solve the problem of the Karens' place in the new union, communal violence erupted between Burmans and Karens (Silverstein 2004). In January 1949, the Karen Forces under the banner Karen National Defense Organisation (KNDO) rebelled. As the violence increased, three battalions of Karen Rifles deserted and joined the KNDO. This was a major crisis for military leadership in Myanmar (Steinberg 1981: 13). Meanwhile, the remnants of the Chiang Kai-Sheikh's KMT had fled and taken refuge in Myanmar. They sought to join the indigenous rebels in the Shan State, and thereby posed a new threat to the 'Union'.

When the diplomatic initiatives to end the KMT build up and to appease Beijing failed, the Burmese government sent the army to the troubled region. The army established a military administration in this region and soon embarked on a massive transformation of the armed forces (Callahan 2001: 417). By 1950, their (KMT forces) numbers grew to around 12, 000. They became a major concern for the Burmese political and army leadership when the KMT forces started receiving airdrops of US supplied arms over the next few years. The KMT threats were not really laid to rest until 1961 (Smith 1999: 155-157).

By 1958 the insurgents appeared to have become demoralised and many responded to government's offer to leave the jungle, lay down their weapons and rejoin society. These measures, however, did not bring peace to the countryside (Silverstein 1977: 27). Shan youths with the help of the Shan dissident leader took arms to fight for greater political autonomy. Similar rebellious activity developed among Kachins, increasing the danger of the existing insurgencies and posing a serious threat to the nation's unity (Fink 2001: 24).

Parliamentary Democracy

The structure of the government adopted after independence followed the British parliamentary model. A primary goal of the founders of independent Myanmar was to create a government blending the values and ideas of liberal democracy inherited from the British with the socialist values and goals expressed in Western Socialism (Silverstein 1977: 54-55). The leaders of the post-independent Myanmar embraced parliamentary democracy as the principal political system but, continued their fascination with socialistic principles as a basis for equitable economic development. The political system exhibited competitive party politics in a democratic setting; state intervention in the economic system was charecterised by an indigeneous interpretation of economic nationalism with socialistic leanings (Than 2007: 49). The Constitution also sought to solve the major problem facing the nation, of constructing an Union in which formerly separate people could join together so as to benefit from unity, while retaining a nominal degree of autonomy (Smith 1999: 27). The Anti-Fascist People's Freedom League (AFPFL) dominated Myanmar's politics for more than a decade after independence. The machinery of government and party overlapped to such an extent that the two seemed to be difficult to distinguish at times.

The parliamentary political system installed by the AFPFL government at the time of independence had encouraged competition and divisiveness among the political elite of the country (Taylor 2005: 16). After independence, various political groups within ruling AFPFL argued over their differences more frequently, by vigorously pushing the party to adopt their preferred policies and to appoint their members to top party and government positions. As a result of this internal turmoil, within first year after independence, the AFPFL government found itself being paralysed by factional and power struggles (Hlaing 2008: 151).

The idea that the opposition could play a constructive role in putting up different points of view had 'no roots in Burma'. It had always been understood as insubordination, and leaders in 1950s found it difficult to negotiate and work together with political representatives from other factions and parties (Fink 2001: 25). As the wave of insurgency subsided, members and supporters of the ruling party struggled for power and privileges. Patronage was widespread with AFPFL and power became personalised. These shortcomings aggravated the centrifugal tendencies brought about by personal rivalries among the ruling elite and led to a decline in the AFPFL's popularity (Than 2007: 51).

After the poor performance in the 1956 elections, League's cohesion began to weaken. The inner party rivalry continued despite a public display of unity among its leaders. Although, the AFPFL continued to dominate the Parliament, but it split into two antagonistic groups in April 1958—'Clean' and the 'Stable' AFPFL (Smith 1999: 176; Hlaing 2008: 155; Silverstein 1977: 28; Fink 2001: 27; Steinberg 1981: 15). Ideology played little or no role in the split, as all were committed to vague socialist goals. Issues revolved around personalities and cliques. Both the groups wanted to retain the official name of the AFPFL, the pre-eminent political designation since 1945 (Steinberg 1981: 15).

After months of months of accusations and revelations of corruption and crime, U Nu sought to end the dispute by calling a special session of Parliament and letting it decide, which faction would govern. He was able to hold on to power with the help of the National United Front (NUF) and the representatives of the minorities (Silverstein 1977: 28). The resulting unstable political situation led to widespread unrest and confusion. In August, as the situation deteriorated the curse of Burmese politics continued to spread. The air was filled with coups and assassination attempts. The matters went out of control by September 1958 (Smith 1999: 177-178). Unwilling to face the regular sessions of the Parliament, U Nu turned to General Ne Win and relinquished his position as commander-in-chief of the armed forces to General Win. He in turn agreed that the military would hold a free and fair election within six months. However, with Parliamentary approval, General Ne Win extended the tenure of his caretaker government from 6 to 18 months (Hlaing 2008: 155). U Nu, announced that the handover had been voluntary, but in reality he was left with no choice in the matter. In anticipation of the impending crisis, the military had surrounded Rangoon. U Nu was, in fact, faced with a coup if he did not act. The coup was characterised as a 'coup by consent' and a 'pseudo-constitutional-peaceful-military coup-d'etat' (quoted in Steinberg 1981: 16). At that stage, according to Steinberg (1981: 16), "U Nu took the constitutional way out, Ne Win the constitutional way in" The takeover was a positive military response to the U Nu's request to the army to bring about conditions that would allow the peaceful and non-partisan holding of elections.

Caretaker Government

Under the Caretaker government, which was also known as *Bogyoke* (General's) Government, Ne Win achieved several successes (Fink 2001: 27). There were three main objectives of military control—to re-establish law and order, to combat economic insurgents, and to prepare for civilian elections (Steinberg 1981: 16). On the eve of the formation of the caretaker government the military leaders held a conference at which they defined the national ideology, as they understood it, and their role in upholding it, declaring that so long as their strength remained, 'the Constitution shall remain inviolate'. They held that the nation's goal was to build a political-economic system on the principles of justice, liberty and equality and to construct a democratic society based on socialist economy. In the 'National Ideology and the Role of Defense Services', published 1960, three main objectives were set out: the restoration of peace and rule of law; the consolidation of democracy; and the establishment of a socialist economy (Silverstein 1977: 77; Smith 1999: 179). They pledged to pursue the aims of national politics as distinct from party politics. The caretaker government gave Ne Win a chance to put the army's ideology and theories into practice; while he followed the letter of the constitution, he violated its spirit (Silverstein 2004).

The military caretaker government sought to clean up the cities which were filled with squatters. Huts lined-up throughout the thoroughfares and covered vacant lots (Fink 2001: 27; Silverstein 1977: 28; Steinberg 1981: 20; Smith 1999: 179). Ne Win kept the food prices low and moved the squatter communities to newly established satellite towns (Fink 2001: 27). The economic activities of the military caretaker government were of greatest importance because of the attitudes they created within the military. The Defense Services Institute (DSI) was vastly expanded. Its main objective was development of national economy; lowering of prices; expansion into new economic fields and propagation of the industrial and commercial knowledge. The military further, perceived DSI to play a significant part in the process of Burmanisation (Steinberg 1981: 17-18).

The military caretaker administration's most important legacy was the continued development of a national political identity for the *tatmadaw* under General Ne Win (Smith 1999: 179). In its effort to deal more effectively with insurgency and lawlessness in the countryside, the caretaker government formed security and administrative committees composed of representatives from the army, police and administration to coordinate and cooperate in establishing or restoring law and order. The Frontier Areas Administration assumed direct jurisdiction over remote border areas and took responsibility for security and improvement in services to the people in those areas. As a result of these changes a more centralised administration developed throughout the nation, and internal security was improved (Silverstein 1977: 78). The Caretaker government, further, led to the integration of the frontier areas and local chiefs with the Union. The government brought pressure on the Chiefs in the Shan and Kayah state to surrender their historic rights and transfer administration to elected leaders (Fink 2001: 27-28). A constitutional amendment, passed in 1959 confirmed these changes and was hailed as an important step in the democratisation of the frontier areas. But, the change did not bring peace to these troubled states. The destruction of the traditional political and economic hierarchy has been a factor in increasing Shan state resistance to the Union government (Steinberg 1981: 18).

In the caretaker government, AFPFL-Stable formed the key component of the military (Hlaing 2008: 155). General Ne Win complied with the election date which was set for February 1960. The military leaders hoped to influence the outcome of the election and the AFPFL-Stable faction flaunted their connection with the high ranking officers (Fink 2001: 28). Backed by senior military leaders, the AFPFL-Stable leaders appeared confident of their electoral victory. They believed that their supporters in the military would do everything to undermine the position of the AFPFL-Clean in the election. The outcome of the election was, however, contrary to the expectations of the AFPFL-Stable because a large number of people, especially, the business elite, who suffered due to caretaker government's regulatory measures were dissatisfied and acted on this animosity by whole heartedly supporting the AFPFL-Clean (Hlaing 2008: 155). Thus, when the third national election was held in February 1960, the Clean AFPFL won an overwhelming majority—203 out of 250 seats.

After the elections, in a third governmental change, the military transferred power back to the winning party—AFPFL-Clean, which was renamed as *Pyidaungsu* or Union Party. The new government under the leadership of U Nu called for strengthening of democratic institutions; establishment of Buddhism as the state religion; creation of new state for Mons and Arakanese within the Union; and development of a plan for promoting social and economic growth (Silverstein 1977: 29). Yet, despite its popular mandate Union Party government could last for just two years. The triumphant return of U Nu to office precipitated events that demonstrated the faults in the Burmese democracy (Steinberg 1981: 20). These faults were well articulated by the military during the caretaker government period.

A major cause was the continued failure of a truly democratic, multi-party system of government to take root (Smith 1999: 187). Factionalism within the Union government was, in fact, conceived and given life in the new *Pyidaungsu* government. Three different factions were created—Thakin group, U group and the Bo group (Hlaing 2008: 156). As the tension between these three groups intensified, party leadership had torn AFPFL apart before (Smith 1999: 187). Continuing economic and administrative stagnation seemed to grip the state as U Nu began to carry out his campaign promises. He tried to appease the Buddhists by making Buddhism the state religion. Further, by espousing a constitutional amendment allowing freedom of religion, he to some extent appeased the Christians. Minorities and ethnic communities, on the other hand, remained unrelieved under the limited autonomy and insufficient economic progress and rewards (Steinberg 1981: 20). The secessionist movement among the Shans and discontent among the other minorities came to dominate the relations between the state and the Union government (Silverstein 1977: 29). On the question of re-establishing harmony among the people of Myanmar, especially Shans, Kachins and Burmans, the government hoped that a final settlement could be worked out at a federal Seminar held in February and March 1962, but as a result of the military coup it was dissolved before it could complete its negotioations (*ibid*). On the whole, the deficiencies in the quality and personnel of the *Pyidaungsu* administration and government's failure to resolve the urgent problems of the day caused U Nu's ultimate downfall (Smith 1999: 187).

Military under the command of General Ne Win witnessed significant changes. The government authorised the recruitment of PVOs loyal to the state, and other former World War II soldiers to form territorial units (*Sitwundans*) to buttress the depleted army. Under Ne Win's leadership, a process of Burman domination in the army began. Despite the loyal support given by Kachin, Chin and Shan battalions, their units gradually were reformed with Burman officers in command and Burman soldiers in their ranks. Aung San's federated army gave way to Ne Win's Burman-dominated and integrated army (Silverstein 2004). The new army became more professional with the establishment of a military academy in 1954, and later a National Defence College.

Establishment of Military Rule: 1962–1974

In the wake of the Federal Seminar in February-March 1962 in which leaders were allowed to put up their case so as to examine various alternative solutions advocated by the participants, that the Parliamentary democracy ultimately collapsed (Smith 1999: 196; Fink 2001: 29; Silverstein 1977: 30; Steinberg 1981: 22-23). The military under General Ne Win organised a bloodless coup on March 2, 1962. A seventeen member Revolutionary Council was established—consisting all the members from the military (Steinberg 1981: 22-23). The coup suspended the Constitution, dissolved the Parliament, abolished the state councils and took control over the state. Although, the causes of the coup have been subject to considerable speculation, Brigadier Aung Gyi, the main spokesman of the Revolutionary Council made it explicit by stating—"We had economic, religious and political crisis with the issue of federalism as the most important reason for the coup" (Quoted in Smith 1999: 196; Silverstein 1977: 30).

The Revolutionary Council led by General Ne Win, which came to power in the wake of the coup attempted to carry out fundamental structural transformations in the country's political and economic affairs by forming the Burma Socialist Programme Party—BSPP and adopting the *Burmese Way to Socialism* (Hlaing 2008: 157). From the outset, the military displaced the institutions created at independence, replaced the civilian leadership with members of their own organisation, and substituted their thought for that of their political predecessors. The Constitution was suspended and became inoperative in areas where the Revolutionary Council, the military governing body, issued decrees and promulgated orders. The courts were reconstituted (Steinberg 1981: 23). Old parties were outlawed and replaced by the military's own new party, the BSPP, the only political party allowed after 1964. Freedom of press eventually was restricted and replaced by an official publication, the *Working Peoples Daily*. Most of all, the federal system, while remaining in name, in fact, became a centralised administrative system. Security Administration Councils, composed of representatives from the army, civil service and police, replaced state political and administrative organs (Silverstein 2004). The new system was organised hierarchically with control located in Rangoon.

Ne Win's vehicle of reform, the BSPP, was announced in July 1962 and military's new ideology was contained in two major policy statements published during the first year of military government—the *Burmese Way to Socialism* and the *System of Correlation of Man and his Environment* (elaborated in the next section). Through his Revolutionary Council, General Ne Win sought to remake Burmese politics and society. Land and wealth were to be redistributed, foreigners stripped of their assets, and self serving politicians and capitalists replaced with loyal army men dedicated to serving the nation. The army ensured its political control of the country by establishing 'security and administrative councils' led by military officers (Smith 1999: 199). General Ne Win started by replacing approximately 2000 civilian members of the country's administration with military personnel and security councils were set up at the divisional, township, and village level (Fink 2001: 32). As BSPP slowly began to evolve, even the BSPP's administrative wings were set up to run parallel to the divisions of the military command.

The military was also able to extend its control over the national economy and the Defense Services Institute (DSI) became the major commercial institution of the country involved in shipping, banking, construction, transport and a variety of other business services. By 1963, all banking, importing and exporting, production and distribution sectors were nationalised (Silverstein 1977: 33). This state led development without adequate preparations ruined the economy. By 1967, there were widespread shortage of rice, cooking oil and other basic commodities. As a consequence black marketing and corruption became rampant (Steinberg 1981: 37).

State led socialist development in Myanmar was largely influenced by ideas and notions closely associated with socialism and economic nationalism endured during the pre-colonial period (Than 2007). These manifestations of 'reactive nationalism' against the colonial power continued after independence and dominated the political landscape by the '1945 generation' of political and military leaders whose credentials were legitimated by their role in the 'anti-fascist revolution' of 1945 (*ibid*). Historically, it was also the result of the economic experience and alienation of the population from the sources of societal control. Socialism along with nationalism was also nurtured with Buddhist traditions. Buddhism, in fact, acquired a new vigour and a more pronounced role because of its close association with both nationalism and socialism (Steinberg 1982: 35). The intermingling of Socialism, Nationalism and Buddhism in '*Burmese Way to Socialism*' disguised the military foundations of Ne Win (Based on interview with. Zaw Aung Win).[1]

All institutions that could challenge the Revolutionary Council were dismantled or neutralised while potential dissidents and pressure groups were either co-opted or emasculated through socio-economic and administrative controls (Than 2007: 112). Mass rallies and support for the Revolutionary Council was more like a ritual deliberately organised to disguise the real character of the politics which was of an exclusionary type. The Burmese Way to Socialism failed both to improve the economy and to gain real support amongst the people. By the end of the decade Ne Win and his co-leaders gradually shifted to a new direction.

By 1971 the BSPP was converted from a cadre to a mass party. Military rulers ordered the BSPP to begin planning for a constitutional form of government. It, therefore, started working for a new constitution (Silverstein 1977: 35). Despite changes in structure, the party remained a political vehicle for the military with General Ne Win as its head and senior military officers monopolizing all sub-leadership posts. In April 1972, while the party pursued its tasks, Ne Win and nineteen senior military officers retired from the Defence Services. At the same time the government changed its name from the Revolutionary Council to the 'Government of Burma'. Ne Win remained Prime Minister and most of the same senior military leaders, thereafter retired, continued as government heads; four civilian cabinet officers were added to their ranks. During this period Ne Win abolished the Secretariat inherited from the British colonial system, and transferred its responsibilities to the ministers. In terms of who led the nation, these changes were more nominal than real as the military retained near exclusive control of power. A new constitution was approved by the people in a referendum in December 1973 (Than 2007: 112). Early in 1974, elections were held to fill the seats in the National Assembly. Subsequently, the military rule entered its second phase—'Constitutional Dictatorship' in which Ne Win and his military officers continued to rule under a Constitution that legally concentrated all powers in the hands of the BSPP (Silverstein 1977: 35).

Constitutional Dictatorship: BSPP Rule: 1974–1988

In March 1974 the second phase of military rule began. On March 2, 1974, the twelfth anniversary of the military coup, the Revolutionary Council dissolved itself, and the new government was officially installed (Steinberg 1981: 65). The constitution institutionalised the power of the BSPP. It was directed to lead the nation; no other parties were allowed (Silverstein 2004). The 'Preamble' of the Constitution provides a prime position for the BSPP. It specifically lays down "We, the working people, firmly resolved that we shall-faithfully follow the leadership of the Burma Socialist Programme Party." According to article 11 of the Constitution, "The State shall adopt a single-party system. The Burma Socialist Programme Party is the sole political party and it shall lead the State." The Party was charged specifically with the responsibility of drawing up lists of candidates for all offices in consultation with its own mass and class organisations and the electorate (Article 179). The Party was also empowered to give advice and suggestions to government at all levels on economic planning, the annual budget, and anything else it chooses to discuss (Article 205). Like the army, government was centralised and hierarchical. The various levels of administration were tied together by the principle of democratic centralism.

The new Constitution codified changes in the military structure related to reorganisation of the administrative structure. According to Article 29 (b) of the Constitution "The different levels of administrative areas of the Socialist Republic of the Union of Burma shall be as follows: - (1) wards or village-tracts; (2) townships; (3) states or divisions; (4) the State. Hence, the lowest administrative level in rural areas was the village tract, a grouping together of several villages for administrative purposes. In urban areas, its equivalent was the ward. The next higher level was of township followed by division or state. At the apex of the system was the *Pyithu Hluttaw*—Peoples' Assembly, the titular source of all power in the state (Steinberg 1981: 69-70). At each of these levels a Peoples' Council was formed which composed of ten to thirty members. Electoral representation at each of these levels was based on BSPP's prerogative of nominating official candidates. Elections, therefore, implied confirmation rather than competition (Than 2007: 161).

Once the euphoria of the constitutional government passed, Peoples' Assembly devoted its time to the major questions inherited from the military government—security, national unity and economic improvement. Ne Win gave a speech on the differences between the two governments he headed. According to him, "under the new government Peoples' Assembly is the source of authority, with the people granted power and encouraged to act with self reliance and independence. In the present one party system, according to him, there was no longer need for inter party strife and struggle for power in the legislature" (quoted in Silverstein 1977: 139). But moralising and lecturing was no answer to the immediate problems of insurgency, national unity and economic decay. The ailing economy, continuing insurgency, thriving black-market and narcotics traffic were some of the major problems that have plagued the Ne Win regime for a greater part of its 26 year life span (Gyi 1983: 225). These problems were inextricably intertwined, but the economy and insurgency were the main issues out of which grew the other two.

Insurgency, which began during the first constitutional period and continued into the military period, remained an important fact of life for the leaders of the new constitutional dictatorship (Fink 2001: 47-48; Smith 1999: 198-354). The problems facing the new government do not come only from the insurgents. The failures of the military such as mal administration, black marketing, inefficient management, and corruption among both civilian and military officials, were as much a part of the new as they were of the old (Silverstein 1977: 140). Both the Revolutionary Council and its constitutional successor could not solve the problem of the inefficiency of the state managed economy. It in fact, became a source of financing state's enemies and creating a self perpetuating series of conflict (Taylor 2005: 17).

The implementation of the new Constitution in 1974 brought no substantial change to Myanmar's economy. Production of basic goods was less than planned and what entered the market was not distributed well, resulting in higher prices, hoarding, black markets and outright shortages (Silverstein 1977: 141, 164). As the state's economic drive deteriorated in the mid 1980s, inflation and shortage of consumer goods brought economic hardship to the populace (Than 2007: 164). National economic performance fell into complete disarray, inflation was uncontrollably high, the manufactured sector showed a negative growth rate and exports and imports dropped to record lows (Hlaing 2008: 161).

Although, there were institutional restructuring and limited reforms during the mid 1970s, in reality it turned out to be dysfunctional. Economic stagnation became deep rooted in the seventies (Alamgir 1997: 343). The post-1974 monetary and fiscal policies were aimed at controlling price inflation, financing state led economic development, and maintaining a favourable balance of payments position. In reality, the financial sector remained undeveloped and the government was unable to prevent persistent budget deficits and recurring balance of payments problems brought about by poor resource mobilisation and export stagnation (Than 2007: 179, 200). Scarce foreign exchange was tightly controlled and centralised. "Constraints such as weak demand, backward technology, poor infrastructure, inelastic pricing, over-valued exchange rate, over centralisation, over concentration on a few commodities, bad weather, population pressure, inhibited export growth" (*ibid*: 201). Another aspect of Myanmar's external trade was the so called informal trade that had considerable impact on the overall economy due to its wide scope and huge magnitude. The cross-border black market not only deprived the state of substantial tax revenues and trading profits but also undermined its authority in terms of the flouting of socialist principles.

Monetary and fiscal reforms were marred by the drastic demonetisation measures taken in November 1985, in which roughly one-quarter of the currency was taken out of circulation, which included 20, 50 and 100 kyat notes. This action was more a politically inspired punitive measure than an effective monetary instrument to rectify the problem of excess liquidity and illegal trading (Than 2007: 193). Thereafter, the money supply continued to grow apace and the state again resorted to demonetisation on September 5, 1987. About 56 per cent of the currency was invalidated, which included 25, 35 and 75 kyat banknotes. Both legal and illegal businesses were affected (Taylor 2055: 20).

All the measures of the Socialist government to remedy the economic problems only worsened the country's economic situation and further contributed to the outbreak of social unrest in many parts of the country (Hlaing 2008: 162). In May-June 1974 a major strike led by workers broke out over food shortages, rising prices, and bad labour conditions. This erupted at the railway workshop in Insein and spread quickly to other state concerns. As rioting continued, troops were called out to restore order and over hundred were arrested and imprisoned (Silverstein 1977: 141). Universities, colleges and educational institutions were closed to prevent further demonstration.

In December 1974, the society exploded once again, this time over the manner in which the government sought to deny any honours to UN Secretary General U Thant, when his body was returned to Myanmar for burial. Because of the long-standing political feud between U Thant and Ne Win, the Myanmar government sent no official delegation to receive the coffin (Fink 2001: 43). The students discontented with an appropriate ceremony and inadequate burial site for U Thant, seized his body in a clear protest against the military. Along with the monks, they attempted to bury it at a former student union building before its destruction by Ne Win in 1962 (Steinberg 1981: 73). The government responded by declaring martial law and sending troops to the campus. They were successful in reclaiming the coffin and reburying it at a cemetery near Shwedagon Pagoda.

In June 1975, a year after the workers strike, both students and workers held a joint demonstration marking the anniversary of 1974 workers strike. As they marched down, more and more people joined the protest (Fink 2001: 44). Sit-down strikes, labour demonstrations and other forms of protest by workers and students lasted for one week. The government subsequently resorted to force to break-up and end the demonstrations (Silverstein 1977: 143). Again the government closed all the universities and educational institutions and they were not to open until January 1976.

On March 6, 1976, yet another demonstration took place, although it was less widespread. It was organised to mark the anniversary of a prominent left-wing leader, Thakin Kodaw Hmaing. In anticipation that the crowd may become rampant, the universities and institutes were closed (Steinberg 1981: 73; Fink 2001: 44; Silverstein 1977: 143). Over more than hundred students were arrested in Rangoon itself and sentenced to an imprisonment ranging from five to fifteen years.

Although, the modus operandi of the BSPP professed the guidelines of 'inner-party democracy' and 'democratic centralism', according to Than (2007: 163), in reality it was centralism which prevailed over 'democracy'. This led to authoritarian practices and rigidities. The centrality of the idea of the party as a political force insulated the BSPP from the socio-economic and political changes occurring beyond the arena of routinised political exercises (*ibid*). The state also lost the ability to reform itself and the economy because of the political necessity to protect a large number of unproductive positions in the bureaucracy, party and state-owned industries. Moreover, the leadership of the BSPP and the bureaucracy came increasingly to be filled by less competent army officers. As a part of the patronising policy of Ne Win, many competent officers were eased out of office or demoted because of their inability to conform to the norms of the system (Taylor 2005: 17-18). Antagonism between those who remained in armed forces and those who remained in party also grew. As a part of the attempt to raise fund and recruit the loyalists, several small economic enterprises were established such as bee farming centres, small food processing factories, orchid plantations, and chicken farms (Hlaing 2008: 160). This style of administration threatened the legitimacy and continuation of the regime. The riots and demonstrations were strong warnings to the party leadership that something very basic was wrong with the system (Silverstein 1977: 144).

The system remained intact, with relatively little change until 1988. The first sign of real change came in August 1987, when Ne Win startled the nation by admitting 'failure and faults' in the management of the economy and called for open discussion about the past and change (Silverstein 2004). On August 10, Ne Win made a speech to senior party and government officials. "Noting that the system over which he presided for twenty-five years was increasingly incapable and that the world and domestic economic and political conditions had changed since the army took power in 1962 and the new Constitution adopted in 1974. Therefore, he suggested that the existing political order was in need of revision" (Quoted in Taylor 2005: 20). Prospects for further change in the economy and politics were promised by Ne Win in a subsequent speech in October. The regime had publicly admitted that the socialist revolution introduced in 1962 had been a failure and the general populace was losing faith it had in the credibility of the regime.

The ultimate collapse of the BSPP took seven months, from March to September 1988 in a series of event. For several months reports of student-led protests over shortages of essential commodities and spiraling rice prices had been circulating. But, it was only in March of that year, that the world first took note of their growing momentum (Smith 1999: 2). As students took to streets in protest, the government replied severely. They clamped down with horrifying force and an estimate 100 civilians were killed. Although, the demonstrations subsided as a result of the army's crackdown and abrupt closure of the colleges and universities, the protests resumed soon after the campuses were opened in early June. In the demonstrations that followed, students were joined by monks, workers and high school students. As the clashes broke out, this time, the security forces opened fire and several demonstrators were killed (*ibid*: 3). Throughout the month of June rioting continued and there were reports of gatherings and protests in Rangoon, Mandalay, Moulmein, Taunggyi, Pegu and a number of provincial towns.

Developments came to a climax in July 1988 while the nation was in turmoil. Government's crackdown worsened the situation. Protests against shortages of supplies in the shops and rising prices of the essential goods such as cooking oil and medicine continued to rise high dramatically. In the midst of this worsening backdrop, the BSPP announced its emergency Congress. At this emergency session, Ne Win announced his resignation as party head and urged the leaders to consider the creation of a multiparty system, among other changes. The resulting change in leadership from Ne Win to Sein Lwin aggravated the deeply deteriorating legitimacy of the BSPP and the State leadership (Than 2007: 164). Subsequently, the elaborate political and administrative superstructure collapsed.

Although the party permitted Ne Win to resign, it did not adopt his recommendations. Instead, it appointed as its new leader General

Sein Lwin, another protégé of Ne Win. He had the reputation of having led his military unit in suppressing dissent on the university campus in 1962, and again in 1974 where hundreds of students were killed and wounded. In response to his appointment people flooded back on the streets. People's main target was the hated Sein Lwin, who had been dubbed as the 'butcher of Rangoon' (Smith 1999: 4). To bring matter under control, martial law was declared on August 3 and was immediately followed by the call for a general strike.

A new mass demonstration was called by the students for the auspiciously chosen '8-8-88'. Across the country, workers laid down tools and took to the streets. This time, the government's crackdown was most draconian. Shootings were reported in many towns and cities across the country. To put down the growing national unrest, which had been building up during the year Sein Lwin ordered the military to suppress the strike of unarmed civilians; it resulted in the death of thousands (Silverstein 2004). On August 12, after a brief but bloody interregnum of just 18 days, Sein Lwin resigned and his place was taken over by Dr. Maung Maung, who was the only non-military man ever to have served in the higher ranks of the BSPP.

The "8888 Uprising", the largest ever national Burmese uprising demanding democracy ended on 18 September 1988. The student leaders promoted a 'set of ten demands' for the restoration of a democratic government in Myanmar. At this critical juncture, when the people felt that they were on the verge of victory, General Saw Maung, the head of the army and very much a loyal subordinate of Ne Win and his protégé Sein Lwin, organised a coup and on September 18 seized power and ordered the armed forces to suppress all dissent (Smith 1999: 15). The BSPP government fell and the military imposed martial law giving absolute power to the commander-in-chief, General Saw Maung, in order to quash the demonstrations. The army established as a government in the form of State Law and Order Restoration Council (SLORC) (Taylor 2005: 21). This resulted in abandonment of *Burmese Way to Socialism* and the eventual dissolution of the BSPP. Thus, the military's carefully constructed constitutional dictatorship crumbled and the army found it necessary to abandon the facade of constitutional government in favour of naked power to restore its leadership (Silverstein 2004).

Military Junta: SLORC 1988–1997

On September 18, 1988, General Saw Maung Commander of Burma Army carried out a coup in support of a tottering military government. Battered by widespread popular riots that had evolved over the previous months into a peoples' revolution, the government was under popular siege (Steinberg 2001:2). Brutal suppression of popular discontent followed the coup. The military instituted a new government called the State Law and Order Restoration Council (SLORC). It re-instituted the old name of the state, the "Union of Burma" dropping its previous socialist appellation, "the Socialist Republic of the Union of Burma." It dissolved the previous single legal party—BSPP—and reconstituted a smaller National Unity Party (NUP) which was in fact, the former BSPP disguised in new clothes without any serving military members (Smith 1999: 20). It made many changes in the government's institutional framework and presented an image of taut, authoritarian administration, bent on change. Also following the coup, the army dropped the original ethnic names of its military units. This was the last step in erasing its original federal structure (Silverstein 2004). Restoration of law and order, preserving peace and tranquillity, facilitating smooth transportation and communications, and providing decent livelihood for the public were the professed objective of the junta. It promised to hold 'multi-party democratic elections', once these objectives had been accomplished (SLORC Declaration No. 1/88).

Although the Burmese coup of 1988 replaced the previous leadership with a new group of officers, it was not intended to shift power even among the military or between military factions. Rather it was designed to continue military rule by other means. It took place with the acquiescence of the authorities. In this phase of regime change, the ruling military junta has been managing a dual transition towards "multi-party electoral democracy", and a market oriented economic system (Than 2007: 340). Since its inception, junta's legitimacy and authority has been contested by the legally constituted political opposition and a number of Western states and non-governmental organisations.

After the upheaval of 1988, multi-party election was a contingent choice to prevent its recurrence and together with the economic openness constitute the military's development paradigm for the 1990s and beyond. Saw Maung in an address on January 9, 1990 vowed that the army would stand by the election result and hand over to the elected government (Smith 1999: 23). A large number of political parties emerged at the close of registration numbering 235. Out of these, 93 ended up fielding candidates. Altogether there were 2209 candidates representing 93 parties and 87 independents. Although 492 single-seat constituencies were established, only 485 were contested in the elections held on 27 May 1990. Out of the elections which followed 479 seats were won by 27 parties and independents won 6 seats. The NLD won 392 seats and claimed victory (See table below).

Table 3.1: Multi-party General Election in 1990

General Statistics of Elections:-		
Constituencies	:	492
Number in which election held	:	485
Eligible voters (485 constituencies)	:	20,818,313
Vote cast (72.6 per cent)	:	15,112,524
Valid votes cast (60.3 per cent)	:	13,253,606
Candidates	:	2,296(2,209 from Parties , 87 independents)
Elected	**:**	**485**(479 from Parties, 6 independents)
NLD seats	:	392
NUP seats	:	10
SNLD	:	23
Other parties	:	74
Independants	:	06

Source: Democratic Voice of Burma Documentation "The 1990 Multi-Party Democracy General Election."

http://www.ibiblio.org/obl/docs4/1990_multi-party_elections.pdf

Elections, which in 1990 gave an overwhelming majority to the pro-democracy National League for Democracy (NLD), have simply been ignored. A stand-off between the military and the NLD ensued. The party, demanding the army convened a meeting of the *Pyithu Hluttaw* (Peoples Assembly) to form a new government under its auspices, was confronted by the army which persisted in stating that until a new Constitution was promulagated, the SLORC would continue to hold all legislative, executive and judicial power (Taylor 2005: 23).

As, such, the 1990 elections did not lead to the formation of a government and the implementation of the election results has been a bone of contention between the junta and its political detractors (Than 2007: 342). Having made a massive miscalculation, the SLORC simply refused to hand over power, claiming in July 1990 that the election had only been for a constitutional assembly, and that a new election would have to be held once a new constitution had been written (SLORC Declaration 1/90).

In the years following the 1990 election, Myanmar's Generals focused on four objectives (Fink 2001: 77). First, they sought to expand greatly the size of the armed forces in order to be in a stronger position against their armed and unarmed opponents. As a result, the number of soldiers was increased and new bases were constructed throughout the country.[2] Second, the ruling generals worked to break-up the organisational structure of the pro-democracy movement and particularly the NLD. Third, they attempted to neutralize the ethnic nationalities by making cease-fire agreement with almost all of the armed groups. And fourth, they tried to improve the economy by opening up the country to trade and foreign investment.

The nationalisation of industries, twenty six years of central economic planning, and the curtailment of almost all foreign direct investment, ensured the destruction of the Burmese economy (McCarthy 2000: 234). Recognizing that the socialist economic policies had been disastrous, the regime attempted to revive the economy encouraging private business and foreign investment (Fink 2001: 77). According to Martin Smith (1977: 23), "if Ne Win's *Burmese Way to Socialism* was not exactly buried, it was most certainly dead." The SLORC undertook reforms in the name of "open door market economy of Myanmar" and has been using this "open door economy" and other measures since 1988 to improve its international image and attract foreign direct investment (Maung 1997: 503). It promulgated a liberal foreign investment law in December 1988. This has been regarded as a major step towards liberalisation and an attempt to redress the capital deficiency caused by the cessation of Official Development Assistance (ODA). A number of institutional, legal and administrative reform measures were introduced over the next fifteen years (Than 2007: 355). These included the revoking of restrictions in agricultural trade and the relaxing of restrictions on production, milling, storing, transport, marketing and pricing of major crops. To facilitate economic development, SLORC initiated infrastructure projects such as roads, bridges and irrigation canals throughout the country, although in many cases they were completed by forced labourers under duress. Fertilizers were imported and efforts were made to make the agricultural sector more productive (Fink 2001: 80). Other measures included—reformulation of corporate procedures; revision of regulations and procedures on domestic and foreign trade; reactivation and reconstitution of chambers of commerce and business associations; and transforming municipal authorities into development committees.

As a part of the cosmetic reform procedure, international renaming of the country as *Myanmar Naing Ngan* (Union of Burma) took place in June 1989. It was followed by Burmanisation of most public names and titles (Smith 1999: 21). This modernisation and expansion was further enhanced by a restructuring of the military bureaucracy. It saw the creation of two new regional commands—Tenasserim Coastal and Kegtung, as well as three regional administrative commands—all in pivotal ethnic minority border areas where military presence had previously been week (Smith 1999: 426). Barring few of these attempts, restructuring of the civil bureaucracy, however, remained a low priority amid the prolonged struggle between the military government and the political opposition (pro-democratic NLD) and the military's attempt at state building and consolidation (Mutebi 2005: 152).

In conjunction with the reformation drive, the military has actively plunged into the new business world through a policy, it termed 'Productive Establishment' (Smith 1999: 426). The main vehicle for this transformation was a new military company—the Union of Myanmar Economic Holdings (UMEH), which had been set-up in 1990. Besides, UMEH, the military owned and operated a number of other conglomerates, the most significant being the Myanmar Economic Corporation. These became a major force in the private sector and are engaged in banking, construction, external trade, manufacturing and gems (Than 2007: 392).

In transition to a market oriented economy, Myanmar experienced the inevitable economic distortions, uncertainties and instabilities (Mutebi 2005: 152). After some modest growth during the mid 1990s, Myanmar once again faced economic problems (Ng May 2008: 58).

The country suffered from declining investments, a severe depletion of foreign reserve and rampant inflation (Fink 2001: 77). Although, in the first few years foreign direct investment flows quickly became significant. Tourism, textiles, mining, gas and oil became major developmental sectors (McCarthy 2000: 244-245). But in the wake of the Asian financial crisis in 1997, these flows mainly from regional powers were severely truncated. Although, there has never been any realistic expansion in export oriented industries under *Tatmadaw*, except for the illegal trade, Myanmar's economy was not directly influenced by the contagion affect of the Asian financial crisis. Nevertheless, the *Tatmadaw's* goal of acquiring foreign exchange reserves by legal means was seriously curtailed by the direct impact of the financial crisis upon its ASEAN neighbours and Japan (McCarthy 2000: 254). This has been supplemented by the pressure from the West and the poor economic management by the regime (Taylor 2005: 24; Ng May 2008: 58; Smith 1999: 432). As a result of the Asian economic crisis, foreign investment approvals fell by more than 70 per cent in the financial year 1997-98. Furthermore, tourists visits fell below significantly from an estimated 1 million in 1996 to a sharp decline in 1997 and continued to decrease in 1998, largely due to the regional instability caused by the Asian depression (Guyot 1998: 93). The regime had no expertise in economic planning and the generals were unwilling to delegate responsibility to trained economists (Fink 2001: 77). Inflation was estimated to have run at the rate of 20-40 per cent per year. Corruption was rampant due to trade, rising prices and foreign exchange controls imposed by the SLORC. The economy remained primarily an inefficient command economy with a nation-wide black market (Maung 1997: 504).

At the same time, the military regimes were scoring victories in the long standing battles with armed groups (Fink 2001: 80). In 1989, the Communist Party of Burma (CPB) collapsed. The ethnic minority faction within the CPB broke off and agreed to cease fire with the regime in return for the minimal Tatmadaw interference in their internal affairs. In early and mid 90s, the SLORC was successful in splitting the armed Democratic Alliance of Burma which included many of the ethnic nationalist armies who had previously agreed to negotiate with the regime only as an allaince. The Pao National Organisation was the first to break with its allies and made a ceasefire deal with SLORC in

March 1991.[3] Others including the powerful Kachin Independence Organisation soon followed, leaving only a few diehard groups to battle on by themselves.[4] Most of the groups felt that they could not compete with the increasingly powerful *Tatmadaw*, and they would be better off signing a deal that would give them continued control over some territory as well as chance to bring development to the civilians in their areas.

In the meanwhile, the junta sought to institute a legitimate role for the military in public life by holding a National Convention to write a new Constitution (Smith 1999; Taylor 2005: 2006; Than 2007). The National Convention was launched on October 2, 1992. The junta first convened the convention in January 1993. By September 1993, a detailed set of 104 basic principles endorsed by the National Convention Convening Committee (NCCC) had been established as a basis for future deliberations. The Convention was aborted in 1996 after NLD delegates walked out in protest, saying it was undemocratic (Taylor 2005: 23). It then went on eight years of long recess after April 1996, the steering committee continued to sit frequently for deliberations (Than 2007: 343). In the intermittent sessions that dragged on through a decade represented SLORC political vision, in which military's dominant role would be formalised in an ostensibly multi-party system of civilian government (Smith 1999: 128). The topic of holding a reconstituted 'National Constitutional Convention' dominated Myanmar's politics for past several years. The advent of National Convention, however, was accompanied by a great deal of international attention as Asian and European governments sought ways in which to assist the process of political reconciliation in Myanmar (Taylor 2006: 6). The convention was resurrected in May 2004 without NLD representatives. It completed its task on September 3, 2007.

The regime continued to face challenges in the late 90s, as it struggled with a weakening economy and sustained opposition from domestic political groups and foreign organisation and government. Foreign investment began declining in the mid 90s due to poor economic management and constantly changing regulations. The Asian economic crisis in 1997 and Daw Aung San Suu Kyi's repeated calls for foreign businesses to stay out also resulted in reduced investment. Throughout the late 90s, inflation was running in double digit numbers eroding the value of fixed salaries and leading hundreds of thousands of Burmese to seek work outside the country (Fink 2001: 94). In spite, of the introduction of the market forces and opening of the economy to local and international private initiatives, the statist legacy and the interventionist role of the state has remained pivotal. The primacy of the state's role in relation to non-state institutions was taken for granted by the ruling elite and has made the attempts by the regime to institute a 'market economy' open to private initiatives extremely problematic in Myanmar (Than 2007: 394).

SPDC Regime: 1998—2008

As a result of the military government's second major shake-up since 1988, in November 1997, the SLORC was replaced by the new State Peace and Development Council (SPDC). Following this a 19 member committee was formed and a new Cabinet was also announced (Smith 1999: 433). The generals in the SLORC and the SPDC have relied on an expansion of military, the staffing of the administrative offices with loyal servicemen, and the creation of a new mass organisation to widen and deepen their control over the general population. The regime increased the Tatmadaw's presence in cities and towns throughout the country, building dozens of new military compounds. If mass protests were to break out again, there would be troops everywhere to take action. The number of military intelligence agents was also increased infiltrating opposition organisations and monitoring soldiers as well (Fink 2001: 94-95). The regime appointed a number of military men to ward, township and regional administrative positions, but it also tried to woo the masses through the establishment of Union Solidarity and Development Association (USDA). USDA was purportedly a social organisation founded on September 15, 1993 (Bowman 2007: 8). But it was headed by Senior Genereal Than Shwe and was often used to defend the interests of the regime. The regime sought to turn the USDA into a counter force against the NLD and students activists working for the restoration of the democracy (Smith 1999: 429). The authorities also gave military training to some USDA youth and used them to initimidate and attack Daw Aung San Suu Kyi and her supporters. The aim was to make it appear that the people and not just the regime were opposed to her and the NLD (Fink 2001: 96). Periodically, the USDA organised mass rallies throughout the country to demonstrate support for military rule and to denounce the NLD.

In parallel, the SPDC also tried to organise political and administrative structure that can pursue its agenda during the latter stages of the roadmap, a structure headed by the USDA, which was being groomed to be the dominant political actor in a future multi-party state (Bowman 2007: 2).

Since its overwhelming victory in the 1990 elections, the NLD has progressively developed and refined its policy position. It was taken further in 1998. In September that year the Committee Representing the Peoples' Parliament (CRPP) - the NLD's answer to the regime's consistent refusal to call the elected Parliament—created 10 smaller committees, each charged with certain policy studies (Sleth 2001: 7-8). On several occasions, the leaders of armed ethnic organisations wrote individual and joint statement declaring their support for Daw Aung San Suu Kyi and the democratic struggle. Despite NLD's efforts to develop closer relations with ethnic nationality leaders, the regime continued to drive wedges between them. The armed ethnic groups were often reluctant to do anything that might jeopardise their ceasefire agreements[5] (Fink 2001: 98-99). Thus, as long as the Tatmadaw was in control, most of the leaders of the armed ethnic organisation felt it necessary to cooperate with the regime.

Ethnic Pao minority in Myanmar has gained considerable economic freedom as result of its accommodation with Burmese junta, who control possibly most repressive state in world. Pao, by agreeing to cease-fire with generals who run country, have won themselves civil rights and economic opportunities all but unimaginable to most Burmese. In addition to Pao, at least 15 other armed ethnic minorities have ended decades of bloodshed and are doing business with the military. For Generals, agreements with minority groups has brought end to series of expensive insurgent wars and freed them to focus state resources on saving themselves with ever-expanding web of repression as key to their continued rule. Deals between Generals and ethnic minorities have weakened hand of country's primary opposition group, whose leader is Daw Aung San Suu Kyi (New York Times 2000).

Meanwhile, on Nov 7, 2005, at an auspicious hour selected by astrologers, Myanmar's ruling junta shifted the national capital from Yangon to Nayipidaw located in Kyatpyae Village of Pyinmana Township of Mandalay Division. Naypyidaw means "Royal City", but is also translated as "abode of kings." Pyinmana in Mandalay Division was chosen as the new capital because "it is centrally located and has quick access to all parts of the country.[6] The location confers the new capital many advantages, which the military regime did not enjoy in Yangon. "There was a real concern that the soldiers were becoming contaminated by the masses in Yangon and being made soft by the increased standard of living in Yangon: the restaurants, the consumer goods," says Larry Jagan. "So this was a way, really, of isolating and insulating the military so they would remain loyal." This may be the world's only national capital without mobile phone service or international flight connections (Indian Express 2007). According to Soe Minn, "Myanmar's paranoid military feels safe in a denuded area nestled among mountain jungle, aloof from the demands for democracy that are popping up elsewhere in the country."[7] Although it had been known for some time that a new strategic command centre was being built near Pyinmana, the sudden announcement in November 2005 that the entire government would start moving soon after came as a shock to the world (Pederson 2007: 4). The move to Naypyidaw has meant that they are now more remote and alienated from the general community and, most importantly, less in contact with the local communities than is the *Sangha*. As a result of this, the shift to Naypyidaw may lead to a more fragile state than they had expected (McCarthy 2008). The civil servants and the military contingents have found themselves frustrated as the shifting has affected their social and family life adversely.

However by 2007, the regime had not been able to raise the standard of living of the majority of the domestic population. While military Generals' families and their friends managed to amass fortunes through virtual monopolies over many of the most lucrative businesses, ordinary Burmese businessmen found that without the necessary bribes and connections, they were not able to participate in the new market economy. Water and electricity shortages became acute in 1998-99, with frequent blackouts in Rangoon, and some rural towns receiving electricity only once every three to five days. Businesses and home suffered alike. The government's decision on 15 August 2007 to cut fuel subsidies, causing a sudden surge in fuel prices, was the spark that ignited a nation waiting to explode (Kingston 2008: 6). The sudden increases in official prices were 66 percent for gasoline, 100 percent for diesel fuel, and 500 percent for CNG.

Four days later, the '8888' Generation student leaders and pro-democracy activists staged a powerful demonstration against this fuel price hike and other mass protests followed throughout the week (McCarthy 2008: 298-314). The crackdown which followed after the peaceful protests over fuel prices has been a setback for the country and had the effect of calling into question the Government's commitment to democratisation (Burma Net News 2007).[8] The protestors pointed out the economic mismanagement of the SPDC regime. Although the military regime claimed as a 'Government of Burma' after a brutal and bloody coup in 1988, it has not played the required roles in an economy as a government (Myo 2007).[9] The protests in 2007 were a consequence of Burma's dire economic circumstances and it was supposed to remain explosive unless the needs of the vast majority remained neglected (Kingston 2008:8).

On 5th September more than 2,000 Buddhist monks staged a protest march in the Myanmar city of Pakokku to fight for democracy in the country. It came a day after soldiers fired teargas and warning shots to disperse a similar demonstration against Myanmar's ruling generals. They were marching very peacefully, just chanting prayers and Holy Scriptures. "No slogans, no demands" (ITN 2007). The increasing involvement of monks, who were key players in a 1988 mass uprising, is a sign that the dissent that broke out in August, over the rise in fuel prices, is intensifying. However, the demonstrators were attacked and beaten by members of the security forces, and possibly the USDA. This mistreatment of the country's highly revered Buddhist 'clergy' (or *sangha*) so outraged some young monks that they immediately began organising their own country-wide protest movement (Sleth 2008: 281-297). News of the beating of monks at Pakokku rapidly spread through monasteries across the country, after which a newly formed group called the All Burma Monks Alliance (ABMA) issued a leaflet giving the SPDC to meet its demands or face a religious boycott by the deadline of 17th September. These demands constituted—apologise to the monks for the Pakokku violence; immediately reduce commodity prices including fuel, rice, and cooking oil prices; release all political prisoners including Aung San Suu Kyi and those arrested during the current protests; and an immediate dialogue with the "democratic forces" to resolve the suffering of the people (HRW 2008: 13). The SPDC ignored these demands (McCarthy 2008: 298-314). Not only did they seek economic reforms to alleviate the suffering of the lay population, on whom they depended, but they also demanded an official apology for the gross disrespect shown to the *Sangha*. The generals have favoured using civilian gangs and members of its feared USDA social network to break up protests.

Myanmar made international headlines, when the military junta ordered a crackdown on protestors marching through Yangon calling for an end to their 45-year rule. A Japanese photographer was shot in front of the Sule Pagoda. Monks were beaten and killed. On 26 September, armed soldiers and police opened fire on a large demonstration in Rangoon. That night, out of the public eye, a number of the city's Buddhist monasteries were raided, and hundreds of monks were forcibly detained. The following day, and for the rest of that week, any protesters who dared to march were met with tear gas, baton charges and, on several occasions, lethal force (Sleth 2008: 281-297).

Myanmar's only Internet server was shut and text and picture messaging on mobiles, stopped. To quote Soe Myint, "Radio is the only means available to the leaders who are in hiding. They broadcast their instructions to the four radio stations that are operating outside Myanmar. At present, all the people of Myanmar are listening to the radio. The military cannot jam the radios as they are on shortwave and if they do so they will affect their own wireless systems. It's an uprising driven by people from all walks of life — except for the police and the military. It's a revolution of the people and has spread to 50 cities since August 15."[10] According to Ashin Panna Siri, "The images of thousands of red robed monks, bare footed and bold quietly standing up to the armed might of riot policemen and tanks were indelible. Somehow their silence seems to be loud and brutal."[11]

These visible protests by the Buddhist clergy, beamed across the entire world have stripped the Burmese generals of the last layer of legitimacy. By overturning their alms bowls and refusing to accept donations from the military, the participating monks threatened to expose the veil of political legitimacy that the current rulers have attempted to maintain internally since the early 1990s (McCarthy 2008: 298- 314). It is clear from the continuing street protests that this time the seeds of dissent may have been sown much deeper than the military estimates. The SPDC has shamed the military as an institution in the eyes of the people and, more importantly, damaged relations with the *sangha*, the repository of moral authority in Myanmar (Kingston 2008: 17). Bertil Lintner predicted that the Saffron Revolution was "the beginning of the end of military rule in Myanmar. It may take time but it clearly will end. The moment an officer stands up and says enough is enough it will all crumble" (quoted in Kingston 2008: 18).

The military regime managed to severely damage the organisational capacity of the pro-democracy movement, but it was not able to a build a prosperous nation. The 'saffron revolution' brought to light, the fact that the generals have lost an enormous amount of legitimacy by committing violence against the very institution they are meant to support and whose traditions they promote, the *Sangha* (McCarthy 2008). The new constitution which took 16 long years to complete has replaced the SPDC regime based on the military engineered Seven-point Roadmap to Democracy in Myanmar in 2003 (elaborated in the next section). The result of Constitutional Referendum held in May 2008 in which 92 per cent of the voters showed their willingness to adopt the new Constitution and subsequently the November 2010 elections have opened a new agenda for reforms and change in the country.

Military Roadmap to Disciplined Democracy

The State Peace and Development Council had been making efforts on all fronts for the Union of Myanmar to become a peaceful, modern and developed nation that can keep abreast with the development of other nations, to strengthen the national economic life and to raise the living standard of the people. This has been popularly termed as "military way of transition." Prime Minister General Khin Nyunt delivered a speech on the future policies and programmes of the State at the *Pyithu Hlattaw* building in Yangon on 30 August, 2003. He explained that "endeavours are being made to develop the best possible democracy in 'future Myanmar' through a thorough study of strong and weak points of the democracy practised in Myanmar in the past and to treat the historical wounds that are not yet well-healed" (quoted from New Light of Myanmar: 2003). General Khin Nyunt who was appointed Prime Minister in August 2003, was a pragmatist, and favoured involving the pro-democracy leader Aung San Suu Kyi in the national reconciliation process and plans for political reform. For this particular reason, he was at odds with country's hard-line leader, General Than Shwe. Khin Nyunt also believed that Burma's future depended on political reform and economic development and that these were linked (Jagan 2006: 30). He also announced seven-point roadmap for movement towards democracy.

As the Union of Myanmar is a plural state, the firmness of Union Spirit is of vital importance for national solidarity. To this effect, the Head of State Senior General Than Shwe had given several guidance, saying, "Union Spirit is the patriotism of the national races, who are the descendants of a single stock, and living in the same land and partaking water from the same source, since time immemorial, to live in amity and unity through thick and thin and weal or woe" (New Light of Myanmar: 2003). Thus, the national policy of non-disintegration of the Union; non-disintegration of the national solidarity and perpetuation of sovereignty - based on Union Spirit, has been laid down as the State policy. In accordance with the national policy, the four political objectives, economic objectives, and social objectives, have been laid down in systematically marching towards the State's goal for emergence of a modern and developed nation in the future.[12]

The 7-step "roadmap" announced by General Khin Nyunt on 30 August 2003 is another major step taken by the ruling junta towards

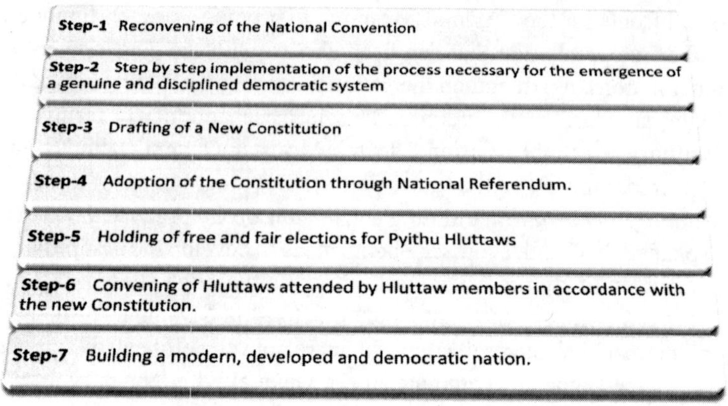

Figure 3.1: Seven Point Roadmap to Military Way of Democracy

democratization. It is identical in all essentials to the National Convention. It contains the seven steps of the political process to develop a modern and developed democracy in the future in accordance with the historical background of the nation, the customs and traditions of the people and the prevailing political, economic and social conditions.[13]

Military began to acknowledge the importance of "national reconsolidation" in the democratisation process. To this end, the rulers in Myanmar have taken measures to reduce the gap between the central and the remote regions as well as making peace overtures to the ethnic rebels. Since 1989, the military regime had developed a multi-sectoral development programme for the ethnic communities residing in the border regions of Myanmar through high powered committees and the Ministry for the Development of Border Areas and National Races. In order to effectively carry out the activities of progress of border areas and national races, "Ministry of Development of Border Areas and National Races" was established on 24th September 1992. The Ministry was reorganised as "The Ministry for Progress of Border Areas and National Races and Development Affairs (PBNRDA)" with the aim of performing urban and rural development measures on 30th January 1994. It placed emphasis on construction projects so as to bridge the development gap as much as possible between border areas and interior regions.

The SPDC regime also tried to improve its image in humanitarian front by demobilising the 'Child Soldiers'. A committee for the 'Prevention against Recruitment of Minors' was formed. Since its inception steady progress has been achieved on this issue.[14] As has been reported, no forced recruitment is carried out and all soldiers join the armed force of their own accord. No one under the age of 18 is allowed to join the military service even out of their own willingness.[15] The regime has denied any recruitment and use of child soldiers. Moreover, they have to pass the prescribed medical examination and must be clear of criminal records. Arrangements were made for United Nations agencies such as the UNDP and UNICEF to meet with new recruits at recruitment units. A Plan of Action has been laid down to scrutinize the procedures to prevent recruitment of minors into the armed forces. It includes procedures on mobilizing raw recruits and discharge from military service, reintegration into society, raising public awareness, taking action against transgressors, reporting, submission of suggestions and recommendations and coordination and cooperation with international organisations. A task force consisting of Ministry of Foreign Affairs, Ministry of Home Affairs, Ministry of Labour and Ministry of Social Welfare, Relief and Resettlement was constituted to oversee the implementation of the Plan of Action.

Off late, the Burmese authorities have accepted the request of International Labour Organisation (ILO) to allow alleged victims of forced labour to seek redressal without fear of persecution. Henceforth, the alleged cases could be reported and investigated without fear of retaliation. The ILO has repeatedly said that forced labour remains a serious problem in Myanmar, with evidence pointing to ethnic minorities being most vulnerable (BBC 2007). This achievement clearly reflects Myanmar's willingness and seriousness to cooperate with the ILO in the eradication of forced labour in the country. According to Dr. Zaw Win Aung, "there are various activists in and outside Myanmar who are working for labour rights and trade union rights advocacy."[16]

Furthermore, the enactment of the law relating to Private Health Care Services for promotion of physical, mental and social well-being; prevention, diagnosis and treatment of disease; and rehabilitation of health and research may be regarded as another milestone towards softening of the authoritarian regime.[17] This law had been enacted, particularly, to systematically participate in and carry out the national health care system and to impart quality services at fair cost and to take responsibility for its non-implementation.

Politically military junta in Myanmar also tried to buttress its role by providing for a 'National Convention'. It pledged to provide a greater voice to the ethnic minorities while the supremacy would remain with the military. The road to Myanmar's third Constitution was a long one and it took the members of the National Convention more than 16 years to the draft it. The National Convention was held from 1993 to 1996.[18] It was temporarily suspended on 31 March, 1996 after NLD delegates walked out in protest, saying it was undemocratic. However, Myanmar's military regime reconvened its National Convention on December 5, 2004 which completed its task of finalising and endorsing Myanmar's draft Constitution on September 3, 2007.[19]

Though convening of the constitutional convention provided an opportunity for the ethnic ceasefire groups to join a process which might eventually ensure a degree of autonomy and legality for their de-facto semi-autonomous zones and businesses, NLD, however, did not participate in it (Taylor 2006: 10-11). Although, the representatives of NLD were present in the first few sessions of the constitutional convention in 1993, 1994 and 1995, during which time Aung San Suu Kyi was under house arrest. But, soon after her release, the party made a decision to withdraw from the Assembly on the grounds that its procedures were undemocratic and its decisions, especially the guarantee of a leading role for the military in any future constitutional regime, were unacceptable.

In this background of the post colonial developments and emergence of military rule in Myanmar, the next chapter seeks to study the authority structure that has developed in Myanmar since independence. The rigid authoritarian authority structure which has emerged in the country has largely shaped the political architecture of the institutions that have developed under military rule since last five decades in the country.

References

1. Interview with Zaw Win Aung, Chief of Bureau, Democratic Voice of Burma and Federation of Trade Union, Burma on October 25, 2008.
2. For instance, the number of soldiers increased from 1,80,000 in 1988 to over 4,00,000 by 1999 (Fink 2001: 77)
3. The Pao people are one of the ethnic minority groups in Shan State. The Christian population among Pao people is less than 1% as they are deeply rooted in Buddhism. The PaO National Organization (PNO) has 300 regular fighters (90 per cent Pa-O, 10 per cent Shan, Kayah, Palaung and others). The Pa-O number approximately 1.6 million.
4. The Kachin Independence Organization (KIO) counts more than five thousand regular soldiers. The Kachin people number some two million persons, who live in northernmost Myanmar.
5. While the ceasefires had not resulted in the granting of ethnic rights and political autonomy, they did mean the end of decades-long civil war and far less suffering for the civilian population.
6. Pyinmana is located approximately 400 Km from Yangon, in the Southern salient of the Mandalay Division. It is a key communication hub with roads and rail leading to the Northeast, Southwest, and Southeast. It also provides easy access to the Shan, Kayah and Karen states, which have been the

scene of powerful minority insurgencies for over five decades. Its historic association dates back to the days of Myanmar's struggle for independence led by Gen. Aung San. It served as the military headquarters of his resistance army. Infrastructure including roads and buildings to house the new capital has been under development for the last four years.

7. Based on interview with Soe Minn, Radio and T. V. Reporter, Democratic Voice of Burma.
8. Accorging to the United Nations envoy Ibrahim Gambari, "These incidents of recent times cannot be seen in any other way than a setback for Myanmar." He further stated that, "They are all the more disappointing as they not only have the effect of calling into question the stated commitment to democratization and national reconciliation by the authorities, but also make it more difficult to maintain support, international support, for engagement with Myanmar at a time when we believe strongly that the country needs international assistance in addressing the many pressing challenges, from political and human rights issues to humanitarian and socio-economic problems." (Burma Net News 2007)
9. Government's first role in an economy is to achieve macro-economic and political stability. Government's second role in an economy is to improve general microeconomic capacity of the economy. Government's third role is to establish the overall macroeconomic rules and incentives governing competition that will encourage productivity growth –For details see Myo 2007.
10. Based on an interview with Soe Myint, at School of International Studies, JNU on October 30, 2007. He is the managing editor of *Mizzima News.*
11. Based on interview with Ashin Panna Siri, a Buddhist monk who participated in the demonstration.
12. The most important four **political objectives** are:
    1. Stability of the State, community peace and tranquility, prevalence of law and order;
    2. National reconsolidation;
    3. Emergence of a new enduring State Constitution;
    4. Building of a new modern developed nation in accord with the new State Constitution.

    Four economic objectives:

    1. Development of agriculture as the base and all-round development of other sectors of the economy as well;
    2. Proper evolution of the market-oriented economic system;
    3. Development of the economy inviting participation in terms of technical know-how and investments from sources inside the country and abroad; and

4. The initiative to shape the national economy must be kept in the hands of the State and the national people.

Four Social objectives:

1. Uplift of the morale and morality of the entire nation;
2. Uplift of national prestige and integrity and preservation and safeguarding of cultural heritage and national character;
3. Uplift of dynamism of patriotic spirit; and
4. Uplift of health, fitness and education standards of the entire nation.

(These objectives are supposed to guide the nation-building process in future Myanmar.)

13. The seven steps of the political reforms are –
    (1) Reconvening of the National Convention that has been adjourned since 1996.
    (2) After the successful holding of the National Convention, step by step implementation of the process necessary for the emergence of a genuine and disciplined democratic system.
    (3) Drafting of a new constitution in accordance with basic principles and detailed basic principles laid down by the National Convention.
    (4) Adoption of the constitution through national referendum.
    (5) Holding of free and fair elections for Pyithu Hluttaws (Legislative bodies) according to the new constitution.
    (6) Convening of Hluttaws attended by Hluttaw members in accordance with the new constitution.
    (7) Building a modern, developed and democratic nation by the state leaders elected by the Hluttaw; and the government and other central organs formed by the Hluttaw.
14. Between 2004 and 2006, 567 persons were discharged from the armed forces as they neither met the minimum age nor the designated qualifications. The Myanmar army released 62 child soldiers August 2013 in its latest bid to meet international human rights standards, although critics said more children still remain in uniform.
15. Based on interview.

16 Based on interview.

17 The Law Relating to Private Health Care Services was enacted by SPDC on 5 April, 2007.

18. The first meeting was convened in January 1993. Of the 702 delegates whom the regime invited, only 99 were elected members of Parliament, out of which 81 were from NLD. The other 603 delegates were all appointed by the SLORC.

19. The six objectives of the National Convention are: (a) Non-disintegration of the Union (b) Non-disintegration of the national solidarity (c) Perpetuation of the national sovereignty (d) Flourishing of a genuine multi-party democratic system (e) Further flourishing of worldly values-justice, liberty and equality in the nation (f) Participation of the *Tatmadaw* in the national political leading role of the future State (National Convention Procedural Code, January 1, 1993).

Chapter - 4

Authority Structure of Military in Myanmar

Authority structure is a significant factor determining the political system and practices prevailing in a country. The authority structures that emerged in Myanmar have influenced the model of state building and modernisation in this country. This is particularly visible in the development of state apparatus—particularly, corporatist structure, political parties and armed forces. The autocratic military framework which developed in Myanmar was characterised by personalistic authoritarian rule of Ne Win and later by the 'junta'. Analysis of this dominant authority structure in Myanmar would, perhaps, explain the reasons behind the hard authoritarian regime that has existed in the country for almost five decades.

Myanmar made its beginning by inheriting the structures and institutions of a free market parliamentary democracy from nearly a century old British colonial rule but was not able to translate these into an enduring foundation for sustainable democratic governance. The politics in Myanmar has been dominated in almost all aspects by military since the 1962 coup. The great hope for transition to democracy that was raised by the 1990 parliamentary elections in Myanmar was dashed almost immediately by the failure of the military regime to seat the elected Parliament. The November 2010 election and the convening of the Parliament in February 2011 was an attempt by the regime to move towards controlled transition and *disciplined* democracy. However, it was November 2015 which for the first time, after a gap of six decades witnessed a free and fair democratic election in Myanmar. Around 91 odd political parties participated in the democratic process where NLD received overwhelming majority and the ruling party gracefully accepted defeat.

Autocratic Military Framework in Myanmar

Military authoritarian rule with command economy and restricted freedom imposed by General Ne Win and his coterie of military officers in Myanmar is expression of an autocratic military framework in Myanmar (Silverstein 1977; Steinberg 1981; Gyi 1983; Alamgir 1997; Callahan 2001; Fink 2001). Myanmar since 1962 has been ruled by military known in Burmese as the *Tatmadaw*. In the leadership vacuum created in 1962 Ne Win seized power and established a 'Revolutionary Council' to govern the state (Alamgir 1997: 438). He subsequently banned all political parties and dissent and organised Myanmar as a one party state under the BSPP, Burma Socialist Programme Party. The elimination of political parties and the severe restrictions on civil liberties and freedoms marked the expansion of authoritarian rule (Silverstein 1977: 100). BSPP, which was established in 1962, was a cadre organisation of military elite for its first nine years and was finally converted into a mass organisation in 1971 (Steinberg 1981: 31). Ne Win ruled till 1988 until he resigned in July 1988 as thousands of students were killed in military firings on demonstrations between March and September. General Saw Maung took over as the new ruler of Myanmar (Callahan 2001: 424). One-party authoritarianism under BSPP rule was abrogated and military authoritarianism was established under the SLORC junta which was renamed as SPDC in 1997 to create a softer image of the ruthless military authoritarianism (Fink 2001: 94). In an effort to control public opinion, political opposition has been systematically intimidated and all media have been censored (Callahan 2001: 424).

Maung Maung Gyi (1983) has studied the Burmese political values as they evolved over the centuries from the monarchical days to modern times. The Burmese monarchy is distinguished by three features: 'the sacro-sanctity and the central position of the kingship; absolutism of the Burmese Monarchy; and undifferentiated function of kingship'. The king was responsible to himself alone (Gyi 1983: 23). The king was not only the chief executive but also the chief judge and the chief legislator of the land. As shown above, there was not only lack of limitation of king's power but, also lack of differentiation of his powers.

In this context, the imposition of the authoritarian regime by military elite dominated by one man, General Ne Win exemplifies a rule pattern not unlike those of monarchical days. Perhaps, Ne Win is not entirely to be blamed for the military coup nor the resultant political system. In fact military coup may be conceived of as the culmination of a political process. The government was entirely dominated by the political cliques and their power crazy leaders engaged mostly in factional fights and it was tempting for a well organised institution such as the military to intervene and impose its authoritarian rule (Gyi 1983: 3). The right soil for the growth of an authoritarian system reminiscent of native Burmese monarchical rule was already there in the society.[1]

Pre-conditions for the retreat to native authoritarian rule patterns were lying dormant in the minds of the majority of the Burmese public. Ne Win's authoritarian political style merely cashed in on this vast store of built in attitudes and values of the Burmese society that are supportive of his rule pattern. Thus, authoritarianism in lines with the old Burmese values returned and has stayed in Myanmar since last five decades.

After the coup, General Ne Win and his Revolutionary Council (RC) immediately set about imposing order, and the universities were one of the first targets. The military regime announced stricter regulations for university students (Fink 2001: 31). The regime tried to stamp out resistance by increasing surveillance and limiting contact between students. Through his RC, General Ne Win sought to remake Burmese politics and society. The RC developed policies that were a product of shared military tradition, common nationalistic aspirations and socialist thought (Steinberg 1981: 27). Land and wealth were to be redistributed, foreigner stripped of their assets and self serving politicians and capitalists replaced with loyal army dedicated to serving the nation. The RC instituted what came to be known as 'The Burmese Way to Socialism'. Between 1963 and 1965, all banks, industries and large shops were nationalised. Most of the businesses were run by Indians and Chinese, by taking state control, the government intended to return profits to the indigenous Burmese. In March 1964, the RC demonetized 50 kyat and 100 kyat notes also with the intention of removing wealth from the foreign hands (Silverstein 1977: 155-157). As a result, hundreds of thousands of Indians and Chinese business people lost everything and left the country. Those businesses that did not collapse came under state ownership (Fink 2001: 32). This lied at the heart of many of Myanmar's problems. The nationalisation of all major industries, including banking and international trade, even though the state lacked the capacity to run them, according to Thant Myint (2007: 31) was a disastrous policy decision.

As the RC expanded its control, most independent associations were either absorbed by the government or forced out of existence. All publications had to pass through a newly formed censorship Board. Private schools were nationalised and a government controlled Burmese language curriculum was imposed throughout the country. Meanwhile, most foreign missionaries, scholars and western foundations were forced to leave and foreigner's access to Myanmar was tightly restricted. Independent trade unions were outlawed and existing political parties were also compelled to disband, with the only legal political party being the governments' Burma Socialist Programme Party (BSPP) (Steinberg 1981: 31). Originally, membership in the BSPP was restricted to the military and the administration, however, the regime later expanded membership and established other mass organisations under state control.

With the development of one party system, General Ne Win sought to use the BSPP to cement the allegiance of the civil servants and others to his military backed regime. In the 1970s party membership was open to all and not joining carried negative consequences. Party officers took over many of the administrative posts at all levels of government and civil servants were expected to become members (Steinberg 1981: 31; Silverstein 1977: 100). The judicial system also offered little hope of a fair hearing. Under the RC, courts were run by a panel of three judges, at least one of whom had to have some legal training. During the BSPP period, the three judges were elected but had to be party members. The chairman of the three judges was generally a military officer, while the other two judges came from the people and frequently included individuals with modest education. From the government perspective a lack of education was not a problem because 'goodness' mainly charecterised by loyalty was more important (Fink 2001: 39).

All associations were controlled by members of the ruling junta; the wives of the generals often lead civic organisations. There were only a few grassroots organisations with very limited mobility. Civil groups or associations were co-opted by the military and there was hardly any room to manouver independent of the military (Alagappa 2001: 494). Despite market reforms since the end of the 1980s, large state enterprises have dominated key economic sectors such as energy and heavy industry. These state enterprises enjoyed competitive advantages and the special protection of the ruling military elite because of their loyalty to the existing regime. There was no state policy on competition and development except some commonly recognised rules. State banks were controlled by the military leaders and they enjoyed special privileges which were not granted to the country's private banks. They were not allowed to conduct business with foreign clients. Foreign trade was essentially limited to the export of natural gas and agricultural products. The government consistently suppressed opposition activities, used extra-judicial killings, disappearances, torture, arbitrary arrests, denial of fair trial rights and more. In addition to restrictions of human rights and freedoms, other factors also contributed to a silent emergency in Myanmar (Sarkin and Pietschmann 2003). Poverty, hunger, disease, sexual violence and insurgency are a few of them.

The military dominated the political and social system for the last five decade. The so called 'free' elections held in 1990 and 2010 could not make much of a difference. The military government was not elected by the people but rather took power in a coup d'etat. It completely controlled all domestic media and blocked independent reporting by foreign journalists. The entire population was denied essential aspects of full citizenship and crippled in its political expression. The country's largest opposition party, the National League for Democracy (NLD) had to suffer extreme repressive measures until 2012 when it was allowed to contest in the April 2012 by-elections. The political leadership and dissenters were either eliminated or arrested arbitrarily and were under permanent surveillance by the secret police. Thus, the autocratic rule of Ne Win provided a framework for the military junta to thrive in later years.

Socio-Political Roots of Authoritarianism in Myanmar

Burmese Political Values

The rule pattern of a government is reflective of the prevailing political culture which is not an overnight creation. It is organic in nature and grows over years absorbing mainly the political experience of the people and the role they are expected to play in the political order vis-á-vis the ruling elite of the country (Gyi 1983: 7). Furthermore, political traditions and folklores, political myths and symbols, social values and customs and religious teachings pertinent to the political system are all interwoven into this complex network of political and social structure. Hence, it is relevant to explore the traditional Burmese values and belief system that underwent little change during the British colonial rule. Many of the traditional values and attitudes that characterised pre-colonial Burma persisted through the period of foreign rule, and continued even after independence (Silverstein 1977: 35).

The authority of the Burmese king was neither distinguished nor circumscribed. The king was the central figure in the old Burmese system of government. He was the pivot around which the wheel of administration revolved. He was the core of whole nation and his palace was referred to as 'the centre of the universe'. He was the embodiment of the highest attainment on earth, and according to Buddhist philosophy, "kingship was a position earned through merits accumulated in the numberless cycle of existence in the past and, therefore, not easily to be achieved. The king claimed to be lineal descendant of *Mahathamada*" (the first king of the world also known as 'Manu') (Gyi 1983: 14). His conscience alone controlled his actions and thus, ultimately, it came to mean that it was the personality of the king that largely determined the character of the government. (ibid: 34). The actual concentration of powers in one person and the manner in which these powers had been exercised led the people to believe that the king and his agents were capable of exercising "any and every function whatsoever" (ibid: 35).

Authoritarian nature of the traditional Burmese state was based on highly personalised concepts of power and central authority. These stem back to the system of semi-divine rule which has sustained it (Carey 1997:3). From 1044 to 1885, for over 800 years, the Burmese lived under absolute monarchy. Its authority was never challenged by any liberal forces during these years until it was overthrown by an alien power in 1885 (Gyi 1983: 13-14). Burmese thought pattern towards the government was molded during this 800 years and the nature of kingship largely determined the pattern of thought. Although, the colonial period effectively destroyed this monarchical tradition in

Myanmar, the centralising processes of the late Burman monarchy were carried on under the British (1826-1948)[2] (Carey 1997:3).

Authoritarianism emerged as the core value in this evolutionary process. Burmese have traditionally identified the government as one of the five elements—others being fire, water (floods and storms), thieves and malevolent people. Ordinary people had never had much control over the political process and felt it was just best to get on with life regardless of who was in power (Fink 2001: 29-30). Although, the government did seek to develop the country, there was little substantive dialogue between politicians and the people in their constituencies. As a result, democracy was only superficially rooted in Burma, and the military was able to take over with little resistance. Burmese reverted to the traditional political system of authoritarian rule, on March 2, 1962, when General Ne Win put an end to the parliamentary system with plurality of parties and free elections (Gyi 1983: 7). Most of the patrimonial elements and the patron client relations that dominated the functioning of the parliamentary democracy continued to persist under the two subsequent regimes. It was precisely due to this persistence of patrimonial nature of the state throughout the post independence period that authoritarianism has continued to dominate in Myanmar (Hlaing 2008: 176).

Under the caretaker government (1958-60), the ideological development of the military was advanced through the publication of the statement on 'National ideology and the role of the Armed Forces'. The document set forth three objectives—restoration of peace and the rule of law; consolidation of democracy and the establishment of a socialist democracy. According to this document, "to establish a socialist economy, democracy is pre-requisite and for democracy to flourish law and order is essential" (Quoted in Silverstein 1977: 77).

Burmese ideas of national unity are based on the Buddhist concept of harmony as a product of mental culture. The 'people of Burma' were described as having experienced 'fusion' under the influence of Buddhism. Given its sudden emphasis on Buddhism, some have dubbed the regime's efforts to inculcate Buddhist values, in particular through the reports of enforced conversions, as 'Buddhification' (Houtman 1999). Buddhism was not only central to the Burman personality but, it became a sanctioned form of nationalistic expression as well

(Steinberg 1982: 43). From the fourteenth century until the annexation of Burma by the British in the mid-nineteenth century, unification progressed rapidly through the spreading of Buddhist culture. The links between Buddhism and nationalism were forged on the British annexation of Upper Burma. The British policy was to eliminate the 'supreme patriarch' of the Buddhist hierarchy in Burma. This created a fear in the mind of Burmans that the Christian invaders were destroying their religion. Secular education made in roads on a field traditionally reserved for the *Sanghas* (Taylor 2005: 10).

Nationalism in Burma was a product of British colonial policy of annexation and, indeed, of the strengthening of the 'Burmese xenophobia'. The British conquest of Burma not only destroyed the traditional regime but also eliminated the seat of secular authority (Steinberg 1982: 36-39). The British substituted an alien administrative machine that had two functions—maintaining law and order and collecting revenue. In this process, it overturned the traditional institutions from the highest level to the village. This change subverted the effectiveness of these institutions in upholding the traditional moral, economic and political order. As the indigenous population was displaced from any significant role in the country's military or administrative affairs, it brought about alienation among them (Taylor 2005: 11). They were dislodged from the control of the economy, and sometimes, even from the ownership of prime agricultural land. This institutional change distanced the Burmans, as they were excluded from the development process. They, thus, continued to be marginal farmers; owner of traditional industries and some remained petty traders in traditional bazaars (Steinberg 1982: 39). Even in the military, British had created barriers between the ethnic minority peoples and the Burmans. Their military potential was seen as a potential threat to British control. Therefore, by keeping the ethnic minority people from the hills divided from the peoples in the plains, they furthered their policy of divide and rule (Fink 2001: 18-19). Not only were the 'minority races' governed under different principles from the 'majority' of the population, but also from the formation of the first Legislative Assembly in 1921, parliamentary constituencies were based on ethnicity and religion (Taylor 2005: 12). Ethnic differences were thus incorporated into the representative structures of the colonial state.

This continued until 1951 when the first general elections took place in Myanmar.

The institutional transformation also resulted in large influx of foreigners into Myanmar, mainly from India. The need for trade also brought in Chinese, who had been in Myanmar from traditional times, but in smaller numbers. Thus, nationalism developed in Myanmar to breed xenophobia as well (Alamgir 1997: 339). The Chinese and Indian merchants centred around Rangoon and other ports. Although, serious clashes occurred in 1930s in between student activists and British officials, growth of nationalism in Myanmar became directly associated with the expulsion of all foreign influence. The aim was, in fact, free Myanmar from foreign capitalist and imperialist dominance (Gravers 1993: 39). The authoritarian government in Myanmar under Ne Win, furthermore, coupled socialism (under Burmese Way) with nationalism in order to wipe out the Chinese and the Indian merchants. Anti Chinese riots began in 1967 following the food shortages. In an attempt to support the indigenous capitalist and reduce the economic challenges against the regime, the government in May 1964 recalled 50 and 100 kyat notes. This caused mass exodus of Indians and Pakistani residents in Myanmar (Silverstein 1977: 160; Steinberg 1981: 35). In addition, the regime passed the citizenship law restricting various privileges for citizens who cannot prove their Burmese ancestry back to 1823. English was also banned as a medium of instruction (Alamgir 1997: 339).

Burmese intellectuals were skeptical of foreign contacts and developed their own approach to social issues, one centred on socialism. Further, there were inextricable ties in Myanmar that eventually linked nationalism, Socialism and Buddhism. In traditional Myanmar, productive private investment was not possible since the king controlled all foreign trade and a considerable amount of the country's production and internal trade as well. As far as economic expansion occurred, it was state controlled. Thus, the existing socialist state was considered both as an effort to create secular modernisation programme and also as a reversion to traditional monarchical practices (Steinberg 1982: 108). As a part of the ideology of Socialism, the great project of Nationalisation began by which all major foreign and domestically owned businesses came into the hands of the state apparatus. Many petty shops and stalls were also nationalised (Taylor 2005: 17).

The rejection of the British parliamentary democracy with all its strength and weaknesses attests to the fact that the alien political institution and values have failed to strike roots in Myanmar. The experience of Parliamentary democracy under U Nu often represented his deeply Burmese religious and cultural sensibilities with the country's politics. Although, the state was officially secular, U Nu was establishing himself as the patron of Buddhism in the same way that Burmese king had in the past (Fink 2001: 26). Military elites infused with traditional values, led the Burmese people and went back to their age old political habits and rule pattern reminiscent of their semi-feudal, autocratic government headed by a king as a real head and mainspring of the whole governmental system. The Burmese continue to accept authority from above and have never widely accepted the idea of authority stemming from the people (Silverstein 1977: 35). Thus, Buddhist values and attitudes are still the major influences on Burmese thought.

From the very outset, the coup leaders never seemed to doubt the legitimacy of their actions (Silverstein 1977: 80). Their publications and speeches demonstrated their belief in the right of the military to intervene and alter the government in the time of national crisis. In order to unite with the people and inform them where and how the military intended to lead the revolution, the coup leaders wrote a new ideology that would become their blueprint. This ideology is contained in two documents—'*Burmese Way to Socialism*' and '*System of Correlation of Man and His Environment*' (Steinberg 1981: 28; 1982: 41-44; Alamgir 1997: 340; Silverstein 1977: 80-85). They represented a new stage in the development and formulation of military's concept of a national ideology.

'*Burmese Way to Socialism*' gave a direction to the Burmese authoritarianism. This model of Socialism was compatible with the traditional Burmese values and Buddhist traditions (Alamgir 1997: 340). In Myanmar, there was a re-interpretation of the Buddhist political and economic ideals—a Buddhist welfare state—and an equating of that ideals with contemporary Burmese nationalist and social needs (Steinberg 1982: 44). This dynamic inter-play of Buddhism and Socialism, in the Burmese context, has been continuous since 1930s (discussed in detail in the next section). Socialism in Myanmar, was thus, fully harmonised with the religious beliefs and cultural background and heritage of the people (Silverstein 1977: 87). The Revolutionary Council also published an ideological proclamation entitled '*The System of Correlation of Man and His Environment*' which tried to blend the Marxist notion of dialectics with Buddhist theological concepts about change (Alamgir 1977: 340). "The Burmese beliefs were not based on the theory of inevitable progress—but on the idea of change as a constant in all material and non-material things, and men and society should progress or regress dependency on their own ideas and endeavours" (Silverstein 1977: 86). This interplay between Buddhism and Socialism in that period was so complete that there was an association of Marxist monks within the Buddhist Sangha (Steinberg 1982: 44).

The authoritarian element was not confined to the political domain. It had its parallel in the social sphere as well. The Burmese social system was conceived in terms of ordered relationship based on moral obligations. The system, thus, established was highly personalised hierarchical system which guided the relationships between the superior and the inferior and older person and a younger person and a person of higher status and a person of lower status. Each was morally bound to fulfill his or her obligation or duties. It was based on will guided by morals rather than an individual system based on positive law. Popular participation in the governance of the country had never been a native concept (Gyi 1983: 39). The ministers were not the people's representative but the king's officers and they enjoyed office during his pleasure. The king and his bureaucracy of courtiers and officials took upon themselves the task of deciding what was best for the people and the country (ibid: 40).

The aforesaid mentioned features of Burmese monarchy along with actual administrative practices such as arbitrary actions, monopoly of power, and use of violence and terror in forcing compliance with royal commands have generated in the minds of ordinary laymen a general attitude of helplessness and resignation against the government that many came to view as omnipotent and omnipresent. Many Burmese saying attest to this conclusion, for example, (*bayen do phone mou thou chone lu pone taw mha ma nay thah*) i.e. the authority of the monarch is like a thunder clap, criminals hiding in the jungle must surrender because they could not stand its terrifying sound and (*min nar ta htaung min myaung ta thein*) a king has 1,000 ears and 1,00,000 royal messengers (Gyi 1983:48). Furthermore, superstition of the courts; its arrogance and pride; and its inefficiency largely reflected an undeveloped and primitive type of administration as well as the political immaturity and credulity of the Burmese people of those days. These governmental and the national traits persist in varying degrees to this day as well.

Theoretical foundation of Military in Myanmar

Attempts were made in Myanmar to establish the legitimacy for military rule based upon historical necessity, cultural imperatives and traditional authority relationships between Burmese rulers and their subjects. Almost immediately after the coup, the new regime began to formulate the ideological basis for the future direction of the state. Three critical documents were published in a short span of time. Each of them complemented the other creating a pattern of socialist policies that continues to be paramount (Steinberg 1981: 27). The first of the trilogy was *Burmese Way to Socialism* (*Myanma Hsoshelit Lanzin*) published on April 30, 1962. Subsequently, the Revolutionary Council formed a cadre party called the Burma Socialist Programme Party—BSPP (*Myanma Hsoshelit Lanzin Parti*) (Than 2007: 112). The leaders of the BSPP issued a pamphlet known as the '*Constitution of the BSPP for the transitional period of its construction*' in July 1962 that set forth the specific differences between their ideology and that of any other fòund in or outside Myanmar. The last of the trilogy appeared in Janurary 1963 with the publication of *System of Correlation of Man and His Environment: The Philosophy of Burma Socialist Programme Party* (Silverstein 1977: 81). This document was the theoretical underpinning for the political and economic system of the BSPP. These three documents together formed the basis for the distribution of political and economic power. Taken as a whole, they articulated the goals of the state, the theoretical bases for such goals, and the administrative means by which the goals were to be achieved (Steinberg 1982: 76). They clearly represented Burmese tradition and melding together of the three central concepts of –nationalism, socialism and Buddhism, in modern Burman life.

The Revolutionary Council announced its ideology as *Burmese Way to Socialism* (BWS). It stated that that parliamentary democracy had failed and that the bureaucracy was an impediment to achieving socialism. It advocated the need for reorganisation of the social services, protection of minorities, and the destruction of capitalism and exploitation (BWS, 1962). After 1962, socialism came to be used as an excuse for army business ventures. The desire to establish socialism was an excuse which the army in Myanmar has used in their establishment of authoritarianism (Alamgir 1997: 339). In Ne Win's concept, as expressed in *The Burmese Way to Socialism*, the army has a special role as it 'will also be developed to become national armed forces which will defend our socialist economy'. Further, it was an instrument for the army to attain control of the State (BWS, 1962).

The BSPP was formed as a transitional political party to carry the leadership in Burma's future politics. It was a cadre rather than a mass party. With the promulgation of the Law to Protect National Solidarity in March 1964, it became the sole legal political organisation (Than 2007: 112). It was created and controlled by the Revolutionary Council and operated under a highly centralised command system. The BSPP was to be built on 'democratic centralism' and membership to the party was subject to the approval of Revolutionary Council. A member of the BSPP could never resign from the party. However, provision was made for candidate members to go through a probationary period of two years during which they could resign prior to acceptance as full member (Steinberg 1981: 28-29). The BSPP was transformed into a mass based party during the First Congress of 1971.

Socialism combined with Buddhist concepts was presented in the book *System of Correlation of Man and His Environment*—SCME (Gravers 1993: 60). According to, SCME the ideology of the Revolutionary Council rests on three basic principles: *change, revolution and socialism.* It draws its ideas from a variety of contradictory sources—the Burmese Buddhist tradition, Marxism, socialism, humanism and pragmatism. The SCME blends the "moral pronouncements, abstract generalisations and utopian goals" (Silverstein 1977: 81). Man, according to SCME is dual—egoistic and altruistic. Man strives for freedom in order to fulfill himself, at the same time, his empathy and concern for others leads him to identify and work with his fellow men to achieve their common objectives. Man's nature has a propensity for evil as well as for good. In order to check and control this evil tendency, we must make our life a living reality, i.e. adopt a socialist way of democratic life (BSPP, 1964).

Socialism, according to the Burmese, is a necessary form of social control to restrict the unbridled freedom of individual man and channel his energy and effort along socially useful and constructive paths.

The socialist democracy envisaged by the military thinkers includes the unity of the will and initiative of the individual man and group on the one hand and the centralised guidance of society on the other. Democratic centralism and individual freedom, therefore, are compatible and when combined produce a progressive and prosperous society (BSPP, 1964). But, however, the concept and goals of 'Socialism' as espoused by Myanmar's military thinkers has been criticized as being utopian and vague for they do not tell us how these goals are to be realised. Instead of following a particular school of thought, they sought to blend the traditional Burmese ideas with the popular western concepts. The ideology provided a theoretical justification for changing the economy and polity of Myanmar, while keeping up with the Burmese traditions (Silverstein 1977: 84). By doing so, they also sought to unite with the anti-capitalist sentiments of most of the newly independent nations of Asia and Africa.

The '*Burmese Way to Socialism*' (BWS) is less theoretical than the SCME. It focuses on the approach that is to be taken in transforming Myanmar. Its immediate goal was to expand production so that the general standard of living could rise, unemployment could disappear and everyone to be assured of a means of livelihood. To realise these socio-economic objectives, the parliamentary democracy was to be replaced by a socialist democracy. Under this system, democratic centralism was introduced to respond to existing conditions by being flexible and non-dogmatic. The immediate objective outlined in the BWS included the re-building of the administrative structure and re-ordering of economic priorities (BWS, 1962). Since the existing bureaucratic machinery was considered as a stumbling block in the path of change, the BWS stated that it must be reformed so that it can contribute to the conversion of society. Modernisation of agriculture and development of industrial infrastructure were given priority in the allocation of new resources. (Silverstein 1977: 86, 87).[3] Mickael Gravers (1993: 61) argue that "central to the programme seems to be corporate thinking: a middle road between bourgeoisie democracy and communism, between right and left, where all classes and ethnic groups unite and function under a central leadership controlled by the army."

This was suppose to create harmony between individual and social forces.

Many of the socialist ideas expounded by the military ideologues were not new to Burma. Socialism, as noted earlier was one of the goals of the first Burmese Constitution and of the coalition of parties and groups in the original AFPFL. Though, vague and incomplete, the military theorists' ideas were part of the continuum in the growth of the Burmese Socialist tradition. They provided a frame of reference for analysing Burma's development under military rule and rationale for the decisions and priorities of the military since 1962.

Justification of Military in Myanmar

Military rule in Burma (Myanmar) has been justified on a number of grounds since 1962, including the army's claims to possess a unique ability in suppressing communist and ethnic insurgencies while effectively managing the economy (Mc Carthy 2007: 2). Silverstein argues that military justified the coup of March 1962 on three grounds: to preserve the union, to restore order and harmony in the society, and to solve the economic problems facing the nation (Silverstein1977:80). The Revolutionary Council started pursuing long term policies and the idea of military rule being established for a temporary phase began to be eroded.

The role of the military under Burma Independence Army during the war and the nationalist movements in 1920s and 1930s is highly applauded as 'nationalist tale of heroism' in modern history of Myanmar (Taylor 2005: 14). The *tatmadaw* is thus, seen as the leading pillars of the nation. Founded seven years before independence, the army preceded the independent Myanmar state and, therefore, its leaders claim a supervisory role in maintaining the state's independence. The role of the military was further enhanced when the military tried to preserve the nation against the ethnic clashes and armed revolt by political rivals (*ibid*: 15). The communist uprising in 1948 split the Peoples' Voluntary Organisation (PVO), with members divided between the government and its opposition. The PVO eventually faded as a military and political force. During this same period the minorities, too, were torn between loyalty to the new state and loyalty to their ethnic groups.

The Karens, in particular, experienced a sense of abandonment by the British to their historic oppressors, the Burmans. This helped raise their ethnic consciousness at the expense of full identity with the new national army. In 1947 the Karens formed a paramilitary group, the Karen National Defence Organisation (KNDO) to defend their villages. At the same time, the other large minorities, the Shans, Kachins and Chins, gave their full loyalty to independent Burma (Silverstein 2004). In the early phases of the rebellions their loyalty to the Union of Burma and their unwillingness to join the Karens and others in revolt was a major factor in saving the union. The KMT crisis forced the *tatmadaw* leadership to begin a course of experimentation and reorganisation that persisted throughout the decade. The process laid the foundation for an institutional development of the military that expanded the role of the army over the next decade (Callahan 2001: 419). The *Tatmadaw's* victory in 1948-1950 civil war has laid the foundations for greater centralisation by establishing the sovereignty of the centre. The military's effectiveness and administrative autonomy in dealing with these hostilities sharply contrasted with the failures of the government bureaucracy and the ruling political party (AFPFL). This has been argued as an important reason of army's growing strength vis-à-vis other institutions within post-colonial state in Myanmar (Callahan 2001: 422).

The Revolutionary Council's policies were informed not only by the legacy of the nationalist movement and its own version of saving the nation during the civil war in 1940s and 1950s, but also due to the failure of the civilian rule in the first decade after independence. The army saw itself as being above politics and acting in the interest of the state as a whole, not the partial interests that elected representatives allegedly represent. This 'self serving argument' provided justification for the attempted re-ordering of Myanmar's administrative and political systems in the name of *Burmese Way to Socialism* (Taylor 2005: 17). During the fourteen years after independence, the political leadership wavered between a federal state and a military-dominated central government. This belief of the military in its own efficacy and capacities to run the government and the economy stems from the effectiveness of the military during the 1958-60 Caretaker government. Steinberg (2005: 96), however, argues that this should have been re-evaluated following the disastrous performance of the economy run directly and almost exclusively by the military after 1962.

As factional struggles grew, the military became increasingly concerned and involved, and by 1958 it had a dominant role in domestic politics (Hlaing 2008). In the midst of the political turmoil caused by the 1958 split in the AFPFL, the military feared that the primary loyalty of the Union Military Police (UMP) and paramilitary forces was to political parties rather than the state and that UMP units might take sides and even displace the army as the nation's defender (Silverstein 2004). It also was alarmed at the divisions in the ranks of the nation's leaders. In this deteriorating environment the army saw itself as the only national institution ready to sacrifice itself to preserve the union and protect the constitution.

Increased economic and administrative penetration into the countryside, military measures aimed at securing border areas, and the resettlement of lowland peoples in highland areas further interfered with traditional practices among the minority peoples (Thompson 1995). The brutal war against ethnicities has helped Burmese regimes to divert attention away from their economic failures. Given the multi-cultural setting of Myanmar, military authoritarianism arose amid various small-scale ethnic insurgencies, which the regime up to the present time has been trying to crush (Alamgir 1997: 339).

Since, the Civilian government failed to solve the Union's social, economic and political problems, military's action to return to power became inevitable (Steinberg 1981: 20). The *Tatmadaw* regards civilian politicians as corrupt, venal and insensitive to the needs of the state, and bureaucrats as too closely associated with colonial power or civilian politicians. This denigration, according to Steinberg (2005: 96), dates back to the caretaker government of 1958. Although, it did use and build on the extensive civil service under military leadership, it has thus, been deeply ingrained in military thinking.

Security was the general concern of the army dominated government. Justifying the coup in the name of the national unity, the Revolutionary Council began a gradual process of restructuring the institutions and the policies of the state (Taylor 2005: 16). According to a '1988 generation' student activist Bala, "the people were told that its purpose was solely to preserve the union, but in reality it misguided them."[4] The regime pursued its approach to governance largely unaided and unadvised by the outside world for the first twelve years of the Revolutionary Council and in 1974 a new one party authoritarianism was established by the name of 'State Republic of the Union of Burma'.

The need to preserve law and order has been the stated justification with which the regime has cracked down on students and the *sanghas*. In fact, SLORC—State Law and Order Restoration Council, derived its acronym from the claimed responsibility to restore law and order (Alamgir 1997: 343). It is this rationale that has also fed its counter insurgency wars against various ethnic groups, and against students and intellectuals. The army is the mainstay of SLORC's strategic survival, therefore, massive resources are channeled into the defense sector (*ibid*). The military budget has rapidly increased and it constitutes more than 70 per cent of the GDP. Whereas, expenditure on social services such as health, education, and social welfare has been relatively low—relatively 5 per cent of the GDP (Asian Development Bank 2005: 30). Thus, although the nature of government structure adopted at the time of independence followed the British parliamentary model and liberal democracy was sought to be established, but authoritarian tendencies have dominated the way politics has operated since the early years in the country.

Institutions of Political Architecture in Myanmar

Myanmar's politics in the post colonial era has undergone tremendous changes. Beginning with parliamentary model in 1948 and after the army seized power in Myanmar in 1962, there has been series of extended power struggles within the different groups in the society. During this prolonged rule of successive military regimes under different nomenclatures, military junta seems to have endured under its often contested institutions and history. The importance of authoritarian institutions, such as party, military, and state apparatuses, in sustaining non-democratic rule is significant. Under this background, this section looks into these structures of political architecture in Myanmar.

State Apparatus

A primary goal of the founders of independent Burma was to create a government blending the values and ideas of liberal democracy inherited from the British with the socialist values and goals expressed in evolutionary socialism. The liberal tradition provided the basic idea underlying the Constitution that power emanated from the people. The socialist basis was reflected by the imposition of certain limitations such as expropriation of the private property in accordance with law (Silverstein 1977: 54-55). The structure of the government followed the British Parliamentary model. For eighteen months Burma experimented with constitutional authoritarian government under the leadership of General Ne Win.

Military rule was established in Burma by the coup in March 1962. Following the coup, all powers were assumed by the Revolutionary Council, which in turn conferred all legislative, executive and judicial power on its Chairman Ne Win. The line between the Revolutionary Council and the government was undefined and the members of the Revolutionary Council were also the ministers in the government. This pattern persisted through most of this phase of military rule (Steinberg 1981; 1982). In 1971, the formal government assumed a more traditional façade. After the first Congress of the BSPP it was announced that a new Constitution would be written which finally completed its task in 1973. Subsequently, a constitutional dictatorship was established under the control of Burma Socialist Programme Party (BSPP) (Taylor 2005: 23). The Constitution sought to continue the goals it undertook following the coup in 1962, i. e. direct control over the entire nation through a strong and disciplined administrative structure (Silverstein 1977: 133).

Since the collapse of Ne Win's personalistic authoritarian military regime in 1988, several attempts have been made to accommodate Myanmar's diverse political forces on the nature of political transition from military to civilian rule, but so far no significant results have been achieved (Pederson 2005: 162). The military government effectively annulled the 1990 election following a landslide victory for NLD, and work on a new Constitution which began in 1993 was abandoned three years later when NLD withdrew from the military controlled National Convention (Taylor 2005: 23). The government has since then announced a seven point 'roadmap' and holding of fresh multi-party elections in 2010. The experience of the two decades in Myanmar shows that the people within the government and the NLD, as well as most ethnic nationalist organisations recognizes that the only viable way forward is a gradual transition, which accommodates vital interests on all sides.

The BSPP's monopoly in controlling the state meant that the singular route to the control of state resources lay with the party. Politics, according to Than (2007: 162) resembled a 'triangle of accommodation' in which the party assumed the pre-eminent position (see the figure below). It relied on military for support in realising its goals through the state apparatus. Personnel were co-opted into the party hierarchy through their selection from state and military establishments. The unabated insurgency also enhanced military's role. Attempts were made to undermine the ethnic conflicts that continued to threaten the unity of the union (Taylor 2005: 18).

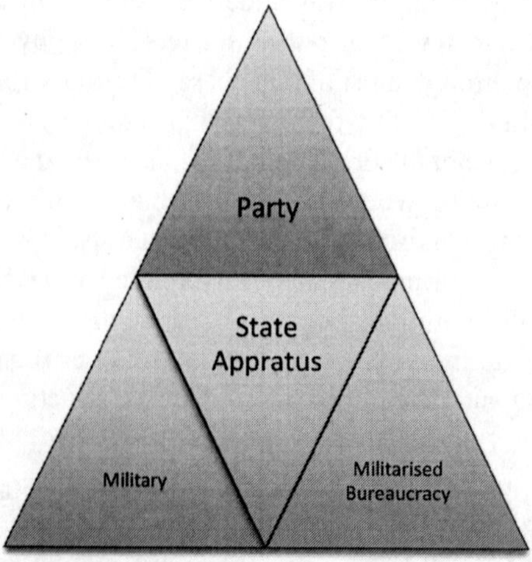

Source: Than, Tin Maung Maung (2007), *State Dominance in Myanmar: The Political economy of Industrialisation*, ISEAS, pp. 162.

Figure 4.1: Triangular Axis of State Apparatus under BSPP Regime

In an attempt to civilianize the government about twenty key military officers were forced to resign and assume civilian titles. However, this effort to govern has been alleged as a camouflage for continued military control (Steinberg 1981: 70). Although, military was devoid of its formal political role, its influence in the governance of the country remained undiminished (Than 2007: 162). In fact, the party and the political leadership comprised of the paramount position of Ne Win as Chairman of the BSPP, the Chairman of the Council of State, and finally as the head of the military (Hlaing 2008: 157). Although, formally subscribing to the BSPP's political role, the party organisation within the armed forces was structured to ensure that the chain of command was not compromised—beginning from ward and village level to township and state level. The military formed an important component of people's council at each level and also is a major element of *Pyithu Hluttaw*—Peoples Assembly, as well as of the BSPP itself (Steinberg 1981: 70).

In order to establish one-party authoritarianism Ne Win sought to use the BSPP to cement the allegiance of civil servants and others to his military backed regime. The party membership was open to all. Party members took over many of the administrative posts at all levels of government, and civil servants were expected to become its members (Fink 2001: 37). Increasing bureaucratisation resulted in a privileged class, even as more professionals and technocrats were co-opted into the system. Although, this trinity of state-party-military appeared to have instituted political stability and ensured regime security by consolidating its political structure, in reality, the BSPP could not forestall the building up of systemic weaknesses associated with one-party dominance in an authoritarian setting (Than 2007: 163).

Another aspect of state apparatus is reflected in the way power has been devolved from the central level to the local units. Legislative and executive power for the first time has been partly decentralised in Myanmar (ICG 2011 a: 6). Regional Hluttaw has been created for each of the fourteen regions/ states. The new President, Thein Sein, has urged for greater government decentralisation while at the same time admonishing lower-level organisations to stay within the policy framework set by the central government (Irrawaddy 2011b). "But we have to build mutual cooperation and understanding between the Union Government and Region/State Government and between Pyidaungsu Hluttaw and Region/ State Hluttaw." (The New Light of Myanmar 2011: Thein Sein's Speech in the Parliament, March 30, 2011)

Based on article 56 of the 2008 Constitution which came into force on 31 January 2011, six self-administered areas have been delineated for certain ethnic groups (the Danu, Kokang, Naga, Palaung, Pao and Wa), giving them a degree of autonomy within the ethnic states concerned (Notification 7/2011). While the legislative and executive powers of regions and states are limited, this shift holds out the prospect that governance can be more informed about, and responsive to, local concerns (ICG 2011 a: 6). All these structures are dominated by the USDP or the military appointees. All the Speakers of the State Legislatures are USDP representatives and all the chief Ministers, except the Kayin State who is a military legislator, are dominated by the USDP (TNI 2011: 2-3). This ensures that the USDP or the military will control decision-making on issues of national concern.

Although, under the constitution, the decentralised powers are rather limited nevertheless, they include a number of areas that can have a significant impact on people's lives: land (including allocation of land and agricultural loans), local business (small business loans and some taxation), cultural promotion, and municipal issues. Moreover, a number of ministerial portfolios in the seven states have been given to legislators from ethnic nationality parties (for details see TNI 2011). Though, it is too early to make any definitive assessment of the prospects for greater decentralisation in Myanmar. How this decentralisation process will function in practice remains uncertain. While the division of powers is defined in general terms in the constitution and in legislation, the detailed implementation – and, in particular, how administrative functions will be divided and coordinated between central government ministries and regional governments – has to be worked out in practice.

Economy

The economic objective of the *Burmese Way to Socialism* was to establish a socialistic economy that entailed "participation of all for the general well-being in works of common ownership……Socialist economy, according to the document, aimed at the establishment of a new society for all, economically secure and morally better, to live in peace and prosperity" (Burmese Way to Socialism, 1962). Self reliance and economic independence were stressed as essential elements of socialist economic strategy. The main thrust of the Revolutionary Council's was oriented towards establishing state control over the 'commanding heights' of the national economy through nationalisation and regulation of the private sector, while attempting to considerably expand state owned enterprises (Than 2007: 114). On the whole rapid expansion of the socialist structure was envisaged.

After the military coup of 1962, General Ne Win's promotion of *The Burmese Way to Socialism* embarked the country upon a catastrophic programme of international isolation and autarchy (McCarthy 2000: 234). The economy was characterised by near isolation from the international system and stagnant growth. Foreign firms were the first to feel the effects of the new policy of Burmanisation of the economy. All foreign and private banks were nationalised. Ne Win further stipulated that the state would nationalize the production, distribution, import and export of all major commodities. The overall economic direction meant state ownership of the basic means of production (Steinberg 1982: 77). The wave of nationalisation was so intense and severe that according to Bala, "it resulted in an army dominated state. Even the pan shops were nationalised."[5] Between 1963-1965, all banks, industries and large shops were nationalised (Fink 2001: 32). This policy of economic nationalism, according to Sundhaussen (1995: 775) resulted in 'economic xenophobia'. In May 1964 currency was demonetized (50 kyat and 100 kyat) forcing large amount of cash out of private control. Most of the businesses were run by Indian and Chinese. The regulation of the currency, trade and production restrictions forced hundreds and thousands of Indian and Chinese people leaving the country (Steinberg 1981: 35; 1982: 77-79). Furthermore, the private sector was emasculated both by regulations on private ownership and exclusion of private sector from institutionalised credit and other resources (Than 2007: 144).

In April 1964, the government established a Socialist Economic Construction Committee (SECC). Nationalisation of trade and industry was one of the steps in the construction of a Socialist State. The rapid action of socializing and nationalizing the commercial and industrial sector of the economy produced shortages, rising prices and black markets (Silverstein 1977: 156). By 1966, the economic situation had not improved and dissatisfaction increased. In spite of the articulated goals of centralised planning and nationalisation of means of production and trade, the policy of economic nationalism failed miserably under Revolutionary Council (Steinberg 1981: 36). Corruption expanded with state control, production fell and imports of these commodities dropped. Black market came to be known as 'Corporation 24', as there were 23 other state corporations (Quoted in Steinberg 1981: 37). Private capital had very few legal avenues of economic investment. Smuggling came to play an important role in the economy and the easiest way to make money.

The economy was largely influenced by the decline state of agriculture. While land reform programmes carried through by the regime gave agricultural plots to many landless farmers, but, the farmers were told from now onwards to sell their produce to the government at below market prices. This frustrated the farmers and they started putting less effort in cultivation which resulted in dramatic reduction in the rice exports from the country (Fink 2001). By 1967, there was a serious crisis in the agricultural sector. Exports fell as a result of poor government procurement, and scarcities arose both in foodstuff and household necessities including clothing (Steinberg1981: 36). At the national level, the denial of the market forces and the marginalisation of the private sector impaired the country's robustness for sustained growth. The slow progress of the manufacturing sector, which had absorbed one-third of state investments and yet whose labour productivity was below the national average, aggravated the problems of economic stagnation in the second half of the 1980s (Than 2007: 275). The socio-economic situation continues to deteriorate in Myanmar. According to Than (2015: 453), "since the early 1960s, Myanmar has followed an industrialisation strategy within a state led developmental approach informed by nationalist and socialist ideologies. The centralised planned economy, severely constrained by the denial of private participation and neglect of market forces, until the mid-1980s. High inflation, unsustainable fiscal deficits, increasing illegal trade, mounting debts, persistent balance of payments problems, and harsh administrative reactions to economic problems drove the weak state to the point of bankruptcy."

The military regime tried to reverse the deteriorating socio-economic conditions and introduced several market oriented reforms. The Union of Myanmar Foreign Investment Law was promulgated on 30th November 1988, as The State Law and Order Restoration Council Law No. 10/88, in order to promote all round development of national economy. This has allowed private sector businesses to engage in external trade and to retain export earnings, and started to legitimize and formalize border trade with neighboring countries, hitherto an activity that had been deemed illegal. Following this, "Myanmar's economy was released from the isolationist foreign policy of the quarter-century long Socialist era and began to re-integrate into regional and world markets" (Kudo and Mieno 2007). However, the benefits have accrued primarily to a small privileged elite and have not translated into broad based improvements in the standard of living (Pederson 2005: 163). According to the Myanmar analysts, growing direct foreign investment, strong economic growth, and economic reforms, in Myanmar, has led to inflation. It has outstripped the rate of GDP growth by three to four times, indicating the lack of genuine reforms introduced by the military rulers.

Through this open trade policy, volume of external trade increased substantially in Myanmar. Imports, however, grew more rapidly than the exports resulting in the trade deficits. In spite of the foreign economic sanctions, Foreign Direct Investment (FDI) in Myanmar has significantly contributed to the development and growth of a liberalised neo-patrimonial economic regime. When taking a closer look at the European sanctions towards Burma, it becomes obvious that they have never had an economic impact. The EU implemented an investment ban on Burma but made exceptions for the oil and gas industries, which constitute Burma's most important sector for international investment. French and German oil companies have a major stake in Burmese energy resources. Despite the European arms embargo, their assistance extends to providing technical assistance and advice with regard to military activities.

The country after the 2010 elections is on a drive to attract investment, promoting tourism, timber, gemstones and its vast oil and gas reserves. In this regard, a "Special Economic Zone Law" was passed on January 27, 2011 to attract much-needed foreign capital to an economy held back by decades of sanctions and mismanagement. On January 31, 2013 the Ministry of National Planning and Economic Development released the new detailed regulations under the 2012 Myanmar Foreign Investment Law. The much awaited regulations are provided under two separate notifications, Notification 1/2013 and Notification 11/2013. The new investment law follows a series of reforms undertaken over the past year, including the privatisation of hundreds of state assets, and plans to expand banking, telecommunications, shipping and agricultural sectors. Even Nobel laureate Suu Kyi has appealed for the support of the Burmese cause and establishment of a just political and economic order in Myanmar. It specifically specifies areas restricted for foreigners, joint ventures, and other restrictions related to foreign ownership and environmental impact assessment.

Party Machinery

Although, the Revolutionary Council had a monopoly of power, it needed to win and hold public support. The Council realised this from the beginning that it had to establish contact with the people and win their loyalty if it was to convert its authoritarian rule into a more democratic form (Silverstein 1977: 100). Faced with this dilemma, the Council announced in July 1962 that it was creating a new party to be known as *Burma Socialist Programme Party* (BSPP—*Lanzin* Party in Burmese). In making the announcement the Council expressed the hope that members of the old parties would be able to discard their partisan feelings and come closer for unity and understanding through intimate exchange of views. As the regime began to solidify its control, the civilian parties were pushed into the background. By March 1964, all political parties except the BSPP were finally banned (Steinberg 1981: 31).

The BSPP was to be a transitional party under the leadership of the Revolutionary Council and its purpose was to lead the country towards the ideological goals expressed in the *Burmese Way to Socialism.* At its early stage of development it was to be a cadre party with emphasis upon identifying, indoctrinating members who assist the military rulers in carrying out their programmes (Silverstein 1977: 101). It remained a cadre party until 1971, when it was transformed into mass national party and given the responsibility of drawing up the new constitution and the opportunity to assume the leadership of the nation.

After the dissolution of BSPP, it was replaced by National Unity Party (NUP) which was formed on September 26 1988, through the intervention of the SLORC. The NUP was intended to serve as an electoral vehicle for SLORC in the polls held in 1990. In the polls that followed, NUP captured only ten seats in the Peoples' Assembly of the 485 seats. Subsequently, in the National Convention that was instituted,

NUP participated as the unpopular instrument of the resented military (Leifer 2001: 199). According to Smith (1999: 20), it was in fact, "the former BSPP disguised in new clothes without any serving military members." Allied to the NUP were a number of smaller satellite parties made up of former BSPP supporters. It also inherited the buildings, property and registration lists of the BSPP (Smith 1999: 21). The party had a distinct financial advantage because it was able to take over many of the BSPP offices and equipments for free (Fink 2001: 63). It soon became clear that the regime hoped to engineer the elections of 1990 so that the NUP could have an outright victory.

The Union Solidarity and Development Association (USDA) was formed by the military to woo the masses on September 15, 1993. Although, purportedly a social organisation, USDA was officially headed by General Than Swe and was often used to defend the interests of the regime (Fink 2001: 95). Since its formation in 1993, however, and particularly in recent years the SPDC has been pursuing an internal strategy intended to make it the post-SPDC civilian political vehicle (Smith 1999: 429). The USDA is also taking a greater informal role in local administration. The military is instructed to work in close cooperation with the USDA on irrigation, agriculture, economic issues and transportation in the regions, and central instructions have been for them to be present at all opening ceremonies of dams and bridges and so on, wearing USDA uniforms (Bowman 2007: 8). Although established in 1993, membership of USDA has quickly rose to several million people. According to Bala, "Less educated people were, particularly drawn towards USDA, believing it was really working for the country."[6] However, in several districts peoples' names were simply added to the membership list without ever being consulted. And it was virtually impossible to become a civil servant without first joining the USDA.

The USDA was transformed into Union Solidarity and Development Party (USDP) on 29th March 2010 in the wake of the general elections in November 2010. The state supported political party with strong military ties – USDP grew out of the USDA, which was a regime-created organisation that has received substantial government support since its formation in 1993 (NDI 2010: 5). In the post election politics, USDP has dominated the National Parliament and the state/region assemblies.

The USDP controls well over half the seats in both houses of the national legislature and the opposition parties really have no political role as such (ICG 2011 a: 6). Even the Election Laws declared ahead of the 2010 General elections resulted in the silencing of many of the most prominent opposition voices (NDI 2010: 5). It required political parties to register or in order to remain in existence and compete in the elections.[7] They were allowed to register only if none of their members were currently imprisoned based on a court conviction. As a result, the political parties could register either expelling prominent imprisoned leaders or declining to register. Under those circumstances, leading opposition groups, including the NLD, chose not to register and was disbanded by 7 May, 2010. However, many political parties met the requirement to submit party membership lists and name their candidates before the deadlines (BNI 2011: 4). By the time of the election, 23 parties out of 37 remained to participate in the elections.

The National Democratic Force (NDF) was formed as a breakaway group from Suu Kyi's NLD party, which was forced to disband following its decision not to run in the 2010 elections. As a breakaway faction of NLD which could not take part in the election, the NDF emerged as the major opposition force along with the other ethnic parties. According to its head Than Nyein, "people should approach politics pragmatically as sometimes when the things that we want cannot happen, we need to think about other ways to achieve our main goal—how to contribute to society in a better way" (Mizzima 2010). Although Aung San Suu Kyi had voiced disapproval of the breakaway faction, still it contested elections. The Party believes that ethnic political issues should be resolved alongside democracy and human rights issues. As a result it allied with other political parties and ethnic groups and took part in the 2010 elections. According to its supporters, "the boycott of elections by Aung San Suu Kyi's party is meaningless and will only aid the military government."

Many ethnic politicians saw this election as a rare opportunity to campaign for ethnic rights and democracy. Therefore, they formed new parties to run in the elections.[8] Altogether 16 ethnic parties took part in the election in 2010. Like NLD the nine ethnic parties in the United Nationalities Alliance that won seats in the 1990 polls also boycotted the 2010 elections.[9] As a result, their future now is highly uncertain, and the new government may well consider their activities illegal.

Various kinds of restrictions were imposed by the Union Election Commission (UEC) on campaigns by the political parties. Even the foreign journalist and media were not allowed to cover the elections. International observers were also debarred from monitoring the elections. Campaign environment was highly constrained and many irregularities were observed on Election Day, still they marked an important step forward towards a more democratic state in Myanmar. Although, parliamentary procedures post elections are crippled, they have full faith in the system. Political parties are forward looking and determined to make best use of the limited resources which is available to them. They have decided to take advantage of the small window of political space that was opened for them.

However, hopes were raised when NLD was allowed to register for the April 2012 by-elections. According to a study made by Peace Research Institute, one of the main challenges faced by the political parties in Myanmar is of split and factionalism both at the Union and regional level (Nilsen 2013). This has been a common issue not only for the leading opposition party—NLD, but several ethnic based parties are also confronting it. They have tried to put forward a united opposition against the "total Bamar domination of the future Union *Hluttaw*." (ibid).

Armed Forces

As the army grew and consolidated its political and economic power during the 1950s in the wake of civil war and divisions among nationalist forces, it became more than a pillar of the post colonial state. As Taylor (2005: 15) argues, it became 'state's guarantor and protector' or as Callahan (2001: 429) argues—transformation took place in the role of the 'military as institution' into 'military as government'. It also developed its own ideology for the future direction of the state. This was profoundly influenced by the three interacting forces of—Nationalism, Socialism and Buddhism—which was enshrined in the three critical documents, *The Burmese Way to Socialism*; *The System of Correlation of Man and his Environment*; and the *Constitution of the BSPP* (Steinberg 1982: 35). Each of them complimented the other creating a pattern of socialist policy that continues to be paramount.

Military junta which replaced parliamentary regime through a coup organised by Revolutionary Council on March 2, 1962, abolished the 1962 Constitution and ruled through decree. The populace was completely depoliticized and socialist revolution became the vanguard of state ideology. The Revolutionary Council's rule was charecterised by unprecedented power and autonomy for the state which became synonymous with the ruling military junta. Ruling by decree, the Revolutionary Council was able to impose its authority over the polity (Than 2007: 111, 113).

Ever since the creation of the State Law and Order Restoration Council (SLORC) in September 1988, the Burmese armed forces have been engaged in an ambitious expansion and modernisation programme. Despite the country's chronic economic and social problems, reduced internal security concerns and lack of external threats, this program is continuing under the SLORC's successor, the State Peace and Development Council (SPDC), which was created in November 1997 (Sleth 2001: 1).

Over the past two decades years, the regime made a major effort to expand and modernise Myanmar's military, consistently reserving about 35 per cent of the national budget to this end. After decades of being a small, lightly armed infantry force geared to regime protection and counter-insurgency, Myanmar boasted for a large, reasonably well-integrated, well-armed, tri-service defence force capable of limited conventional military operations. These increased capabilities raise the stakes faced by a hostile neighbour and help act as a deterrent against invasion (Sleth 2008: 281-297).

The militarised State had near total control over all other non-military institutions – from the economic and cultural sector to civil society, industry and media. Even the educational system—both higher and a secondary level and the market forces—the Chamber of Commerce and think tanks were all working under the close supervision of the military. The state engulfed by military was in its pre-modern stage dominated by feudal and patrimonial tendencies. Recognised by class formations which were primarily feudal, the military had cut across all the levels of the society. After the end of the BSPP regime, the country moved towards 'marketisation' which was in stark contrast to the '*Burmanisation*' programme of the Ne Win era. This economic reform carried out by the military junta had given rise to 'crony capitalism'. According to Maung Maung Zarni, 'the pie is to divided amongst the cronies who, inter alia, serve as the generals portfolio managers' (Zarni 2010). Institutionally, since the early 1990s, "the military had its hand in virtually every economic pie, from poultry farms, small factories, real estate, tourism, transportation, construction, rental business of regimental facilities to shipping, power, banking, export and import, agriculture, energy and mining" (ibid). No business entity of commercial significance can operate without being linked to the military, institutionally or to individual commanders, thereby bringing the market forces of the society under the *Tatmadaw's* effective control.

Although, the country has moved towards a civilian government with junta handing over power to the newly elected Government on 30th March 2011, still its grip over the power continues. With a quarter of all seats in national and regional legislatures reserved for serving military officers, and the overwhelming number of USDP candidates, the military has over three-quarters of all seats necessary to enact legislation, marginalizing the small number of genuine opposition or independent members of parliament (HRW 2011). Symbolically, though army has stepped into the background, but the military elites constituting USDP continues to wield authority (Bangkok Post 2011).

Despite the convening of the newly elected Parliament, Myanmar's 'democratically-elected' regime is nothing more than a disguised version of the military dictatorship that has ruled Myanmar for the past five decades (Altsean 2011 a). The military's power rivals that of the President. They hold 25 per cent of reserved legislative seats, ensuring that they can block changes to the constitution (ICG 2011a). The military-dominated Parliament has placed high-ranking SPDC officials at the top of the country's political system (Altsean 2011 a). SPDC PM Thein Sein is the new President. SPDC's former third-in-command Shwe Mann and the junta's Minister of Culture Khin Aung Myint are the Speakers of the People's Assembly and National Assembly respectively. Twenty-six of the 30 newly appointed cabinet Ministers are either retired military officials or outgoing SPDC Ministers. All State and Division Chief Ministers are MPs from the USDP or the appointed military bloc (TNI 2011).

The legislative power of the military has been somewhat weakened, at least on paper, by the USDP's landslide. But, USDP is indeed a disguised form of the military and it is unlikely that the interests of the military and the USDP will diverge significantly. The military also has considerable executive authority, since it appoints one of the presidential/vice-presidential candidates, and the commander-in-chief appoints serving military officers to be the ministers of Defence, Home Affairs and Border Affairs. In addition, the commander-in-chief will have effective control of the National Defence and Security Council (ICG 2011 a). Junta chief Senior-General Than Shwe had revealed that he would personally lead a newly created council called the "State Supreme Council," which will be the most powerful body in the country. The eight-member State Supreme Council is the highest body of the state assuming an advisory role to guide the future governments. Senior-General Than Shwe's leadership over the State Supreme Council will ensure that he retains final say over the military (Mc Coy 2011). The Council comprises of General Than Shwe, Vice Senior-General Maung Aye, *Pyithu Hluttaw* Speaker Thura Shwe Mann, President Thein Sein, Vice President Thiha Thura Tin Aung Myint Oo, former Lt. Gen Tin Aye and other two senior military generals (Irrawady 2011 c). Out of the two Vice Presidents, Sai Mauk Kham is an ethnic Shan. It is believed that here will be no conflict among the new President and the vice-presidents because they represent the same party, the USDP (Irrawaddy 2011 a).

In order to further strengthen the military power, since October 2010, General Than Shwe issued a series of laws designed to maintain the military's grip on power. By enacting these laws before the newly-elected Parliament convened, he ensured the lawmakers had no say with regard to key policy issues that are vital to the military. These include election laws and by-laws passed for restricting parliamentary procedures (Irrawaddy 2011d). A draft law for the military was enacted making it compulsory for all the males and females to serve in armed forces for two years (Altsean 2011a: 3). General Than Shwe signed a law that gives the commander-in-chief of the military the absolute authority to use unlimited "Special Funds" in performing his duties of protecting the Constitution and preserving national sovereignty. It gives the military chief absolute power and discretion in the use of unlimited "special funds" that are not included in the country's defense budget. (Irrawaddy 2011 e). The military budget for the fiscal year 2011-12 was 23.6 per cent of the total budget or 1.3 trillion kyats (US $ 2 bn). Meanwhile the allocation for healthcare was just 1.3 per cent which is equivalent to 99.5 billion kyat ($110 mn). The fund used by the commander-in-chief under the Special Funds Law is over and above those allocated to the military in the defense budget. In addition, the 2011-12 budget allocated 20 billion kyat ($22 million) to the office of the SPDC (ibid).

Country's political reforms are now encroaching on the economic interests of its powerful armed forces (Wall Street Journal 2012). The military, however, has shed some of its businesses through a series of privatisations shortly before the elections that brought the reform-minded Thein Sein to power in 2010. The armed forces have also agreed to receive a smaller-than-usual share of the national budget in January 2012, down to 14 per cent in fiscal 2012-13 from 24 per cent in the previous period.

The power from the junta was handed over to the civilian government after the November 2010 elections but the presence of the military on 25 per cent of the seats alongside 80 per cent of elected seats won by the USDP, which is backed by the ruling junta, means that prospects of a true civilian government has a long road ahead. Although a cosmetic change has occurred towards civilianised democracy, but still, the power is wielded by the armed forces. Above the Parliament exists a President who is not accountable to the Parliament. Above him is a military council—the National Defence and Security Council—and over and above it is the military, which is constitutionally not accountable to the government or to the Parliament. For anything real to change in Myanmar, these structures need to be entirely dismantled.

In spite of the rigid authority structure and the militarised institutions in Myanmar, several forces have operated at various levels, both internally as well as externally for bringing about transition and change in Myanmar. These crisis and contradictions form the subject matter of the next chapter of this book. Various factors responsible for the delayed democracy in the country have also been analysed.

References

1. The cultural elements of the pre-colonial Burma kept the junta's determination to keep things unchanged. They draw on very old anxieties, deeply rooted in their cultural history (Mathews 1999: 79).
2. This was evident in the imposition of modern system of communication, law and order and rational government.
3. The document emphasized five specific characteristics that had been explicit in the Burmese ideological statements. These are as follows:
    1. Their ideas came from several sources—marxist and non-marxist;
    2. It recognized freedom of conscience and religion;
    3. The party was not the leader of any single class but rather a vanguard of all the people except those who exploited others;
    4. Regardless of race of religion, the leadership of the party belonged to the working people;
    5. The Burmese beliefs were not based on a theory of inevitable progress—either unilinear or dialectic—but on the idea of change is something which is constant in all material and non-material things, and men and society could progress or regress depending on their own ideas and endeavours.
4. Based on interview with Bala, '1988 Generation' Student Activist.
5. Based on interview with Bala, '1988 Generation' Student Activist.
6. Based on Interview.
7. Pyithu Hluttaw Election Law, SPDC Law No. 3/2010
8. Some of the main ethnic parties are Shan Nationalities Democratic Party (SNDP), the All Mon Region Democracy Party (AMDP), the Rakhine Nationalities Development Party (RNDP), the Chin National Party (CNP) and the Phalon-Sawaw Democratic Party (PSDP). For details see (TNI 2011: 4).
9. List of ethnic parties that boycotted elections: Arakan League for Democracy, Chin National League for Democracy, Kachin State National Congress for Democracy, Kayah State All Nationalities League for Democracy, Kayin (Karen) National Congress for Democracy, Mon National Democratic Front, Shan Nationalities League for Democracy, United Nationalities League for Democracy and Zomi National Congress (TNI 2011: 4).

Chapter - 5

Delayed Democracy in Myanmar

Internal Crisis and Contradictions

In Myanmar the 2010 elections held after a gap of twenty years has paved the way for a transition from military rule to a supposedly civilian administration and democratic opening. But the fact that the polls were swept by the pro junta political party—Union Solidarity and Development Party (USDP) and its allies exposes the myth of democratisation in Myanmar. In the absence of any clear opposition with National League of Democracy being disbanded, the election has widely been seen as an attempt to legitimize military rule behind a mask of civilian government. Civilian dictatorship sought to be established in the post election Myanmar charecterise an illusion of multi-party democracy at the local and the national level while effectively stripping the legality and efficacy of the elections. The regime alleges that it is preparing for a transition period from military rule to a supposedly civilian administration popularly conceived by the leadership as *Disciplined Democracy*. Various forces and events in the internal politics of Myanmar have created spark for democratisation and liberalisation of the political system. Some of these internal crisis and contradictions have been analysed in this section. These include—role of monks and sanghas; students and protests movements; 1990 general elections and the role of Aung San Suu Kyi and NLD; generational shift in military; role of the civil society; and the introduction of the military roadmap to democracy.

Monks and Sanghas

Buddhism and *Sanghas* are an important political force and source of leadership in the nation. Even during the constitutional period,

U Nu and the AFPFL used Buddhism to build cohesion among their adherents by staging a revival of building and restoring pagodas, holding examinations, and giving prizes for monks who showed exceptional ability in learning and reciting the scriptures (Silverstein 1977: 50). In addition, they strengthened the authority of the religious leaders in the maintenance of discipline in the Buddhist order. U Nu was also establishing himself as the patron of Buddhism (Fink 2001: 26). The revival and propagation of Buddhism antagonised the religious minorities. Despite constitutional protection, the adherents of other faiths felt threatened and secure. Notwithstanding, U Nu's effort to make Buddhism a state religion and attempt to woo other religious minorities, religious issues inflamed the nation (Steinberg 1981: 20).

The *Sangha* has played a central role in organizing opposition to the regime, since all political parties were banned in 1964. The strategy of both Ne Win and SLORC has been to simply repress such organisations (Alamgir 1997: 343). On numerous occasions soldiers have fired upon demonstrations by monks. They have invaded monasteries and pagodas to cleanse the clergy of political elements.

Immediately after seizing power, the Revolutionary Council asked all monks to register with the government, which they refused to do in 1964. The conflict between the government and the monks led finally in April 1965 to the arrest of ninety two monks and an open effort to suppress their political activity (Silverstein 1977: 50-51). For nearly ten years the monks did not take any public stands or offered open resistance to the government. They remained close to the people in the villages and cities and reverted to their more historic role as religious leaders and teachers. Demonstrations against the burial of UN Secretary General U Thant brought monks back into action (Fink 2001: 43). In the riots of December 1974, the monks with the students led the popular response to the brutality of police and soldiers (Alamgir 1997: 343). The event demonstrated that the monks are still a potential source of leadership if the military's hold on power weakens or if the people are pushed too far by the soldiers and civilians who exercise authority.

In 1988, the monks too took part in the demonstrations. Since the beginning of the public protest, monks were on the forefront of demonstration (Mathews 1993: 419). They took over administration of Mandalay and many surrounding villages. People from outlying districts ventured into the city to ask the monks to come out and administer their areas until peace was restored (Fink 2001: 214). Young Monks Association (YMA) of Burma played an important role in the organizing the protests. According to Bruce Mathews (1993: 422), "Buddhism has afforded an essential patience and endurance to its followers in Burma, and this imbues them with a quality of steadfastness that remains undiminished, even if it is not always apparent in daily life."

The Saffron revolution which is supposed to have begun on September 5, 2007 began as a result of attack by junta on a group of monks in Pakokku (Sleth 2008: 281-297; Kingston 2008: 6, 16-17; McCarthy 2008: 298-314). This was in direct violation of Buddhist teachings, something of which the military had long been cognizant, largely due to the massive public support that the clergy holds in Burma. The SPDC has shamed the military as an institution in the eyes of the people and, more importantly, damaged relations with the *Sangha*, the repository of moral authority in Burma. Desperate attempts by the government to brand the protesting monks as convicts and hooligans badly resented (Kingston 2008: 17). Six months after the Saffron Revolution began, the All Burma Monks Alliance (ABMA) continued to boycott Burma's military families, all the while urging the Burmese people to continue resistance against military domination. This resistance has taken several forms. On January 17, 2008 demonstrators in Taungkok, including a handful of monks, attempted to gather near a local market, where they were met with a large number of armed personnel and forced to disperse (Ng May 2008: 26). On the occasion of the anniversary of Burma's Saffron Revolution, the International Burmese Monks Organisation gave the voice to the monks and nuns inside Burma who have been silenced by a cruel military dictatorship. They vowed to keep the struggle for freedom and human rights alive in Burma (IBMO 2008).

Students and Protest Movements

Student activism in Myanmar was a product of a long and illustrious tradition of anti-colonial struggles. The leaders of Burma, military and civil, had sprung from and received their training in nationalist agitation of the 1930s and 1940s. Students had been on the vanguard of the movement (Steinberg 1981: 23). University and high school students played an instrumental role in developing a new political consciousness which combined a commitment to Buddhism with a desire for independence and a progressive form of government (Fink 2001:19). They were an important element of Burma's elite; they knew of their potential role in Burmese society.

The protest by the students against the military coup d'etat in 1962 has been one of the significant demonstrations by this community. The bloody suppression of the student discontent accompanied by the destruction of the Rangoon University Student Union Building demonstrated a willingness to exercise force and symbolised hardening of the regime (Steinberg 1981: 25). Subsequently, the students came to streets on several occasions between 1962 and the late seventies. These include military's handling of U Thant's funeral in 1974; the joint demonstration by the students and workers in 1975 to mark the anniversary of the 1974 workers strike; demonstration in March 1976 to honour the centenary of Thakin Kodaw Hmaing's birth; and attempt to launch '7-7-77 movement' which was the anniversary of the military crackdown on the 1962 student demonstrations (Fink 2001: 42-44; Silverstein 141-144).

From the late 1970s until 1987, fighting continued but there were no more large protests. In 1988, pro-democracy demonstrations broke out nationwide, shattering the silence that had charecterised political life for so many years (Fink 2001: (1) Students, professions and civil servants and even some soldiers took to streets to celebrate their new found freedom. After over six weeks, of public demonstration, the state apparatus became paralysed as unrest spread from Rangoon to major cities and towns all over the country (Than 2007: 340). The military was, however, able to re-establish control in part by promising multi-party elections for a new government.

The demonstrations in September 2007, dubbed the 'saffron revolution' due to the participation of many Buddhist monks, were the most significant civil protests seen in Burma since the ill-fated pro-democracy uprising of 1988 (Sleth 2008: 281). The mass demonstrations of September 2007 in Burma attracted worldwide attention and, in many cases, international condemnation. In contrast to previous protests and demonstrations, technological advances allowed the events to receive widespread media attention and they were well documented by various international organisations (McCarthy 2008: 698). The pro-democracy protests began in September 2007 as the government abruptly hiked fuel prices, pushing up transport fares that triggered a sharp rise in the price of consumer goods. Such public defiance has not been seen for nearly 20 years as the generals usually adopt a zero-tolerance policy towards the slightest criticism. Myanmar's military masters thought the protestors' momentum would eventually die down. However, to their own disappointment, the protests intensified day by day across the country and the issue was whether they will eventually fizzle out, or if this really marks the 'beginning of the end for military rule in Myanmar' (Kingston 2008: 18). The courageous step taken in September 2007 by the peace-loving monks in the streets walking for freedom and chanting the *mantra* of *metta sutta* (unconditional well-being to all) was seen as a sign of extreme crisis in Myanmar. According to Tint Swe, "although, Burma's 'saffron revolution' is down, but not out."[1] It symbolises the weakening grip of junta's top leadership, General Than Shwe over the Burmese as public took to the streets to defy the dictatorial regime. By overturning their alms bowls and refusing to accept donations from the military, the monks were determined to expose the ruthlessness of the military regime (McCarthy 2008: 56).

The sustained international interest since 2007 uprisings have also allowed the monks calls to be heard with greater strength around the world. Over the past several years, International Burmese Monks Organisation has been opened 14 international branches in countries like India, Bangladesh, Sri Lanka and several other countries in West and throughout Southeast Asia (Ng May 2008:57). Since the September uprising, students unions, activists groups and youth wings belonging to NLD have continued spreading underground pamphlets and posters.

NLD and Political leadership of Aung San Suu Kyi

Military junta, by opposing the results of the election, has destroyed its own credibility, which has resulted in pro-democratic movements and demonstrations. "Other than those espousing the extreme hard line in the regime, no one would like to see the main opposition organisation totally excluded" (Win 2007: 22). However, NLD was allowed to continue as a legal political party until the 2010 elections when failing to register, it was disbanded. However, it was allowed to register as a legal political party in the wake of 2012 by-elections. It has now emerged as the largest opposition party with 43 seats and commanding a total of 6.4 per cent seats in Parliament.

The NLD, an organisation as old as Myanmar's current military regime was a loose coalition of anti BSPP, anti-army, pro-change students, veteran politicians and former army officials who had served in, and fallen out of with, the government of Ne Win over previous quarter century and more. According to Taylor (2006: 12), it rose like a phoenix from the ashes of the old socialist order around its charismatic leader Aung san Suu Kyi. As the daughter of national independence hero, General Aung San, Aung San Suu Kyi became a magnet for those opposed to military, thus contributing significantly to the success of NLD in the polls in 1990 (Taylor 2006: 12). Her out-spoken public criticism of the regime and its predecessor, including General Ne Win, drew the ire of SLORC, which attempted to limit the newly found political freedoms of the country. In July 1989, Suu Kyi was placed under house arrest the day after she and her supporters in NLD attempted to demonstrate in Yangon by organizing a mass parallel ceremony to honour General Aung San and other assassinated national leaders (Taylor 2005: 22).

The military and the NLD did not trust each other, especially after the party's leader, Aung San Suu Kyi, became publicly critical of the army and its former leader, General Ne Win. As a result, they sought to undermine each other's position. The military government often used the state-controlled media to openly attack the NLD and its leaders. It also restricted campaigning and other political activities. When opposition party members broke the rules, severe action was taken against them and they were detained for long periods without trial. On its part, the NLD also tried to delegitimize the government domestically and internationally. They tried to expose all the anti-democratic actions taken by the military by distributing anti-government propaganda throughout the country. They also informed the international media and foreign governments of their version of the latest developments within the country. In response, the military government took severe action against the NLD (Hlaing 2005: 239). Confrontation between the army and the NLD reached a climax when Aung San Suu Kyi was placed under house arrest in July 1989.

The 1990 elections was one of the significant events in the transition process in Myanmar. Although more than 90 political parties contested the 1990 elections, only the NLD, the National Unity Party (NUP) and the Shan National League for Democracy (SNLD) remained active. Among them, the NUP, which was labeled as the government-backed party, acted neither as an opposition party, nor as a ruling party. It merely functioned within the framework of the rules and regulations adopted by the junta and rarely criticized the government. The NLD and the SNLD, on the other hand, functioned like major political parties (Hlaing 2005: 239). The fact, however, is that the presence of Aung San Suu Kyi is seen as the single biggest deterrent to any feeling of long-term confidence the military regime might have. The military junta feared that if she had the opportunity to present and explain herself to the Burmese public, latent popularity would revive. It was widely assumed that if anything untoward happened to her, the result would be an uprising on the scale of 1988, possibly leading to political spasm (Mathews 1998: 22).

Generational Transition in the Military

At the centre of continuing tension within the military leadership is the issue of transferring power to the next generation of officers. A new generation in the military is coming to the fore (Win 2007: 27). According to Larry Jagan (2006: 36), "there were clear signs that a new younger officer class was being groomed to succeed the old men currently in charge." With the two top generals advancing in age and declining in health, the prospect of a generational transition in the military leadership cannot be very far in the future, thus increasing the stakes of the current state of play in the internal competition. Many private institutions for advanced education have sprung up and the younger generation is eagerly reaching for modern skills (Clapp 2007: 12). "The regime's top generals have also taken keen interest about the need to transfer power within Myanmar's military leadership to the next or younger generation."[2]

There are, however, extreme elements within the establishment who would like to return to a neo-authoritarian system, but there are also other elements who oppose this and who are unhappy with unfettered authoritarianism. This is quite a positive sign for future of democratisation in Myanmar. There is also a necessity that with the passage of time the army should provide satisfactory career paths for officers as they seek advancement (Taylor 2006:17). This places inevitable pressure on the top leadership to give way to those rising from below. "Most military regimes, lacking mechanisms for orderly succession, fail to manage this dilemma satisfactorily" (*ibid*). In the new era of transition in Myanmar, General Than Shwe has handed over power to the next generation of leaders (ICG 2011 a:15). This offers a larger avenue for critical thinking and openness in Myanmar.

Civil Society

Before a future democracy can take root and be meaningful to local communities, it is necessary to transcend the barriers created by the cultural and structural legacy of repressive, autocratic rule, and build a more vibrant civil society (Pederson 2005: 170). At the societal level, economic development, industrialisation, and urbanisation have worked together to create and strengthen interest groups and voluntary associations (Shin 1995: 152). Many of these organisations and associations, which are considered as the building blocks of democracy, became alternative sources of information and communications. They directly challenged authoritarian regimes by pursuing interests that conflicted with those of the regime and eroded the capacity of authoritarian rulers to dominate and control their societies. But, the total domination by the military of the 'State' left no space for political and civil society in Myanmar (Alagappa 2001: 493).

In the post Cold war era when the values of democratisation and civil society were being promoted by much of the international community, the political relationships and language inside Myanmar were still very loosely charted (Smith 1999: 424). Annihilation of contending political forces and its extensive surveillance and intimidation networks that penetrate and control society through fear and coercion was extensive. According to Muttaiah Alagappa, "civil society framework in Indonesia may well be under the stage of transition phase whereas in the case of Myanmar, they are still in the liberalisation phase. Civil society groups there are still seeking to carve out spaces in various spheres of public life."[3] Zaw Win Aung who works for the Federation of Trade Union of Burma argues that "GONGOs, or government-organised non-governmental organisations, are prominent in Myanmar. The largest and most prominent of these organisations are youth, child welfare and women organisations, largely controlled by military generals' wives."[4] Organisations such as the USDA, the Myanmar Red Cross Association and the Auxiliary Fire Brigade, for example, have been organised as 'auxiliary forces' of the *Tatmadaw*, while other 'NGOs' such as the Myanmar Maternal and Child Welfare Association and the Myanmar Medical Association are located under the umbrella of the *Tatmadaw*, through the patronage of senior military personnel and their spouses, for the purpose of 'national defence' (ICG 2000: 25).

During the 1988 public demonstration, however, there was a flowering of all kinds of independent civil society groups and media outlets that reflected a release from stringency of authoritarian rule. Since then, there has been a growth in NGO activities of various kinds; both indigenous and international NGOs have mushroomed. They supplement state-provided services, or offer services that the state has found it impossible to provide. These groups assist the people to improve the quality of their lives and the state to achieve some of its longer range social plans (Steinberg 2006: 156-157). With the military losing its grip on surveillance and population control, there is now more space for civil society to expand its own organisational base especially in the present era of transition. They have begun to take more control of villages and neighborhoods. Some of this is already apparent in neighborhoods and villages, where self-help organisations are relatively widespread (Clapp 2007: 26-27). There is evidence that since 1988, there has been a growth in civil society in Myanmar (Fink 2001; South 2004; Alagappa 2004; Hlaing 2004).

The first beginning of civil society emergence, according to Christina Fink was "during this chaotic, violent and exciting time of 1988" (2001: 58). After the retreat of the soldiers, independent organisations sprang-up everywhere. "Artists actors and civil servants and housewives organised unions and marched in the streets. Large group of people resigned from the BSPP and other military controlled organisations, holding 'bonfires' where membership cards were thrown into fires in front of local BSPP offices" (*ibid*). Since several groups were organised everywhere to denounce the government, maintenance of law and order became rather difficult. In order to handle the daily affairs regarding security and food distribution, several committees were set-up which was usually run by teachers, lawyers, doctors and intellectuals. In many places monks also played the leading role. According to Soe Myint, "Although civil societies are working at a meek level, but still we find a network of journalists, humanitarian groups and environmentalists are working in close cooperation with neighbouring countries. Even Pagodas and house tuitions are acting as mobilizing agencies."[5]

The emergence of civil society and mass students led demonstrations in Myanmar in 1988, jolted the military that had ruled the country since 1962 compelling the leadership to organize multi-party elections (Alagappa 2004: 3). This emergence is a complex phenomenon, owing much to the political space created by the ceasefire process since 1989 (South 2004: 246). Besides, the increased presence of international NGOs (INGOs) and partial opening of the economy in the early 1990s are among other factors responsible for the 're-alignment of state and civil society relations' during this period (*ibid*). Confidential advocacy with national, state and local authorities has helped to build a more protective environment, especially in the fields of control and reduction of HIV/AIDS issues, trafficking and child rights. Examples of these include the establishment of an inter-agency government committee to stop recruitment and facilitate demobilisation of child soldiers and International Committee of the Red Cross (ICRC) and UNHCR training programs for police and other government employees (South 2007). Many of them are also involved in the Community Development Programmes, Empowerment of Youth for Development and Urgent Recovery Programme for Cyclone Nargis affected area.[6] In the field of humanitarian development, numerous CSOs are engaged in areas such as welfare of women, proper care and nourishment of under five children, income generation activities and vocational training. A large number of organisations are also focusing on Civic Education Programmes, Youth leadership, capacity building and creating awareness about the long standing political stasis, unbalanced development, unending armed conflict and sustainable development.[7]

Hlaing (2004: 389) on the other hand, argues that most of these organisation, to which he refers as 'Social Movement Organisations' (SMOs), that emerged after the "8888 Democratic Movement", were not the organisations that emerged after the breakdown of the socialist government. These groups, formal and informal, were those that survived the military's cleansing campaign (ibid: 390). These are largely, welfare and development oriented, as against explicitly, political.

Ever since 1988, most of the civil society networks have begun to expand in the non-government controlled areas as a result of the mounting insurgent groups, fighting for democracy in Myanmar (South 2004: 244-245). Ironically, the decline of the old insurgent paradigm opened the space for the emergence of new and more participatory forms of social and political organisation among opposition ethnic nationality communities.[8] In the 1990s a number of local NGOs were organised by Chin, Kachin, Shan, Lahu, Karenni, Karen, Tavoyan, Mon and all Myanmar student and youth, women's environmental and human rights groups in the border areas (*ibid*: 245). These began to occupy the political space created by the declining influence of mainstream armed groups.[9] In the wake of the 2010 elections, many of these CSOs were involved in providing training and awareness campaigns in the rural as well as the border areas (*ibid*). Since the regime failed to provide voter education training to ordinary citizens, the gap was filled by the Burmese NGOs and INGOs such as Myanmar Egress, the Vahu Development Institute, Shalom Foundation, and various political parties. This was done under the name of 'capacity building initiatives' because they want to avoid problems with the regime.[10]

Representing new models of organisation, these networks constituted one of the most dynamic aspects in an otherwise bleak political scene. The emergence of civil society networks is not in itself sufficient to bring about national level political transition. This will require concerted and explicit political actions. The challenge according to Karl Dorning (2006: 209), therefore, "is the creation of what could be called an 'enabling framework' for civil society which must ensure trust, transparency, openness, accountability and modes of operation."

Delayed Democracy in Myanmar

Although there has been a cosmetic change in Myanmar since 2010, but even after more than forty-nine years of army rule, political power in Myanmar still remains in the hands of the ruling junta. Noted military analyst, Mary Callahan observes persistence of military rule in Myanmar is largely due to the "comparative durability of the *Tatmadaw's* (military) command relationship with its society."

Since 1962 military coup, *Tatmadaw* have come to dominate state and society for more than four decades (Callahan 2001: 413, 416; May Ng 2008: 58). Democratisation continues to be at a farce with a military apparatus clinging on power through democratic facade denying legitimacy to a popularly elected Parliament. This section, in particular, highlights the following factors for delayed democracy in Myanmar.

The military regime managed to severely damage the organisational capacity of the pro-democracy movement, but it was not able to a build a prosperous nation. The 'saffron revolution' brought to light, the fact that the generals have lost an enormous amount of legitimacy by committing violence against the very institution they are meant to support and whose traditions they promote, the *Sangha* (McCarthy 2008). The new constitution which took 16 long years to complete has replaced the SPDC regime based on the result of Constitutional Referendum held in May 2008 and the November 2010 General Elections. Characterised by ethnic conflict, economic stagnation and political oppression, Myanmar has been unable to achieve—the ideal of peaceful, happy and prosperous society. Antagonism to democratisation still thrives in the country. Ethnic insurgencies and communal violence has posed fears for democratic transition in Myanmar.

Economic Mismanagement

Chief among the internal factors weighing on the military leadership is the abysmal state of the economy. Burma's reliance on imported fuel, its energy shortages, trade deficits, the huge cost of maintaining its unprofitable state-owned enterprises, and many other deficiencies resulting from decades of inept military management have left the economy in a constant state of instability and uncertainty (Clapp 2007: 12). Although, the SLORC-SPDC regime tried to reverse the deteriorating socio-economic situation, which saw Myanmar designated as "Least Developed Country" by the United Nations in 1987 and led to a popular uprising in 1988, the benefits of new market economic reforms, however, have accrued primarily to a small privileged elite and have not translated into broad based improvements in the standard of living (Pederson 2005: 163).

Existence of an 'extra legal economy', at least as large as the 'formal economy' has posed a significant challenge for the regime transition in Myanmar (ICG 2000: 19). According to the US State Department's International Narcotics Control Strategy Report, Myanmar continues to be the world's largest source of illicit opium and heroin, although production and cultivation began to decline from 1997. The report identified money laundering in Myanmar and the reinvestment of narcotics profits laundered elsewhere as 'significant factors in the overall Burmese economy'. Added to this was the country's underdeveloped banking system and lack of enforcement against money laundering which has created a 'business and investment environment conducive to the use of drug-related proceeds in legitimate commerce (Quoted in ICG 2000: 19-20)

The clearest indicator of the economic plight of ordinary people in Myanmar is reflected in the escalating cost of rice, the staple that makes that 50 per cent of the consumption expenditure of an average family (Maung 1997: 507). For several years, inflation has greatly outpaced increases in wages and other income opportunities, thus, eroding the purchasing power of many households. This situation was compounded in 2003 by a major banking crisis and new US economic sanctions, which disrupted trade, caused widespread job losses in cities, and resulted in a significant contraction of overall economic activity (Pederson 2005: 163). Under increasing strain and extreme conditions, many affected families have migrated in countries across the borders to Thailand, India etc.

Democratisation may be the likely satisfactory answer in dealing with deep-seated economic problems in Myanmar. For any economic reform programme to be successful and sustainable the political structures must be changed first. In other words, economic reform requires a transition to democracy because cronyism, nepotism, and stop-and-go policy cycles, as evident in Indonesia, could derail the reform process. National task of economic revival, argues Oo and Grieg (1999: 131), is more likely to succeed under a democratic political framework due to several reasons. First, for any austerity measures to produce results, the government needs to restrain expenditure and increase revenue. Democratisation can facilitate stabilisation because a democratic regime may help reduce the economic burden of unproductive spending and limit the scope "for *ad hoc* decision-making, for rent seeking, for undesirable preferential treatment of individuals or organisations." Second, the implementation of economic reforms must be underpinned by the credibility and trust that only a democratic regime can provide. Tough stabilisation measures and economic reforms incur social costs and only a regime enjoying the confidence of its citizens stand a chance of sustaining the process. Third, mobilising domestic and foreign private capital is a critical component of economic recovery. Sustaining the private capital flows and creating a climate conducive to investment requires the rule of law, transparency in public administration, and above all, political stability (Oo and Grieg 1999: 131).

Myanmar government today generates less than 3 per cent of GDP in revenue, one of the lowest levels in the world. This greatly limits its capacity to carry out necessary social investments, and contributes to corruption and other violations of human rights. In fact, the pressure for market economic reforms from the international financial institutions could make the situation worse (Pederson 2005: 169). Politically, the extra-legal economy is also causing problems for Myanmar's neighbours, with both Thailand and India expressing public concern over the export of drugs from Myanmar to their territories (ICG 2000: 20). Steinberg (2005: 94) argues that there has been virtual uniformity of opinion on needed changes in economic policy and performance in Myanmar.

Refusal to accept the Popular Mandate

Prospects for democratic and social consolidation in Myanmar seemed to be imminent in 1990 in the wake of multi-party elections. But, the refusal of the military junta to accept the popular mandate dismissed all hopes of early transition in Myanmar. In May 1990, multiparty elections were held for a new National Assembly as per the promise of the new regime. According to ICG Report (2000), "the primary motivation appears to have been the resumption of Western aid cut off after the 1988 coup; it was also apparently assumed that no single party of the plethora of new opposition parties could win a workable majority and that the SLORC-sponsored National Unity Party would be the dominant party." But, in the result that followed, NLD, the major opposition party achieved a landslide victory –led by Aung San Suu Kyi, the daughter of the independence hero and 'martyr', General Aung San, who had been assassinated in 1947. With

52.9 per cent of the vote, the NLD won 392 seats out of 485 in the new assembly – as against ten seats for the NUP with 25 per cent of the vote.

With the victory of NLD change seemed in the offing (Fink 2001: (1) But the regime refused to transfer power and instead began arresting some of those who had been elected including their leader Aung San Suu Kyi. The people of Burma demonstrated their desire to restore democracy and basic human rights by pushing for a political opening towards a democratic transition, which the military regime has resisted at all cost by suppressing the implementation of the popular mandate (Oo and Grieg 1999: 93). Military junta, by opposing the results of the election, destroyed its own credibility, which resulted in pro-democratic movements and demonstrations as a whole (Win 2007: 22).

The relationship between the NLD and the army has always been fraught with hostility. Thus, the military and the NLD did not trust each other, especially after the party's leader, Aung San Suu Kyi, became publicly critical of the army and its former leader, General Ne Win. As a result, they sought to undermine each other's position (Hlaing 2005: 239). Shortly after the election, the SLORC declared that the elections were not for a Parliament that would itself legislate or form a government but simply for a constituent assembly which had the task of drafting a new constitution, thus, rejecting the popular mandate (ICG 2000: 4). The recent November 2010 'controlled' elections organised by the 'Junta' have also been charecterised as a sham and an attempt to establish a *disciplined* democracy controlled by the military under the façade of electoral democracy and civilian rule.

Though, the November 7, 2010 elections held after a gap of twenty years has paved the way for a transition from military rule to a supposedly civilian administration and democratic opening in Myanmar. But the fact that the polls were swept by the pro junta political party—Union Solidarity and Development Party (USDP) and its allies exposes the myth of democratisation in Myanmar. The Electoral Laws of 2010 was in itself discriminatory and further perpetuated authoritarianism. The Burmese electoral process itself was an enormous task to ensure military dominance. Its ingredients were rigged electoral laws interpreted by a pro-military electoral commission. It laid down that parties must declare that they will "safeguard the Constitution."[11] As a serious human rights violation, the Constitution lays down that the President is above the Law;[12] it further provides for impunity for past crimes by government officials;[13] and a total suspension of "fundamental rights" during indefinite and undefined states of emergency.[14]

The Law also authorised the election commission to withhold elections in areas deemed to be "insecure."[15] This dashed the hopes of ethnic-based parties to contest and win in border regions where they have strong constituencies (Than 2010). This is particularly discriminatory against members of the Rohingya ethnic minority, who are already denied citizenship. Rohingyas were issued temporary identification cards, which allowed them to vote—but which do not afford them citizenship (according to the new Election Laws) (Amnesty International 2010). This subsequent provision suggested that they could not contest elections and serve in the legislatures.

The technical regulations published by Union Election Commission in Myanmar for political parties favoured wealthy and elite candidates (Aung 2010; ICG 2010). The party registration regulations stipulate that all political parties have to register by filing a 300,000 kyat fee (US $300). It further lays down that parties may spend a maximum of 10 million kyat ($10,000) for each candidate running for a seat in parliament. The expenditure can come from either the party's funds or from a candidate's private funds. In one of the poorest countries in the Southeast Asian region, such a policy favours elite, well-off candidates who could benefit by greater access to advertising and organizing meetings with voters. According to many Myanmar analysts, these processes are likely to be deeply flawed, and seem to be aimed mainly at consolidating military rule behind the facade of a parliamentary government.

Twenty three out of 37 registered parties participated in the election, including parties representing all major ethnic groups. The Government launched a sustained and conscious effort and carried out media campaign to persuade people of their "duty" to vote. Non-participation by the NLD, the Karen National Union (KNU), SNLD and some other groups associated with the NLD, was a significant negative factor for the electoral process. Moreover, 2,200 political prisoners remained in custody, despite reports that there would be a general amnesty before the elections. The exclusion of sensitive areas from voting in a few border regions meant quite a number of people could not vote and the voting process was far from inclusionary.

In the absence of any clear opposition with National League of Democracy being disbanded, the election has widely been seen as an attempt to legitimize military rule behind a mask of civilian government. International reaction also seems to be split-up in between its neighbours and supporters in the region and the critics in the Western World. Civilian dictatorship sought to be established in the post election Myanmar would charecterise an illusion of multi-party democracy at the local and the national level while effectively stripping the legality and efficacy of the elections. It has dashed all hopes for democratic change in Myanmar. The election though, was just a sham to adopt the new Constitution as drafted by the National Convention. The regime alleges that it is preparing for a transition period from military rule to a supposedly civilian administration popularly conceived by the leadership as *Disciplined Democracy*.

Ethnic Conflict

Restoring democracy in the country has likelihood that the peripheral minorities will get a better deal from the Centre. The successful management of centre-periphery (ethnic) conflicts requires institutional structure for bargaining for the assertion and resolution of demands.[16] The practice of managing inter-communal relations through normal administrative channels symbolizes neglect by the centre of the claims of distinctive status and the special problems of the peripheral communities, to organize politically, or in extremes, to mount insurgencies in order to enhance their negotiating position. In their aspirations for national unity, those in control of the centre prefer to treat all their subjects following the methods and criteria used for the dominant community (Burmans). This, however, is seldom satisfactory to the peripheral people. It requires a consensual arrangement such as the establishment of formal and informal institutions for regulating communal relations, thus, legitimizing pluralism. Democratisation requires an acceptance and a commitment to respect pluralism reflecting the diversity of religious affinity, provincial identity, as well as linguistic and ethnic origin. Five decades of continuous conflict, compounded by the often confrontational positions assumed by both the military governments and pro-democracy forces since 1990, culminating in the September 2007 attack on monks and pro-democracy demonstrators, have created atmosphere of alienation, distrust and a lack of basic understanding and empathy. These conflicts, according to Pederson (2005: 167), are a result of racial, ethnic and religious tensions, reinforced by an intensifying struggle over scarce resources.

Although, Myanmar faces a complexity of challenges today, it is the question of national reconciliation and ethnic inclusiveness which is most noteworthy in the process of democratic reform. In this respect, changes in the ethnic landscape have been most significant since the SLORC-SPDC assumed power in 1988. Martin Smith (1999: 39) attributes these changes to two major developments—first, an ethnic ceasefire movement that was instituted by the military government in 1989; and second, the 1990 elections in which nineteen ethnic minority parties also won seats, forming the second largest block of pro-democracy parties after NLD. It is important to note that the cease-fires were accepted by the various ethnic organisations in part because they promised a process of economic development and political dialogue. Bruce Mathews (2001: 11) alleges that, "regrettably there is little of the former and none of the latter. This will likely compromise the integrity and durability of the cease-fires."

Military dictatorship and human rights violations have destroyed the myth of the unity between various ethnic communities in Myanmar. Until democracy is re-established, there will be disunity, warfare and economic decline in Myanmar. The minorities have concluded that their future lies in union with the Burmans and not outside (Silverstein 2004). They are willing to lay down their weapons and join the Burmans in forming a viable federal state, based on equality, autonomy and self-determination. They want modernisation and development to come to their areas and people, but on terms they can accept and live with. Both the Burmans and the minorities want to see the military return to the barracks, leaving politics to civilian elected representatives.

Under the 2008 new state constitution, all armed forces in the union are to come under the command of the government's Defense Services. Ethnic ceasefire organisations are currently under heavy pressure to join the electoral process and hand over control of their military wings to the government as part of a new Border Guard Force. While some have agreed to participate others are stepping up military preparations in light of increasing military pressure from the Burmese army (Mizzima 2010). However, this concept of BGF has been abrogated and a new process of political dialogue and reconciliation has begun (elaborated in the next chapter).

Military Purges and Strategies

Most attention focuses on power struggles within the uppermost reaches of the regime. Until the 2004 sacking of Secretary-1 General Khin Nyunt, along with nearly all the senior officers closely associated with him, regime affairs reportedly were widely explained through a unilateral power struggle between Khin Nyunt and State Peace and Development Council (SPDC) Vice-Chair, Maung Aye. According to Mary Callahan (2007: 37), "the intransigent latter was said to counter every 'baby step' by Khin Nyunt at least marginally in the direction of reform, including the dialogue with Aung San Suu Kyi and the negotiation of cease-fire arrangements with more than 20 former rebel organisations." With the sidelining of Khin Nyunt, so-called hard-liners are said to have resoundingly defeated the soft-liners. After the defeat of Khin Nyunt, the struggle was said to pit Maung Aye against his boss, junta chair, Senior General Than Shwe who had spent 13 years as Than Shwe's deputy and was thought to be aspiring to ascend to the top position (Callahan 2007: 37; Jagan 2006: 33).

A second set of intra-military tensions that has received ample attention in the past has been tensions rooted in the enormous power and influence that regional commanders have attained in the past 20 years. In charge of all military and administrative affairs in their regions, they at times have acted like incipient war-lords, particularly in the early 1990s. While they remain very powerful, the junta and the War Office in Yangon have established formal and informal mechanisms to rein them in, starting in the early 1990s with moves to require regional commanders to serve as members of the junta and, subsequently, regular reassignments of regional commanders to War Office and Cabinet positions. Several major reshuffles have occurred since then, without producing any significant challenges to the regime. Although, the regional commanders remain powerful, the junta chair retains ultimate authority.

General Than Shwe's approach is largely drawn from his mentor, Burma's former strongman General Ne Win (Jagan 2006: 33). Frequent purges were a major characteristic of his rule. Over the past few years there has been a growing division within Burma's military leadership on how to maintain army's political role in the future development of the country. Than Shwe's approach in recent years has been to revitalise the army and strengthen the military. This is in contrast to the view of the state, where army plays second fiddle to a civilian administration. This has been institutionalised in the draft constitution, according to which, the President must be a military top general, while the defense minister must also be an army commander (Constitutional Principles Approved by the National Convention 2008). General Than Shwe is also renounced for being cautious and xenophobic, as well as authoritarian. In 2004, he ordered all senior commanders in the army to learn how to use computers and access computers.[17] This is all part of Than Shwe's vision to revitalize the army and ensuring that it has an enduring role in Burma's political life.

Despite overwhelming support for Aung San Suu Kyi and NLD military junta has been able to cling on power largely because of the system of surveillance and intrusiveness. The "house check system" is one of the most infamous strategies of the military."[18] This system ensures that every household must register their members and visitors with the local authority. They can also come for random checking in the middle of the night. Mathews (1998: 15), alleges that there are several military intelligence units and often the civilian's travel between Myanmar's fourteen states and divisions are monitored.

An analysis of the factional struggles in the post independence Burma has led Hlaing (2008: 149-177) to conclude that regime transformation has taken place only in the absence of a powerful hegemonic figure at the apex of the state. The existence of a hegemon, who is able to mediate between factions, yields a good possibility of a stable government. Conversely, the absence of such a hegemon results in an unstable government (*ibid*: 176-177). Internal factionalism and conflict was one of the main reasons for the establishment of military caretaker government in 1958—rift in between AFPFL stable and clean faction.

Until 1952, there was no real opposition party in the Parliament. The Burma Worker's and Peasant's Party (BWPP) formed in 1950 assumed the role of opposition after the first general election held in 1951-52 (Silverstein 1977: 27). After the second general election in 1956, a more durable opposition in the name of National Unity Front (NUF) emerged in the Parliament. But, in Myanmar, the concept of legal opposition was relatively new and was often resisted. The parties sought to monopolise power and eliminate the opposition (Fink 2001: 24). The armed forces are a loyal and disciplined ally to the regime in everyday life. Despite rumours of inner-cabinet struggle and possible intrigue among the regional commanders, the regime has shown a considerable durability (Mathews 1998: 13). According to Martin Smith (1999: 424), "although, there are deep differences of opinion between senior commanders, but they make sure they never develop into conflicts of interest. This is the key to their system."

Internally, the purge of General Khin Nyunt and his supporters has exposed strong fault lines within the military leadership that were previously blurred by the trilateral balance of power. The competition between the faction of the senior ranks aligned with Senior General Than Shwe and that aligned with his deputy General Maung Aye is quite perceptible, but it is not strong enough to threaten the stability of the regime. The dissent in the military has also been exposed by a new documentary called "Burma Soldiers." The 4, 00,000 strong army in Myanmar is although, known for its cohesion, cemented by a system of rewards and punishment, has shown signs of rupture. "There are many soldiers serving in the military who secretly support the opposition but, cannot expose their feelings" (Mydans 2011). Since these soldiers come from the lower strata of society who need to earn money for their daily survival and steady employment and status it offers, they do not have any option, but to silently cooperate with the ruling junta. This silent majority has contributed to the growing cohesion in the military with little sign of dissent in its ranks. These soldiers who shot down civilians in pro-democracy demonstrations in 1988 and 2007 in Myanmar were drawn from distant battlefields where they had been fighting separatist ethnic armies. According to Myo Mint, "they are uneducated and do not understand politics" (ibid). "They are told that everyone who supports the demonstrations and opposes the government are enemies of the people and that they have the right to kill these people."

There are also reports of infantrymen from Yangon and Bago divisions participating in the celebration of Ms Suu Kyi regaining her freedom on November 13 (BBC 2010). "We went there to greet her because we believe the hardships the lower rank and file is facing can be solved if Ms Suu Kyi and the military commanders work together. We have high hopes for Ms Suu Kyi," a soldier told the BBC Burmese service (ibid). It follows reports in September, 2010 that soldiers in many areas were refusing to carry out routine tasks in protest at short rations and lack of access to their pay. In a series of BBC interviews, soldiers in garrison towns said their rations had been cut for weeks. In spite of these instances, Burmese authorities have denied any disquiet in the military. According to Tint Swe, "As a result, of isolation of junta, existence of fractions and splits within the regime is not visible. In spite of disagreements within the regime, the chances of military revolt in Burma are doubtful."[19]

The Closed Media

Media in Myanmar has seen a complete 'U-turn beginning with the complete press freedom during the era of Parliamentary democracy under U Nu. Myanmar had one of the least restrictive and relatively sophisticated press environments in Asia before independence. But, the restrictive press laws invoked since the military coup of 1962 forced the government to shut down private publications. Myanmar is ranked 151 out of 179 nations in the world Press Freedom Index 2013, marking Myanmar as one of the few most press-restrictive nations in the world.

The roots of Burmese press freedom date to the colonial era when several newspapers played a significant role in the rise of the nationalist movement in the 1920s. There were around three dozen newspapers, including English, Chinese and Hindi dailies under a civilian government. Journalists were free to set up relations with international press agencies. The establishment of military rule under Ne Win in 1962 led to the establishment of a completely restricted and highly controlled media regime in Myanmar. When General Ne Win seized power in March 1962, one of his first steps was to establish the draconian Printers and Publishers Registration Act, which, required the approval by a censor of anything that is written and distributed in the country, including all books, magazines, other periodicals, song lyrics, and motion picture scripts before it was printed and circulated. The government also created the Press Scrutiny Board to oversee the process of censorship. The Press Scrutiny and Registration Department (PSRD) and the authoritarian model of mass media brought about a total control over the press freedom in Myanmar. The government retained strict control over TV and radio as well. In 1985, the Ministry of Communications, Posts, and Telegraphs enacted a special Television and Video Law that required compulsory licensing of TV sets, video machines, and satellite television. While it was more difficult to get access to foreign TV channels, those in Myanmar still had limited access to Burmese-language broadcasts of BBC Radio and Voice of America.

After the 1988 people's uprising, the junta introduced more media restrictions such as the 1996 Television and Video Act, the 1996 Computer Science Development Act, the 2002 Wide Area Network Order and the 2004 Electronics Transactions Law. Time and again activists and international community had advocated the government to repeal restrictive laws including the 1962 Printers and Publishers Registration Act and the 2004 Electronics Act–described as vague and draconian legislation that has been used to jail journalists and curb Internet freedoms. The government was more successful in taking advantage of the 'old media model,' which was relatively easy to control. The government could achieve this through strict oversight, nationalisation of media outlets, and strict censorship laws. There are numerous accounts of journalists who have been jailed, tortured, killed, or exiled using the 1962 Printers and Publishers Registration and 1985 Television and Video Law.

However, with respect to online media, the case is different. The Internet allowed users to become creators of content instead of just consumers of information. With the emergence of the Internet during the early 1990s, the military government's media policies began to evolve in reaction to the challenges posed by the online environment. With no easy way to stop the information flow in cyberspace, the military government began to actively promote its own views online. Exiled media in this regard played a significant role in dissemination of information to the outside world and exposing the true character of the regime. Nonetheless, internet slowdowns, cyber attacks and tampering have been a common instrument of the military regime.

The recent and relative opening of the Burmese regime has resulted in information being more freely circulated on the Internet, despite continued close monitoring. The international community and Burmese human rights activists need to remain vigilant and keep striving for more freedom. Local journalists say the battle for true media freedom in Myanmar is far from over. While they no longer have to submit the articles to the state's Press Scrutiny and Registration Board, they can still be punished if what they write which offends the powerful. However, notwithstanding the reforms, the Press Scrutiny and Registration Board still exist. The Electronics Act, which was used to prosecute journalists and bloggers, also remains in force.

In a major reform initiative, the government has abolished pre-publication censorship of the country's media after a span of nearly five decades. The new regime in August 2012 announced that the news and religious publications would no longer be required to submit stories for review to state censors before publication, ending one part of its decades-old grip on information. President Thein Sein's reformist government has significantly relaxed media controls over the last two years, thus, allowing reporters to print material that would have been unthinkable during the era of absolute military rule.

There are now some positive signs of momentum in the country. Journalists who were once forced to write about their country from exile are now welcome to travel to Myanmar and to interview its leaders. One of the main opposition news websites, Mizzima.com, now has a Rangoon office and prints a magazine distributed inside Myanmar, M-ZINE. Photos of opposition leader Aung San Suu Kyi – long banned – and articles that report approvingly on her National League for Democracy are now daily affair. Another positive development has been that foreign journalists who once had to sneak around Myanmar on tourist visas are now welcomed and given remarkable access to decision-makers. In another significant move, the Associated Press has become the first international news agency to open a bureau in Myanmar.

Privately run newspapers hitting newsstands in the streets for the first time in five decades has created history and opened a new chapter in the transition from authoritarianism to democracy in Myanmar. The government announced in December 2012, that any Myanmar national wishing to publish a daily newspaper was welcome to apply and could begin publishing from April 1. As a result of this move four private dailies have gone on sale for the first time in fifty years in Myanmar. This has opened a new door for media in Myanmar. Nonetheless, in the name of freedom of press the country faces innumerable challenges due to underdeveloped and immature media practices. Besides, there are significant bottlenecks such as those related to distribution rights, poor infrastructure facilities, outdated printing equipment, advertising and editorial issues. This act as a significant caveat for comprehensive media reform and before freedom of press becomes a reality in Myanmar.

It was under this background of delayed democratic practices that the regime remained in isolation for half a century. The seven point roadmap to democracy (elaborated in chapter-3) and the multi-party elections in November 2010 set the stage ready for democratic transition and change in Myanmar. This has been elaborated in the next chapter with a focus on the reform agenda of the new regime.

References

1. Based on Tint Swe's lecture in School of International Studies, JNU on October 30, 2007. Tint Swe is a NLD MP staying in exile in New Delhi.
2. Based on Interview with Soe Min, correspondent, Democratic voice of Burma.
3. Based on an interaction with Muttaiah Alaggapa, December/January, 2005-06 at Centre for Policy Research, New Delhi.
4. Based on interview with Dr Zaw Win Aung, Chief of Bureau, Democratic Voice of Burma and Federation of Trade Union, Burma.
5. Interview with Soe Mynt, Editor, Mizimma News.
6. Based on interaction with Nan Mya Thida, who is an ethnic Karen and an Advisor of Karens' student Centre, April, 2011.
7. Based on interaction with Khin Zaw Win who is Director of Tampadia Institute, April, 2011
8. Based on interaction with Nan Mya Thida.
9. Based on interaction with Daw Seng Raw who is the Executive Director of Metta Foundation. She is an ethnic Kachin, April 2011.
10. Based on interaction with Aung Naing Oo, Deputy Director, Vahu Development Institute, Yangon (March 2-3, 2011)

11. Political Parties Registration Law, SPDC Law No. 2/2010
12. The President shall not be answerable to either any Hluttaw or to any Court for the exercise of the powers and functions of his office or for any act done or purported to be done by him in the exercise of these powers and functions in accord with the Constitution or any law. However, the exemption does not deal with the provisions relating to impeachment of the President under the Constitution (Constitution of the Republic of the Union of Myanmar, 2008, Chapter V, Art. 215).
13. All policy guidelines, laws, rules, regulations, notifications and declarations of the State Law and Order Restoration Council and the State Peace and Development Council or actions, rights and responsibilities of the State Law and Order Restoration Council and the State Peace and Development Council shall devolve on the Republic of the Union of Myanmar. No proceeding shall be instituted against the said Councils or any member thereof or any member of the Government, in respect of any act done in the execution of their respective duties (Chapter XIV, Art. 445).
14. The President, in promulgating an ordinance and declaring a state of emergency:
    (a) shall specify in the said ordinance the areas and the duration that the state of emergency is in operation;
    (b) may, if necessary, restrict or suspend as required, one or more fundamental rights of the citizens residing in the areas where the state of emergency is in operation (Chapter XI, Art. 414(b)).
15. Pyithu Hluttaw Election Law, SPDC Law No. 1/2010
16. For details see Smith 1999.
17. Army officers of the rank of colonel and above were recently told to buy their own personal computers. Several hundred junior military officers have been sent to Russia and India for computer training.
18. Based on interview with Bala.
19. Interview with Tint Swe.

Chapter - 6

Democratic Transition and Reconciliation

Although change has occurred in Myanmar and it is embarking on a new era of democratic reforms on the path of 'disciplined democracy', very few are optimistic about what it might bring. With the elections being held on Nov 7, 2010 and release of Aung San Suu Kyi on November 13, 2010 there is a ray of hope for democracy and change in Myanmar. On 31st January, 2011 a new Parliament was convened and on 30th March, 2011, the erstwhile junta was dissolved handing over power formally to the new successor civilian government. Myanmar's former Prime Minister Thein Sein was sworn in as the country's new President, marking the end of the military junta that governed the country for decades. Tin Myint Oo and Sai Muak Kham took charge as the two Vice Presidents. The President named 30 ministers and 39 deputy ministers to his government.

Efforts are being made by the newly convened Parliament and leadership to establish a façade of constitutional democracy. The new regime through various articles and speeches is trying to convince its citizens about move that cements the military's control of a new political system. Given below is an extract from an article published in the National Daily, New Light of Myanmar.

> "The State is like a large boat. It must have a government like the captain, the administrative machinery like the boatmen, party organisations like the navigator, people like the passengers, economic forces like the rudder and the sails and economic infrastructures like the hull. Only with these characteristics plus concerted efforts, can the boat reach its destination smoothly.

According to a political term, working harmoniously with the characteristics of a nation means being politically united........... In Myanmar, 98.12 percent of all eligible voters cast their ballots, and there has been a constitution approved by 92.48 percent of all the voters. There have been people's representatives elected through the elections held systematically in accord with the constitution. The Hluttaws at various levels formed with those representatives and a government will emerge soon, and Myanmar will reach the new democratic era" (New Light of Myanmar, December 8, 2010)

Progress and Prospects: 2008 onwards

The new Constitution approved ostensibly by the overwhelming majority of the population in May 2008 referendum not only enshrines the junta's hold on power, but effectively excludes Suu Kyi from office. According to Constitutional Principle approved by the National Convention, the President should be an indigenous Burmese. The Constitution lays down that "the President shall be a person who has stayed in the state continuously for a minimum of 20 years at the time of the election of the State President. Further, either of his parents, spouse, any legitimate child shall not be a loyal subject to any foreign government or a person under the influence of a foreign government or citizen of an alien country." This has disempowered NLD leader Aung San Suu Kyi from contesting Presidential election as her husband was a British national.[1]

Under the Charter, a quarter of seats in both houses of new Parliament would be guaranteed for the military—at the National as well as regional and State Assemblies i.e. in a newly created 440-member House of Representatives there would be 330 elected civilians and 110 military representatives. In view of the upcoming elections, leaders of Myanmar's ruling junta including Prime Minister General Thein Sein and 22 other Cabinet ministers gave up their uniforms and allegedly resigned from their military posts. This meant that those who resign from military positions would not be counted in the military's quota. These additional seats outside the quota for the military (filled by loyalists out of uniform) will help ensure the military's power and influence in the Parliament.

The draft Constitution further, makes it virtually impossible to amend the clauses because more than three quarters of the members of both the houses of the Parliament need to approve any amendment. Given that the military holds at least one quarter of the seats, their representation will be significantly higher and hold an effective veto. The President, the future head of the state, will also have to be a member of the military. In addition, the army retains control of the key ministries, including defense, economy and border affairs (Jagan 2008: 18).

The Political Parties Registration Law, enacted by the military junta in March 2010 ahead of the November 2010 general elections, was aimed at keeping Aung San Suu Kyi out of the electoral process (Amnesty International 2010). The junta had barred anyone convicted of a crime from being a member of a political party.[2] Further, parties that wanted to register under the new law must expel members who are "not in conformity with the qualification to be members of a party." This meant that Suu Kyi could not contest the elections, and the National League for Democracy (NLD) would expel her if it wanted to be eligible to participate in the election process. The junta also offered a carrot to the NLD by removing the seals on the regional offices of the party. They wanted the NLD to contest the election in order to give the polls some credibility. Henceforth, 300 NLD offices were allowed to reopen. But the junta also wanted a very weak NLD, with Suu Kyi completely out of the picture. This posed a dilemma before NLD whether to participate by expelling Suu Kyi or to completely boycott the elections. The party was, however, disbanded for failing to register under the new election law.

Authoritarian rulers may deploy a wide range of strategies to keep control over their agents, as well as their adversaries, in various institutional arenas. In electoral authoritarian regimes, election constitutes the central arena of struggle (Schedler 2010: 71). They have at their disposal a broad array of manipulative tools for reducing the uncertainty that elections can bring such as disempowerment, market restrictions, preference alteration and vote distortions (ibid:73). The 2010 elections in Myanmar, were the fifth step of the "Roadmap to Democracy" as announced by the military junta in 2003. The electoral administration was appointed unilaterally by the regime on March 11, 2010, and soon showed itself to heavily favour the regime and its allies.

The Union Election Commission (UEC) lacked independence. It was appointed directly by the SPDC with no public input. Political parties had to register with the Union Election Commission and request permission to run. The election laws were developed by the military government and effectively prohibited longstanding opponents of the regime from contesting the elections (as mentioned in the preceding paragraph).

Eventually, 47 political parties attempted to register. The UEC initially approved 42 to contest the elections. However, the commission then dissolved five of the parties, leaving 37 approved parties and over 80 individual candidates. By Election Day, 23 parties remained to participate in the elections. Many ethnic politicians saw this election as a rare opportunity to campaign for ethnic rights and democracy. Therefore, they formed new parties to run in the elections. Some ethnic armed groups agreed to be transformed into members of the junta-controlled Border Guard Force (BGF).

On 16 September 2010, the UEC issued notification No. 99, No. 100, No. 101, No. 102, and No. 103. In these notifications, the Union Election Commission announced that, according to Article 8 (f) of the Union Election Commission Law, voting will not be held in some areas in Kachin, Shan, Karenni, Karen and Mon states because they are in no position to host free and fair elections in the Multiparty Democracy General Elections to be held on 7 November 2010. This affected about 300 village-tracts in 32 townships in 5 States. Therefore, hundreds of thousands of people could not vote in this election, thus depriving the ethnic political parties of several thousand votes in these areas.

The Censorship Board (The Press Scrutiny and Registration Board, or PSRB) issued a directive prohibiting all weekly publications in the country from publishing any commentary or analysis on the electoral laws. Also, the approved political parties needed to apply for permission from the PSRB within 90 days after registering with the UEC for permission to print their own campaign materials. Each party had also to deposit 500,000 Kyats (USD 500) with the PSRB. The UEC announced nine restrictions for campaign speeches, while also limiting each party to 15 minutes of media airtime each. Media organisations and political parties faced numerous obstacles, such as only having

15 minutes of airtime for the entire campaign, restrictions, communications and internet slowdowns, threats of punishment, and cyber attacks. The SPDC's Union Election Commission held the elections on November 7, 2010. During the election period, it became increasingly clear that the use of advance votes obtained through coerced voting or outright fraud was a major problem. These advance votes were often taken before the official advance voting period of November 5–6. This advance voting seems to be part of a systematic operation to give the USDP an insurmountable lead before Election Day. These ballots were generally collected in every manner possible, often relying on proxy voting, ghost voting, or coerced voting using threats and intimidation. Allegations of fraud counting and advance voting irregularities were common. The voter turnout was 76.48 percent, in which a vast majority of the seats in Parliament were won by the USDP.

The 2010 elections installed a nominally civilian government which in practice is mostly a 'constitutionalised' façade for ongoing military rule (Turnell 2011: 148). The election was rigged giving military's USDP around 60 per cent of the contested seats, over and above 25 per cent of the seats reserved for the military. The President, Vice President, head of the USDP all are former generals (Economist 2011). The results of the elections are presented in the following table.

An analysis of the election result shows that the military-dominated Parliament has emerged out of the recent General elections held after a gap of twenty years. The junta's political vehicle, the Union Solidarity and USDP, had a landslide victory with 76 percent of the total votes. Twenty-three out of 37 approved parties successfully contested the elections. The USDP won 129 out of 168 seats in the House of Nationalities, 259 out of 325 seats in the People's Assembly, and 494 out of 661 seats in Regional and State Parliaments. It had 79 percent of lower house seats, 77 percent of the seats in Upper House and a 75 percent stake in the seven state and seven regional assemblies. The National Unity Party (NUP) which is supposed to have close links with the military stood at the second position like in the previous election of 1990 with a total of 64 seats. The poll was marred by allegations of fraud and intimidation. The main opposition party, a splinter group of the erstwhile NLD—National Democratic Force (NDF) got twelve seats in both the houses and in total just 16 seats.

The three major ethnic parties were however, able to make their position in the top five slots. They are the Shan Nationalities Democratic Party (SNDP), with 58 seats; the Rakhine Nationalities Development Party (RNDP) with 35 seats, and All Mon Region Democracy Party (AMRDP) with 16 seats.

In addition, 25 percent of the seats in all legislative chambers are reserved for serving soldiers. A total of 166 mid-ranking officers were notified about their appointment as parliamentarians. The military and the USDP, which is mostly constituted by the retired soldiers or junta cronies, jointly control 84 percent of the National Parliament. Rest of the parties such as the NUP, SNDP, RNDP, AMRDP, NDF and others constitute just 16 per cent of the seats in the legislature. The biggest pro-democracy party, the National Democratic Force, has less than 2 percent, with just 12 seats.

Table 6.1: Results of 2010 Election

<table>
<tr><th>PARTIES</th><th colspan="2">House of Nationalities (Amyotha Hluttaw) A</th><th colspan="2">House of Representatives (Pyithu Hluttaw) B</th><th>Total Seats in both the Houses C (A+B)</th><th colspan="2">Regional Parliament D</th><th colspan="2">Total (C+D)</th></tr>
<tr><td>USDP</td><td colspan="2">129
(76.7 per cent)</td><td colspan="2">259
(79.6 per cent)</td><td>388
(78.7 per cent)</td><td colspan="2">494
(74.8 per cent)</td><td colspan="2">882
(76.4 per cent)</td></tr>
<tr><td>NUP</td><td>05</td><td rowspan="6">39</td><td>12</td><td rowspan="6">66</td><td rowspan="6">105</td><td>47</td><td rowspan="6">167</td><td>64</td><td rowspan="6">272</td></tr>
<tr><td>SNDP</td><td>03</td><td>18</td><td>37</td><td>58</td></tr>
<tr><td>RNDP</td><td>07</td><td>09</td><td>19</td><td>35</td></tr>
<tr><td>NDF</td><td>04</td><td>08</td><td>04</td><td>16</td></tr>
<tr><td>AMRDP</td><td>04</td><td>03</td><td>09</td><td>16</td></tr>
<tr><td>Others</td><td>16</td><td>16</td><td>51</td><td>83</td></tr>
<tr><td>Total Elected</td><td colspan="2">168</td><td colspan="2">325</td><td>493</td><td colspan="2">661</td><td colspan="2">1154</td></tr>
<tr><td>Appointed (military 25 per cent)</td><td colspan="2">56</td><td colspan="2">110</td><td>166</td><td colspan="2">222</td><td colspan="2">388</td></tr>
<tr><td>Grand Total</td><td colspan="2">224</td><td colspan="2">435</td><td>659</td><td colspan="2">883</td><td colspan="2">1542</td></tr>
</table>

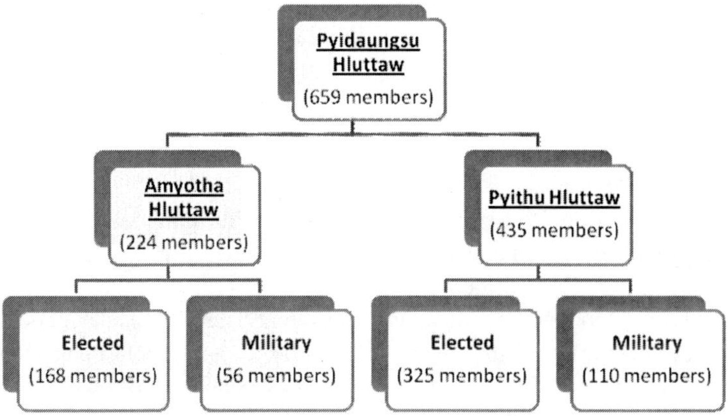

Figure 6.1: Composition of Pyidaungsu Hluttaw

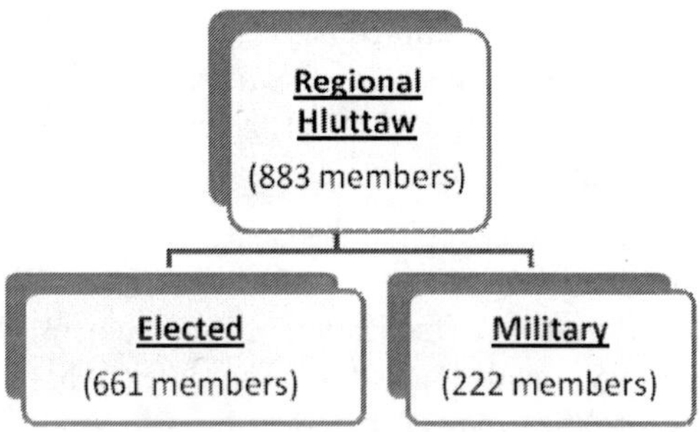

Figure 6.2: Composition of Regional Hluttaw

The release of the Nobel laureate Aung San Suu Kyi after seven years of house arrest in November 2010 just three days after the Elections has been a welcome step for the pro-democracy movement in Myanmar. But the fact that the restrictions were initially imposed over her movement demonstrated that the authorities have just released her as a symbolic gesture. The release has however, came at a time when the entire Western world was opposed to the way elections had been conducted and the new Constitution imposed upon the people of Myanmar. The leadership as goodwill sign wanted to show to the world that they are genuinely moving towards democracy and probably, this was the time when they can easily engage with the rest of the world under the garb of democratisation. At this stage, they really don't anticipate any threat from the 'Lady' as the Burmese Nobel laureate is popularly called, since her political party was officially disbanded and the new Constitution restricted her from contesting any future elections in Myanmar.

The political transition and transformation completely took a different turn with the new regime allowing the NLD to register as a political party before the April 2012 by-elections. It further allowed the Lady to contest election as any other candidate. The results marked a new beginning in the history of regime transition and change in Myanmar as the NLD was able to sweep the election results by winning 43 of the total 44 seats it contested. This constitutes 6.4 per cent of the total seats in the Parliament. With this, it has emerged as the largest opposition party in the Parliament trying to consolidate its position by uniting with other ethnic based marginalised opposition. The Lady's victory from Kawmu township constituency enabled her to take her rightful place in the Parliament 22 years after the landmark victory in the 1990 general elections. This is an indicator of a new Myanmar focusing on reforms and transformation.

Nonetheless, military regime has achieved a multi-party elected Parliament for first time in 50 years. According to Trevor Wilson (2010), "it also achieved quasi-'civilianisation' of government, albeit run by the same people without their uniforms. The elections have also created a new level of political power to reflect quasi-federal nature of the Burmese nation, but the prospects for effective functioning of the new regional assemblies is not clear."

In Myanmar, the elections held after a gap of twenty years in 2010 has paved the way for a transition from military rule to a supposedly civilian administration and democratic opening. But the fact that the polls were swept by the pro junta political party—Union Solidarity and Development Party (USDP) and its allies exposes the myth of democratisation in the country. In the absence of any clear opposition with National League of Democracy being disbanded, the election has widely been seen as an attempt to legitimize military rule behind a mask of civilian government. Civilian dictatorship sought to be established in the post election Myanmar charecterise an illusion of multi-party democracy at the local and the national level while effectively stripping the legality and efficacy of a free and fair election. The regime alleges that it is preparing for a transition period from military rule to a supposedly civilian administration popularly conceived by the leadership as *Disciplined Democracy.*

Reform Agenda of the New Regime

In the light of regime change and transition in Myanmar, a new kind of political system is emerging in the country. The newly elected civilian regime has emphasized on the fundamental rights of the citizens and the need for a clean and corruption free society. The President in his inaugural speech used the words like 'good governance' and 'democratic reforms'.

To quote the President Thein Sein,

> In transition to democracy, it is obligatory to promote democratic practices not only among the *Hluttaw* representatives but also among the people. To do so, I promise that our government will cooperate with the political parties in the *Hluttaws*, good-hearted political forces outside the *Hluttaws* and all social organisations…
>
> Democracy will promote only hand in hand with good governance. This is why our government responsible for Myanmar's democracy transition will try hard to shape good administrative machinery…
>
> To safeguard the fundamental rights of citizens in line with the provisions of the constitution in the new democratic nation is high on our government's list of priorities. We guarantee that all citizens will enjoy equal rights in terms of law, and we will reinforce the judicial pillar…
>
> We will fight corruption in cooperation with the people as it harms the image of not only the offenders but also the nation and the people…
>
> (New Light of Myanmar, 30 March, 2011)

The new regime is also trying to convince the international community of the political changes and reforms that are taking place in the country. The leadership has endeavoured to end its international isolation by promoting the democratic icon Daw Aung San Suu Kyi and allowing her party NLD to participate in the by-elections in April

2012 and play an active role in pushing forward the reform agenda of the new regime. Since her release from house arrest in late 2010, she has traveled to Thailand, Norway, England, USA and India advocating the cause of removal of restrictions and easing out sanctions on Myanmar. This has given the new regime a degree of international acceptance, reduction of sanctions and the possibility of aid from international financial institutions. These cosmetic changes have helped to shift image perceptions, seen in the EU's dropping of some of its punitive measures in March 2011 and its coincident praise for the regime's "greater civilian character." United Nations official Vijay Nambiar followed this, saying the regime has demonstrated "very encouraging" signs after his visit in May 2011. The same has been reiterated by United Nations Human Rights Envoy to Myanmar Tomas Ojea Quintana who has described it as the 'key moment in Myanmar's history'. Most analysts believe the openness being shown by Myanmar's leaders is aimed in part at improving their image abroad with a view to ending decades of Western sanctions and consolidating power at home.

Although, failure of regime performance in the economic front had delayed democracy in Myanmar but the new regime has taken all the possible steps for rebuilding the economy. President Thein Sein in his inaugural speech in the Parliament has focused on the 'economic might' for growth and development of the country. He has focused on agricultural development as well as industrialisation to transform country into a developed, rich one with a lot of employment opportunities and high per capita income. The new regime invited a delegation from the International Monetary Fund (IMF) to visit in October 2011 to advise policymakers on how to tackle problems with the kyat currency, which has appreciated 20 percent in a year, hurting farmers and exporters and bankrupting businesses. After months of inaction and simmering anger, the government in July 2011 cut taxes for exporters and has promised agriculture loans and price guarantees for millions of farmers, suggesting it may be concerned that any mishandling of bread and butter issues could see a repeat of bloody uprisings in 1988 and 2007 that were sparked by soaring inflation and fuel prices.

New laws are expected to come out in the subsequent sessions of the Parliament, such as a labour law and social security law. The MPs have agreed to discuss promulgation of new comprehensive Social

Security Insurance Law which is more comprehensive in its coverage than the 1954 Social Security Act.[3] This is in accordance with the art 24, 26 (b), 28 (a), 31, 32 (a) of the new Constitution. President Thein Sein has also mentioned that "In particular, we will create employment opportunities, stabilize commodity prices and encourage welfare and social security for the convenience of workers and labourers. And we will ensure that minimum pay scale meets current living costs. We guarantee that national workers inside and outside the nation enjoy all rights." The new law protects employees' rights, allows the formation labour associations and establishes procedures for holding a workers' strike. The Labour Organisation Law was enacted in accordance with the provisions of the International Labor Organisation (ILO) and its recommendations.

Health care has also been a major area of concern for the new government. In order to implement better health care facilities, government is committed towards improving the existing health care facilities-both in urban and rural areas at the same time it is also disseminating knowledge about seasonal and other fatal diseases such as AIDS, Tuberculosis and malaria. President has focused on this issue in his inaugural speech and the MPs have also raised their concern in the Parliament about public health care, disease prevention and prevention and control of the epidemic.[4]

Myanmar is taking initiative to carry out education reform soon after the new government took office. President Thein Sein vowed to promote the national education up to international standard and work for the development of human resources in all seriousness.[5] The Vice President Sai Mauk Kham has also called for mending the country's education system in order to meet the international level. Myanmar has been implementing a 30-year national education promotion plan since 2001-02 academic year, guaranteeing that every school-age child can receive good access to education and every citizen complete basic education under a plan being implemented with the cooperation of regional authorities, social organisations and parents of the students. It has also geared up for the launch of compulsory primary education plan in 2011-12 academic year. Meanwhile, Myanmar authorities have started to draft law related to private school education as part of its move to open up education sector to private run and strengthen administration. In its recent attempt after a gap of almost two decades undergraduate students have been allowed to seek admission in various courses in Yangon and Mandalay University from the academic year 2013.

The 'environmental issues' is moving into a more high profile position in Myanmar these days, with political parties making it a priority in the new Parliament and more civic groups taking up the cause. The new government is drafting a new law for environmental conservation for proportionate development of the economic, social and environmental development. One of the latest signs of environmental activism is the formation of an environmental protection subcommittee by the National League for Democracy. Formed on April 27, 2011, the committee's mission is to represent environmental interests in the area of dam construction, irrigation projects and the agricultural use of chemical fertilizers and pesticides. In his inaugural address to Parliament, President Thein Sein talked about conservation of the environment at length, saying that he would weigh the need for economic development and the conservation of environment.[6] Vice President Dr. Sai Mauk Kham has also stressed the need for environment conservation in terms of trees and forest so as to hand down the existing good condition of natural environment of the country to new generations. The government has also bowed to environmentalist and social activists by cancelling two high profile state projects: the Myitsone Dam hydropower project, and a coal-fired power plant in the Dawei deep-sea port project and industrial zone.

Human rights which had been given low priority for decades have also been advanced. It has set up a National Human Rights Commission which will safeguard the rights of its citizens. The panel would comprise 15 retired bureaucrats and academics. The latest human rights committee was formed on the advice of the United Nations Human Rights Envoy to Myanmar Tomas Ojea Quintana. The move follows steps by the newly-installed civilian administration to improve Myanmar's international reputation as well as relations with the country's Democracy movement. Although, the issue of the release of political prisoners and the concern about the ethnic conflict zones remains unresolved, but the process to review and possibly amend or revoke arbitrary national legislation is underway. Tomás Ojea Quintana concluded at the end of his five-day mission to the South-East Asian nation, "This is a key moment in Myanmar's history and there are real opportunities for positive and meaningful developments to improve the human rights situation and bring about a genuine transition to democracy."

Myanmar's once watertight censorship board has in recent months undertaken reforms. President Thein Sein mentioned in his inaugural speech that media is the fourth pillar of the nation and media laws needs to be amended in line with the provisions of the Constitution and that 'it is getting more and more developed'. The Information and Broadcasting Minister has also highlighted that there would be more freedom of press and the government has offered strong indications that it may relax media restrictions. Under the proposed changes, coverage on mostly benign subjects, including sports and entertainment, would no longer have to pass through the office of the censor before hitting news-stands.

In September 2011, pro-democracy icon Aung San Suu Kyi published her first article in the Burmese media for 23 years on the front page of *Pyithu Khit News Journal*, while *Messenger News* also ran an exclusive interview with the Nobel Laureate as its cover story. *Pyithu Khit* (People's Era) was permitted by the Burmese censorship board—the Press Scrutiny and Registration Division under the Ministry of Information—to publish Suu Kyi's article entitled Holiday-1. It also carried a piece by one of her close aides—veteran journalist Win Tin's old article on Suu Kyi's father Aung San. For the last 23 years, even Suu Kyi's name or any symbols indirectly referring to her—such as "the lady," "the mother" or "the rose"—was banned in publications. This move is a part of the recent relaxation of control over media, seen as part of the new, nominally civilian government's effort to reach out to the democratic opposition in a bid to win greater international recognition. In a significant move, in August 2012, the government eased the pre-publication censorship law and finally in December 2012, registration for private daily publication was announced. In this regard, a historic beginning was made on 1 April, 2013 when four private newspapers hit the newsstands in the streets of Myanmar after a gap of five decades. As Myanmar enters a new political phase, the international community should seize the opportunity to encourage greater openness and reforms.

The new regime has also tried to shed its pariah image by appointing U Myint as the economic adviser to the new President.

He is supposed to be liberal minded and close to the democracy icon Aung San Suu Kyi. His appointment is being hailed by the newly appointed civilian regime. In a country whose economy is being controlled by cronies, U Myint faces a major challenge of rebuilding the economy amidst the dismal economic performance of the past five decades. It is believed that his appointment is suppose to send positive signals to the international community for liberalizing its attitude towards Myanmar and encourage investment opportunities in the country. The regime has also shown signs recently that it is seeking to improve its image by reaching out to the opposition leader Aung San Suu Kyi. She has been appointed as the Chairperson of the government led investigation commission for the Copper Mine Project at Letpaudang.

Thein Sein's government has capitalised on the reform agenda through a carefully choreographed public relations campaign that began with November 2010 elections and the release of pro-democracy leader Aung San Suu Kyi and has continued with recent 'liberalisation reforms'. He has sought to dilute his hardline image with somewhat reformist rhetoric. Although there are skepticism about the parliamentary procedures and rules of conduct are yet not established properly, but these sessions are likely to give us a better indication of the direction we can expect the country to take over the next four years. Many of the sessions are so curtailed that the critics call it a '15 minute Parliament'. Opposition members are not allowed to submit their questions and most of them seem to be disillusioned by its style and method. Nevertheless, we find beginning of a parliamentary tradition for the people to voice their concern. It has at least opened up the space for different actors and parties to engage in the political process. Recently, the new regime has released about 200 political prisoners along with more than 6,000 other inmates in October 2011 as a part of its amnesty scheme. Furthermore country's Independence Day on 4 January, 2012 was marked by commuting sentences and apparently releasing more than 30 prisoners. This was followed by the announcement of the release of 651 political prisoners as a positive signal and an important step towards the full release of all political prisoners and a factor in the national reconciliation process (Telegraph 2012). Around 56 political prisoners were released in Myanmar following the European Union decision to lift last of its sanction (BBC 2013).

The first stage of the reform (political reform centered on the restoration of civilian government and multi-party system) has concluded its initial stage, and the goal for the next stage is to advance the people-centered development. The second stage of reforms has been outlined in the "Framework for Economic and Social Reform" (FESR). This indicates that Myanmar's reform has entered the second phase which focuses on economic and social reform. It aims at enhancing the marketisation of its economy and strengthening the role of civil society. These include long-term goals such as building Myanmar into a developed country by 2030. Development of the mobile telecom industry is considered as an important task of the government to quickly turn Myanmar into an information society. The government intends to increase the penetration rate of cellphones in Myanmar from the current 9 per cent to 80 per cent Poverty alleviation and job creation are also important tasks for the second stage of Myanmar's reform. In accordance with this task, the government launched "Framework for Poverty Alleviation and Economic Development" (FPAED). The reform in its second stage also includes "social reforms." It recognizes the important role of civil society organisations in national building and state building.

The third stage of the reform process in Myanmar includes the administrative and constitutional reforms. In this regard, the Office of the President of Myanmar has announced formation of a nine-member anti-corruption committee under the chairmanship of Vice President Dr. Sai Mauk Kham as a part of efforts for the emergence of good governance and clean government."[7] In the meanwhile, Parliament has agreed to review the pro-military 2008 Constitution that could eventually change the political landscape of the country.

The civilian government of President Thein Sein has been working hard to show a new face to the world and to improve its relations with its critics at home and abroad. But there are many analysts who believe that the effort towards reform by the militarised government is just a 'survival attempt'. The regime has been accused for creating a façade for liberalisation to prompt western countries to lift sanctions imposed over the country's political and human rights record. It is a means of cementing their hold over the regime with a view towards long-term control. Opposition member on the other hand, see the new government as merely a front for the military. It has raised hopes for change with a major 'charm' offensive.

All's said and done, the new democratic regime in Myanmar is just born and it is taking its baby-steps. In this stage, it has to face a number of teething troubles. It still has a long way to go from infancy to adolescence. It is hoped that as it moves forward in its growth and maturity, these problems would be overpowered by the emergence of a more open and matured democracy in future. However, President Thein Sein in his address to the Parliament has promised that reforms would continue and "that our country with democracy still in its infancy will not collapse."[8]

Challenges of Democratisation in Myanmar

After five decades of authoritarian rule in Myanmar, the country faces a plethora of challenges both in the domestic as well as external front. On the one hand, the need for building up democratic institutions and re-invigorating faith in Parliamentary procedures, multi-party democracy, reforms in the armed forces and national reconciliation demands attention. On the other hand, the international isolation of this 'hermit kingdom' needs to open itself to the outside world and move forward on the path of economic growth and development. Some of these major challenges have been outlined in the following section.

Political and Ethnic Reconciliation

Although, the regime has witnessed transition but ethnic nationalities are unable to have their say in the governance. Though, they have signed a peace truce with the military, but they have a lack of understanding of the changes brought about by the ceasefire process (Kramer 2010: 70). National reconciliation with the ethnic nationalities has to be more inclusive and political dialogue must be initiated to see how to guarantee these different ethnic minorities equal rights and conditions of economic development that are also as egalitarian as possible. Addressing the issue of ethnic nationalities and resolving their decade long conflict is one of the most important challenges facing the country. The counter insurgency methods used by the armed forces in the border areas have increased their alienation. Further, the pressure on ceasefire groups to join the controversial Border Guard Force (BGF) aggravated their already existing grievances.[9] Furthermore, the use of Army's operation in Shan state has resulted in abuses against local citizens (EBO 2011: 2-3). Conflict also erupted in Kachin State since May 2011. The conflict in Kachin state began after a 17-year ceasefire broke down between the government's army and the Kachin Independence Army (KIA), a rebel group fighting for greater political autonomy and basic rights for the Kachin people. Fighting escalated again in January 2013, with the government's army launching offensives and air raids despite a call from President Thein Sein for a unilateral ceasefire. Peace talks began in February 2013.

After resumption of violence in the Kokang region in February, emergency has been imposed for three months in the affected areas (Kipgen 2015). When Kokang rebels attacked and killed nearly 80 members of the armed forces in February, anti-Chinese wave swept all across Myanmar (Bhaumik 2015). It has been held responsible for encouraging the armed groups along its border (Clapp: 2015). On the other hand, China has accused Myanmar's armed forces of dropping bomb on its side that killed four villagers and injured others. The incident has marked the most serious spillover of the conflict in the border region of northern Shan State.[10]

In accordance with the 2008 Constitution, the power were decentralised to the region and state level, now each of these seven ethnic states having their own state legislature and governments. But in practical terms, after the 2010 elections, each of these structures of authorities is dominated by the members of USDP (TNI 2011: 2-3). The situation is thus, very far from the federal autonomy or self governance as demanded by the ethnic nationalities. In addition, the overwhelming role of the military, in the legislature may help in promoting their own interest, rather than the local population. However, there seems to be little to suggest that the situation has improved for ethnic nationalities after elections. While some limited political space has been created, but it will hardly have any immediate impact.

The formation of the military alliance by the ethnic groups to assist each other in the event of attack by the army has posed a practical challenge before the new regime.[11] The use of violence in the Myawaddy region during November 2010 elections is a lesson which the new regime must always remember. In fact, it has been alleged that this was a part of the government's policy of eliminating ethnic opposition including ceasefire groups that have refused to be under its direct control as BGF, as required by the 2008 Constitution. Overcoming of sixty year old ethnic conflict will not be easy and the government will have to do a great deal to build the trust necessary to move beyond temporary ceasefires to resolve the underlying political issues (ICG 2011 : 5).

The government has entered into a three step process for entering into a political dialogue with the ethnic nationalities (Mizzima 2012)[12]. The first step is to agree a ceasefire between each armed group and the respective state or region government, which is seen as essential for building trust and confidence. The second step involves broader discussions between each group and the national government can begin to address other issues of concern, including socio-economic, cultural and political issues. The third stage is intended to bring together representatives of all armed groups and other stakeholders to discuss the shape of a lasting political agreement on ethnic issues. This would include issues such as constitutional change to give greater autonomy, provisions for greater resource sharing with ethnic communities, and the future integration and demobilisation of members of armed groups (ICG 2012: 5).

"The history of Myanmar is complex and getting involved in endeavors such as peace or politics requires absolute or large amount of optimism", says Aung Naing Oo (Myanmar Times 2015a). On March 31, a tentative deal was reached in Yangon between representatives from 16 Ethnic Armed Organisations (EAOs), the Army, and the government in Myanmar. The draft National Ceasefire Agreement was reached over several rounds of formal negotiations between the parties beginning from November 2013. The goal of the National Ceasefire Agreement is to pave the way for political dialogue, similar to the 1947 conference held in Panglong, to find solutions for the decades-old, ethno-political problems in the country, including the ethnic minorities' demand for autonomy under a federal structure (Kipgen: 2015).

Social and cultural rights of the ethnic minorities in Myanmar deteriorated rapidly after the coup of 1962. Nevertheless, in the new political era, the rise of Buddhist nationalism has become a significant socio-political force in Myanmar (TNI 2015). Tensions are particularly strong in the Rakhine state, where the Rohingya Muslim faces ethnic and religious discrimination. During 1991-92 about 250,000 Rohingya fled to Bangladesh following an army campaign (Kramer 2010: 74). In the wake of the alleged violence and repression (since 2012) in the Rakhine state, more than 200 Rohingya have been killed and approximately 140,000 have been displaced as a result of the communal clash between the Rakhine Muslims and the Rakhine Buddhists. This historic conflict between the Muslims and Rakhines in the Rakhine state has further complicated the religious landscape and tension. The relations between Buddhist and Muslim communities remain strained and potentially volatile. The outburst of Buddhist nationalism in recent times may have long-term implications and the impact is going to be widespread, influencing the security of the entire region of Indo-Pacific (Trivedi: 2013).

International Isolation

The new regime, although took steps to normalize its relation with the West, nevertheless, several thorny issues remain bilaterally, regionally and multilaterally. The issue of nuclear non-proliferation and growing closeness of Naypyitaw and Pyongyang had been a cause of growing concern for United States before 2010. However, the visit of the South Korean President in May 2012 sent strong indications to North Korea. Relations between Seoul and Yangon are only now showing signs of recovery. However, cautious optimism has charecterised the response of the international community to the new regime in Myanmar. The US, United Kingdom, EU have become more pragmatic in its orientation and have launched a substantial review of their policy.

The reform agenda led by the new regime in Myanmar aims to convince the military that the process would be gradual and controlled and that the military's role as envisaged in the new Constitution would be respected. The leadership is trying hard to end its international isolation by promoting the democratic icon Nobel Laureate Aung San Suu Kyi. National League of Democracy (NLD) after participating in the by-elections on April 1, 2012 rejoined mainstream politics. The party has moved to revive and open new branch offices, reorganize its top brass and accept new member applications. The bye-elections has been the biggest political test for the NLD since it last contested in elections in 1990, when it earned an overwhelming victory against the ruling military junta but was prevented from taking power. NLD remains a minority in the Parliament but its landslide victory inspired many citizens who are hoping for the country's full transition to democracy. The junta-backed USDP is still the dominant force in the local politics.

As a victory for the new government seeking international legitimacy after a series of reform moves, Myanmar successfully chaired ASEAN in 2014. The ASEAN leaders are now convinced about the significant changes and developments taking place in Myanmar and those changes have made it more conducive for Myanmar to carry out this responsibility. This would encourage the present government to step up the momentum for reforms. It has been alleged that by giving Myanmar the chance to chair ASEAN, the grouping was trying to ensure that the momentum of democratisation in Myanmar was maintained, as it would put a bigger spotlight on the country, requiring it to be more open and transparent.

Political change in Myanmar is being perceived as an opening of fresh opportunity to expand business by the international capital. Political and economic opening has led United States and European Union to drop sanctions and allow Myanmar to compete in the global economy instead of relying on China for support. Furthermore, the new rapprochement marked by the landmark visit of US President Barack Obama who became the first President to set foot in Myanmar demonstrates that the process of reforms have gained momentum and recognition.[13] This was followed by his second visit in November 2014. The United States eased certain financial restrictions on Myanmar in April 2012, to allow non-governmental groups to operate in the country as it undertakes democratic reforms. It would no longer restrict Americans from financial transactions in Myanmar if they are working for projects that "meet basic human needs" or promote democracy. Such projects include assistance to internally displaced people, delivery of clothes, food and medicine, as well as educational programs such as English-language instruction and promotion of literacy. United States growing engagement with the nascent democracy has been a part of Obama's new foreign policy of 'pivot' to Asia-Pacific, which envisages its active role in the region and forging a deeper partnership which yields both economic and security benefits (Diplomat: 2014).

British Prime Minister David Cameron was the first British Prime Minister to visit the country in more than 60 years. Foreign Secretary William Hague, who visited Myanmar in more than 50 years, said that reforms undertaken so far by President Thein Sein raise hopes that democracy is within reach in the Southeast Asian nation.[14] David Cameroon also made an announcement that his government would push for the suspension of European Union sanctions. The question however remains, how far and how fast the process of reform will develop (BBC 2012).

Minister of Foreign and European Affairs of France, Alain Juppe during his visit in January 2012 was convinced about the total agreement between the different authorities to move forward along the path of the regime's democratisation and liberalisation. The visit by French Foreign Minister has been a sign of Western approval of recent reforms by the new civilian government in Myanmar, after years of authoritarian rule (VOA 2012). In addition, the release of hundreds of political prisoners is seen as **Myanmar's** most significant step towards ending its isolation and securing the removal of European Union and **US** sanctions.

Human Rights Abuse

The government has shown willingness to target the human rights concern, but the issue of ongoing detention of political prisoners is a major challenge before the process of national reconciliation. One significant development in this regard has been the establishment of Myanmar Human Rights Commission on the recommendation of United Nations Human Rights envoy to Myanmar. But how far this independent body is going to be free and effective remains to be seen from the political space it would enjoy in the system of the newly established militarised regime. Despite efforts to present itself as a legitimate and reform oriented administration, the arbitrary punishment and human rights abuse continue in Myanmar (Altsean 2011b). As a matter of concern, in the areas dominated by ethnic nationalities, armed conflict continues such as Kachin, Karen and Shan states. Here, military continues to target civilians during ongoing military offensives. The enduring mistrust between the democratic forces and military establishment and the growing ethnic splits have given impetus to the cultivation of opium crops and the drug trade, making Myanmar the world's second largest exporter of opium and a leading manufacturer of methamphetamine. According to Dittmer (2010: 3-4), "national fragmentation has also contributed to egregious human rights violations with spillover effects complicating relations with neighbouring countries."

Furthermore, reports of child soldiers and forced labour continue to remain serious issue of concern. Human rights groups have reported that there are around 5000 child soldiers presently employed in Myanmar. However, no exact official figures are available on the total number of child soldiers. The Myanmar army released 62 child soldiers in August 2013 in its latest bid to meet international human rights standards, although critics said more children still remain in uniform (*Los Angeles Times* 2013 b).

Political prisoners have been denied rights under imprisonment with continued torture, inadequate medical care and ill-treatment. As a part of Presidential amnesty several political prisoners have been released in different phases. Nevertheless, a significant number of them are still undergoing rigorous sentence. However, President Thein Sein has promised that there would be no 'prisoners of conscience' in the country's jails by the end of the year. The military junta, which ruled the country with an iron grip for decades, has been notorious for arbitrary arrests and detention which led to imprisonment of thousands of pro-democracy activists in jails. This has amounted to serious violation of human rights and rule of law in Myanmar.

Besides, for the development of infrastructural projects, arbitrary confiscation of land and forced displacement has also led to serious political and human rights abuse in the country. In the South-western part of Myanmar due to the construction of the Chinese pipeline project, indigenous community has been displaced eroding of their livelihood and basic facilities. Similar case of confiscation and land acquisition has been reported from Copper mine project at Letpadaung near Monywa in Sagaing division. Violent crackdown on the peaceful protesters using water cannons, tear gas, and fire bombs to disperse protesters, including Buddhist monks and local villagers have been criticized. Despite recent reforms, land grabbing, forced evictions, environmental degradation and other related human rights abuse have continued in the country.

The ongoing sectarian violence and the issue of statelessness of the Rohingya Muslims in the Rakhine state have invariably added to the already existing woes and human security in Myanmar. For around one million Rohingyas in the country, life is only getting worse. Thousands have been displaced from their homes in the Rakhine state by mob violence and are now transferred to camps for displaced persons. The United Nations has declared the Rohingya among the most persecuted groups in the world (*Los Angeles Times* 2013 a). Though, they have been repatriated to Rakhine State by the UNHCR and been rehabilitated in IDP camps, but they face limited freedom of movement, forced labour and administrative barriers to marriage and many are not recognised as citizens of Myanmar (Krammer 2010: 74).

Owing to their stateless status, they are vulnerable to various kinds of prejudice and abuse. The plight of their women and children has been deplorable. Deprived of basic human rights and livelihood opportunities, they have been subjected to all kinds of exploitation and extreme discrimination. Due to lack of proper education, healthcare, sanitation and other social security measures, they remain the most excluded social group in Myanmar. According to UNHCR, the conditions of IDP camps are deteriorating, and the ability of humanitarian agencies to deliver assistance has been severely limited. It is assisting more than 800,000 people without citizenship in the Rakhine state. The levels of human sufferings in these camps are also worsening bit by bit.

In April 2015, **Myanmar's Parliament passed a law that gives regional governments the right to restrict how many children a woman has, legally enshrining a human rights breach.** The new legislation is known as the Population Control Bill (Myanmar Times 2015b). This is highly abusive as it takes away a woman's right to choose when to have children and gives authorities new powers to control women's bodies against their will.

Economic Reforms

Evolution of a market oriented economy from 1989 onwards implemented by SLORC and later carried forward by SPDC and privatisation of a number of state economic enterprises was geared towards strengthening military's own commercial interest and growth (Than: 2007; Brown: 3013). Had the economic adjustment and stabilisation programmes been well designed and implemented properly, then Myanmar would have been able to lay the foundations for solid economic growth. Unlike this, the seriously flawed economic strategy implemented by the military for over a quarter of a century brought Myanmar to bankruptcy (Brown 2013: 192).

Subsequent, failure of regime performance in the economic front delayed democracy in Myanmar. Nevertheless the new regime has taken all the possible steps for rebuilding and bolstering up the economy. President Thein Sein in his inaugural speech in the Parliament has focused on the 'economic might' for growth and development of the country. He emphasised on agricultural development as well as industrialisation to transform country into a developed, rich one with a lot of employment opportunities and high per capita income. The new regime had invited international delegations to visit in October to advise policymakers on how to tackle problems with the kyat currency, which has appreciated 20 percent in a year, hurting farmers and exporters and bankrupting businesses.

The country after the 2010 elections is on a drive to attract investment, promoting tourism, timber, gemstones and its vast oil and gas reserves. In this regard, a "Special Economic Zone Law" was passed on January 27, 2011 to attract much-needed foreign capital to an economy held back by decades of sanctions and mismanagement. The new investment law follows a series of reforms undertaken over the past couple of years, including the privatisation of hundreds of state assets, and plans to expand banking, telecommunications, shipping and agricultural sectors. Even Nobel laureate Suu Kyi has appealed for the support of the economic reforms and establishment of a just political and economic order in Myanmar (Kyi, 2011).

Nevertheless, major reforms are required by the new regime to restructure and re-invigorate the economy. It has to become more competitive before its entry into ASEAN FTA in 2015. Another major issue which needs to be focused is the rapid increase in the value of the local currency kyat. Myanmar's modest rate of growth at around 3 per cent is sufficient to finance the spending on health, education, and crucial infrastructure needed for transformational growth, but these revenues, unfortunately, are not utilised in constructive ways and have been channelised for arms and military infrastructure spending (Turnell 2011: 152). Its large fiscal deficit with a double digit inflation around 20 per cent is a matter of grave concern.

One of the primary challenge before the regime is Myanmar's rural financial system which is in poor shape. A vast majority of farmers are not able to access formal financing of any kind resulting in reliance on informal money lenders whose high rate of interest results in an indebtedness cycle causing increasing landlessness. Transfer of technology and foreign direct investment beyond the resource extraction primarily in the field of construction of gas pipeline, mines and hydro-electric dams needs to be expanded. In addition, the quasi privatisation drive which began after selling off numerous state assets has been devoid of public tenders and transparency. They are primarily associated with regime connected conglomerates. In this background, domestic hurdles in the economic field need to be targeted for implementing deep and lasting reforms. It has to really work hard for reversing the decades of economic mismanagement.

Battleground for Capitalist Penetration

Myanmar is seen by many investors as the next regional frontier market with its huge natural resources, large population and strategic location between China and India. A wave of reforms have seen the international community roll back many of the tough sanctions put in place to punish a brutal junta that ruled with an iron fist until it was replaced by a quasi-civilian regime in 2010. Considered the last, large and untapped market in Asia, investors are eager to explore investments in Myanmar. As the sanctions have loosened, a rush for firms is looking to tap a potential 62 million consumers and a young workforce. It has turned out to be a new battleground for foreign investors and capitalist penetration. No one is talking about the human rights abuse and the hardship caused by the ethnic nationalities at the borders. Western intervention in Myanmar is moving away from humanitarian issues towards supporting capitalist penetration where MNCs from powerful countries are central players. Global corporate giants from Coca-Cola to General Electric have already started their operation for a share of an expected economic boom in the so long isolated country. However,

Parliament has approved the new foreign investment law which seeks to attract foreign capital in the country. It has come as a part of a series of economic and political reforms as **foreign** investors and governments begin re-engage with **Myanmar.**

Many scholars have regarded it as the beginning of 'scramble for Myanmar' in the light of the changing stand of the Western powers and easing of the more than decade long sanction on the country (Singh 2012). Since 2011, Heads of states, diplomats, experts, business groups from Europe, America, Japan, Australia and South Korea have visited the country. Since then, various conferences, public events, official meetings and business forums are all geared towards fiscal liberalisation. This has opened a new chapter in the history of Myanmar, where the country has become an economic battleground of capitalist penetration. This calls for the rise a critical left thinking and strengthening of the civil society groups for fostering a critical social movement in the country.

Environmental Hazards and threat to Bio-diversity

Just as Myanmar seeks to emerge from isolation and encourage investment in new infrastructure for electricity generation and transport to catch up with other Southeast Asian countries, it faces numerous environmental challenges and health hazards. Critical environmental issues are being raised and it is believed that developmental challenges will speed up environmental destruction and is also likely to lead to more human rights abuses. As of now, the authoritarian regime and foreign companies that have invested in the country since the 1988 transition to a market-driven economy have destroyed the livelihoods of much of the population. The transition to a market economy has been crippled by the absence of the rule of law. Government policies and increasing globalisation have lessened economic, social, cultural and environmental rights and contributed to an increase in poverty. Accountability, rule of law, freedom, transparency and security is what is required presently in Myanmar.

As foreign investments begin pouring in Myanmar in the wake of political reforms in 2010, Asia's last bastion of bio-diversity could be further lost and deteriorated. Virtually non-existing environment laws and lack of a democratic social movement, has made environmental conservation a casualty of openness in Myanmar. Pro-democracy reformers and civil society groups associated with conservation have urged the government to put more stringent laws and safeguards into effect. The influx of investment threatens both ethnic minorities and the environment, according to a new report by the Burma Environment Working Group (BEWG). The report highlights how Myanmar lacks any meaningful frameworks on environmental protection and sustainable development that would enable citizens to take part in decision-making about their country's development, despite a recent transition to a military-dominated parliamentary political system. Unless a sound policy framework for environmental protection and sustainable development are in place to ensure that investment does not lead to unnecessary destruction of the natural environment and local livelihoods, Myanmar's environment will continue to be a source of conflict and the concept of sustainable development would remain a mirage.

The country lies at risk of serious environmental crises and high exposure to natural hazards. Development of sea ports, special economic zones and road-rail connectivity projects poses grave environmental challenges which demands immediate intervention. In this regard, environmental activists have called for new and existing investors to stop immediately all project-related works until satisfactory safeguards are in place to ensure investment does not lead to unnecessary destruction of the natural environment and local livelihoods. The new measures are brought in to ensure sustainable development and multi-ethnic participation. In this regard, mention may be particularly made of the suspension of the Myitsone dam in September 2011, which was being constructed on the Irrawaddy River in the northern state of Kachin in Myanmar with the help of Chinese company.[15]

Changing Power Dynamics in Myanmar

The handing of power by General Than Swe denotes the changing dynamics of power structure in Myanmar. Although, the regime change and transition has been a constitutional façade and denotes just a cosmetic change in the power structure, but still it has a major implication for the emerging political scenario in Myanmar. It seems that very soon tussle between the military and the civilian administration would be apparent. It is expected that 'Military' and 'Party' would emerge as the two main power centres and would try to out power each other in the 2015 elections. The so called military leadership holding the position of Party (USDP) General Secretary, the Speaker, two Vice-Presidents and the President himself will have to win the confidence of the people through popular vote, if they want to be elected in 2015 elections. The following section looks at the main political forces and emerging power dynamics in the internal politics of Myanmar.

Hardliners and Reformists

Almost invariably, O'Donnell and Schmitter (1986: 16) argue that "authoritarian regimes in transition are divided between hard-liners....and soft liners." Carothers (2002) observes that "democratisation primarily occurs due to the opening, a period of democratic ferment and political liberalisation in which cracks appear in the ruling dictatorial regime, with the most prominent fault line being that between hardliners and soft liners." According to Larry Diamond, in the context of political opening in Myanmar "if there is to be a transition to democracy, it will have to be a negotiated one, in which regime soft-liners and more pragmatic and flexible leaders of the democratic opposition come together to agree on new rules" (2012: 139).

Accordingly, reform process in Myanmar is scared by the reformists and hardliners in the army. According to Harn Yawnghwe, director of Brussels-based Euro-Burma Office (EBO), the country's top leadership is made up of two factions, divided by conflicting personal feelings and ways of thinking. He believes that the 'Gang of Four', i. e. the Vice President #1 Tin Aung Myint Oo; the Upper House Speaker Khin Aung Myint; the Information Minister Kyaw Hsan; and the Finance Minister Hla Tun constitute the military minded hard core supporters of the previous regime. "They have reportedly urged the Senior General (Than Shwe) to stage a comeback, but unless Thein Sein makes a big blunder thereby giving him sufficient excuse, it is unlikely he will return." On the other hand the "Reformists", i. e. the President Thein Sein; the Lower House Speaker Thura Shwe Mann; the Railway Transport Minister Aung Min; and the Industry #1 Minister Soe Thein are all bent towards introducing Parliamentary practices and reforms for the new regime. However, the fence sitters are still the majority in the top echelon. "They are naturally waiting to see which direction the wind is blowing before they make up their minds", reaffirms Harn Yawnghwe.[16] The battle between reformers and hardliners has been gaining momentum with the liberals led by President Thein Sein and Speaker of Parliament Thura Shwe Mann.

The hardliners have become more concerned after the last bye-elections when military backed USDP could just get one out of the 45 seats. These party members are coalescing into the main anti-reformist noise. This outcome is causing "disarray" within the ranks of the former ruling military and raising speculation about a backlash by hardliners. The reformist minded President Thein Sein has given a signal by saying that "conservatives who do not have a reformist mindset will be left behind, while the country is on its path to change." Even the Vice-President Sai Mauk Kham has also emphasised that "not only political, economic, administrative and social reforms are needed but there also needs to be a change to our mindset" (Irrawaddy 2012). On the other hand, there are some who do not see a rift between hard-liners and soft-liners, but rather they regard it as 'just different points of view' (New York Times 2011a).

However, resignation of the Vice President Tin Aung Myint Oo, a former four-star general, and a close associate of retired dictator Than Shwe almost marks ending of the hardliner's role in the reformist government. He was considered as a leader of the hardliner group in the government which is opposed to the liberal reforms of President Thein Sein. He has been replaced by Nyan Tun, a former Navy Chief, who is supposed to be belonging to the reformist camp. The development has been seen by many as another reformist move by President as he seeks to court the West and develop business ties and diplomatic ties after decades of estrangement. The information minister U Kyaw Hsan belonging to the hardliner group has been replaced by U Aung Kyi of the reformist camp. In the similar move to strengthen reform Finance minister U Hla Tun has been taken over by U Win Shein. Industry Minister Soe Thein and Railways Minister Aung Min have moved as Ministers in President's Office and they have been replaced by U Myint Aye and U Zayar Aung respectively.

Furthermore, appointment of a new negotiating team by President Thein Sein, to reach a ceasefire agreement with the KIO reflects a changing stance by the military, which is being involved in a newly restructured peace-negotiating process with the ethnic nationalities. The team would be led by Vice-President Sai Mauk Kham (who is a reformist and an ethnic Shan). Another liberal minded Minister U Aung Min, is also one of the chief negotiators of the team.

However, amid the biggest political shake-up since the end of military rule in mid August 2015, President Thein Sein seems to have been taken a complete 'U' turn. In a dramatic move Thura Shwe Mann, was removed as Chairman of the ruling Union Solidarity and Development Party (USDP) by President Thein Sein on 12th August, 2015. However, he continues to be the Speaker of the lower house. Shwe Mann's growing closeness with the democratic leader Aung San Suu Kyi had antagonised the hardliners in the military and led to further deterioration of his relationship with the power centre in Myanmar. It is however noteworthy that Shwe Mann, has been considered a leading contender for the presidency in the upcoming elections.

The latest purge in Myanmar shows its fragile experiment with democracy which still depends upon the relics of the previous regime. The thin line between the conservative and reformist forces is widening given the political turmoil in the recent past.

Aung San Suu Kyi and the Military

The complicated and delicate relationship between the military and Aung San Suu Kyi has been the bedrock of the current reform process in Myanmar. Any strain in this relationship is going to hurt the national reconciliation process in the country. The leadership is trying hard to end its international isolation by promoting the democratic icon Nobel Laureate Aung San Suu Kyi. The regime has allowed her party National League of Democracy (NLD) to participate in the April 2012 by-elections and rejoin mainstream politics.[17] The entry of the democratic icon and her party in the recent elections was a means of legitimizing newly established civilian regimes mandate to govern and enhance its own reform credentials. NLD under the leadership of Aung San Suu Kyi had a landslide victory in April 2012 by-elections. This has also influenced the emerging power dynamics in Myanmar.[18] According to Than (2012), "since the NLD has entered the Union Assembly it must quickly transform into 'player' mode away from the 'dissident critic' mode." In order to carry out its campaign pledges it needs to strategize its moves carefully and develop tactics to progressively advance its main causes within the current political structural constraints. It is believed that the success of the NLD in the by-elections is a strong indicator that the NLD will be able to challenge the ruling USDP in the 2015 elections. This will then give both the NLD and ethnic parties a chance to contest and eventually amend the 2008 constitution and a least to some degree ease the military's control over the political processes of the country (BCES 2012: 2).

Aung San Suu Kyi had promised during her by-election campaign to push for amendments to the constitution, including the article that allows the military to appoint 25 per cent of the members in the two houses of parliament – including the regional assemblies (The Hindu: 2012 a). Comments by Aung San Suu Kyi regarding "unelected representatives" as an example of an undemocratic component of the constitution have already distressed military representatives in the Parliament. Nevertheless, the Union Parliament has unanimously approved a proposal on March 20, 2013 allowing for the formation of a committee to review the military-backed 2008 constitution.

Although, the regime needs Suu Kyi in Parliament to bolster the authority of its political system and spur on easing western sanctions but her party's newly elected members were refusing take the swearing in oath that requires them to safeguard the Constitution promulgated in 2010, under the junta. They had appealed to the authorities to change the wording of the swearing-in oath from "safeguard" to "respect" the Constitution. This was the first sign of serious discord between Suu Kyi's NLD and the reformist regime since April 1 bye-elections that gave the mandate to the democratic icon and her party. However, it remains to be seen whether it can successfully work together towards a common goal in balancing the NLD's aspirations with the practical aspects of governing Myanmar and providing a stable political environment for pursuing economic development.

Almost invariably, Aung San Suu Kyi needs the military perhaps more than anyone else if she is to advance politically. She is barred from the presidency under the 2008 Constitution because her husband, who died in 1999, was English. The military controls one-quarter of the seats in Parliament, enough to block the amending of the Constitution. Therefore, any effort to amend the Constitution cannot disregard the role and support of the military officers present in the Parliament. The recent show of strength on the occasion of Armed Forces Day in the capital city along with Aung San Suu Kyi attending the ceremony as one of the VIPs reinforces the political role of army in the politics of the country.

NLD vis-à-vis other Opposition Parties

NLD is the largest opposition party in the national legislature with 43 seats and 6.4 per cent of the overall seats in the parliamentary Union Assembly's Lower and Upper Houses. Regardless of this meager number, there is sufficient optimism that NLD would have a strong presence felt in the upcoming elections in November 2015. It will, at least have an official voice in government for the first time, and the chance to challenge and influence public policy from within. The second-largest opposition party is the Shan Nationalities Democratic Party, with 22 seats in the Union Assembly.

The popular mandate of the by-election is a clear demonstration of the widespread popular support for Aung San Suu Kyi and the NLD. Despite the small number of seats that were contested, the extent of the party's victory gives it an authorisation as the voice of the people in the Union Parliament. Aung San Suu Kyi has described the results as a triumph of the people and welcomed all parties to join Myanmar's national reconsolidation process.

> "We hope that this will be the beginning of a new era, when there will be more emphasis on the role of the people in the everyday politics of our country. We hope that all other parties that took part in the elections will be in a position to cooperate with us to create a genuinely democratic atmosphere." (Reuters 2012).

Furthermore, being the leader of the largest opposition party, the dynamics which she shares with other opposition party is going to be a significant factor so far as the results of 2015 elections are concerned. Several ethnic and minority parties have also embraced the NLD in the legislature as its presence will boost overall confidence in the opposition. Together, they may take issues such as health, education, social security and environmental issues in the Parliament. During her campaign, Aung San Suu Kyi called for "reconciliation" with ethnic groups to bring an end to a long-standing conflict. NLD plans to work with the smaller ethnic parties in the Parliament to push their agenda of reform. Other opposition parties along with Suu Kyi and the NLD may take up the issue of the remaining hundreds of political prisoners, national reconciliation including ethnic peace deals, the rule of law and the thousands of Burmese refugees living in the border areas of neighboring countries.

Aung San Suu Kyi and the Internal Crisis in NLD

Given the ongoing tussle emerging within the NLD, the political scenario at present seems to be in a pandemonium. The NLD party suffers from lack of professionalism, centralised structure and leadership vacuum. One of the most challenging exercises at this point of time is to revitalise the party and introduce inner-party democracy which has so long been dominated by the 88 generation and aging political leaders. As the leader of the party, Aung San Suu Kyi has to reinvigorate faith in the party which suffers from internal splits and schisms due to the ongoing cleavage between the radical and the reformist forces within the NLD.

Subsequent to the rejection of the constitutional amendment procedure by the legislators, all hopes of Daw Aung San Suu Kyi running for the post of Presidency has been dashed off. This puts her into a 'catch 22' situation and in the present scenario she is taking on a path of 'cautious optimism' supporting the reform process at an incremental level for political restructuring and institution building in Myanmar. Amidst the limited political role she is expected to play in the next Parliament, she needs to take calculated steps in this democratic re-engineering and re-structuring.

Her critics also appear to be at loggerheads for not having come out openly on the issue of worsening sectarian violence. The widening 'majority-minority' divide has been an unfortunate development in Myanmar. This historic religious conflict has flared up sectarian violence complicating the socio-religious fabric and aggravating tensions. She appears to have failed to act, given the possibility of alienating voters before the forthcoming elections. Thus, consolidating her position amidst the waves of sectarian violence and widening rift between Buddhist majority and Muslim minority is another formidable challenge faced by her and NLD before 2015 election.

Ethnic Nationalities

Resolving the ethnic issue will be Myanmar's biggest challenge now. An overwhelmingly Burman dominant polity will resist sharing power since both the military and democratic parties are predominantly Burman. It has been argued that a more fundamental gulf is that between the Burmans and the "nationalities" — Kachin, Chin, Shan, Rakhine, Karen, Mon, Kayah and other ethnic groups. While the Constitution of 2008 makes way for regional assemblies, but ethnic leaders have emphasised that these were "powerless" bodies. In practical terms, after the 2010 elections, each of these structures of authorities is dominated by the members of USDP (TNI 2011: 2-3). The situation is thus, very far from the federal autonomy or self governance as demanded by the ethnic nationalities. In addition, the overwhelming role of the military, in the legislature may help in promoting their own interest, rather than the local population.

Overcoming of sixty year old ethnic conflict will not be easy and the government will have to do a great deal to build the trust necessary to move beyond temporary ceasefires to resolve the underlying political issues (ICG 2011 : 5). To fulfill their agenda, some ethnic groups like the Shan Nationalities Democratic Party (SNDP), the Chin National Party (CNP) and the Rakhine Nationalities Development Party (RNDP) have decided to take the parliamentary route. Others like the Karen National Union (KNU), engaged in the world's longest running war with the Myanmar regime, have decided to finally enter ceasefire agreements and initiate talks as a result of the government's peace initiative. But there are still others still waging an armed rebellion — particularly the Kachin Independence Army (KIA) fighting in the north-eastern Kachin State. The conflict has resulted in displacement of thousands of people. Thus, peace and reconciliation with the ethnic nationalities is an important necessity for rebuilding the economy.

These developments, therefore, have a significant implication for the dynamics of power struggle and future road map to the Presidency in Myanmar in the 2015 elections. The issue of ethnic peace has, nevertheless, been a high priority of the government, which has signed preliminary peace deals with rebel armies as part of its three-stage process towards peace (Mizzima 2012). The re-emergence of the National League for Democracy into Myanmar's political arena can open the way for tri-partite dialogue and a genuine reconciliation process between the Government, the NLD, and ethnic parties that may finally lead to a lasting sustainable peace and an end to human rights violations (BCES 2012: 3). Aung Suu Kyi is quite outright in her support for the national reconciliation process with the ethnic nationalities. She underlines the need to develop the trust and confidence, which is lacking at present towards them. Ethnic based political parties, perhaps, may play a greater role in this regard. They require a government, which can understand their aspirations and fulfill their desires. The 2008 Constitution fall short of satisfying the desire of the ethnic nationalities in Myanmar. The reform process therefore, requires being inclusive for establishment of a federal democratic polity in Myanmar. Unless the government recognises the need of ethnic national unity and accepts the principles of federalism, the trust deficit would not be bridged. According to her, "federalism does not mean cessation", it is a means of ethnic reconciliation and integration of the minorities on a country wide scale.[19]

Future Roadmap of Presidency

Aung San Suu Kyi, Myanmar's opposition leader, seems to be more affirmative now and is giving signals to the present leadership that they should now take her more seriously. Suu Kyi's open announcement at the World Economic Forum for East Asia recently that she is a possible candidate for the presidency in 2015, along with her condemnation of the "two-child policy" for Muslims in the Rakhine region and criticism of the government for the slow pace of reforms, is a significant caveat for the existing regime. She has openly stated "I want to run for president.....If I pretended that I didn't want to be president I wouldn't be honest. And I would rather be honest with my people than otherwise."

The entry of Suu Kyi and her party to the Parliament has been a means of legitimizing newly established civilian regime's mandate to govern and enhance its own reform credentials. The regime needs Daw Suu Kyi in the parliament to bolster the authority of its own political system and spur on easing Western sanctions. However, Suu Kyi needs the military if she is to advance politically and amend the constitution, given a quarter of seats are reserved for the military. These developments, therefore, have a significant implication for the dynamics of power struggle and future road map to the presidency in Myanmar in the 2015 elections.

As for the possible leaders to appear in 2015, three are prominent: the reformist U Thein Sein, determined U Thura Shwe Mann and the charismatic Suu Kyi. Who heads the executive and who controls the legislature is an important issue vis-à-vis the current political landscape and the cleavages that exist between the reformists and hard-liners. The scenario, however, is complex.

The incumbent President Thein Sein has given indications of not ruling out a second term for Presidency. Meanwhile, Speaker of the Lower House Thura Shwe Mann, though being projected as a strong contender for the Presidency have been asked to step down as the Chairman of the ruling party—USDP. Given the determination and strong conviction of Shwe Mann, the hardliners had no option but to resort to the old tactics of purges and expulsions. In the given situation Aung San Suu Kyi will have no option but to compromise by becoming the Speaker herself or leading the coalition, probably with the help of the ethnic based political parties. But given the fractured mandate in 2015, she will have a tough time in controlling the house. There are worries that the demand for federal and ethnic reconciliation will be stronger by 2015.

One of obstacles Aung San Suu Kyi faces now is the absence of able administrators and team members in the leadership of the NLD, which at present is facing a generational crisis. It would be difficult for Suu Kyi to run the cabinet with inept colleagues in the already degenerating party. There are fears that she will be able to manage the executive and pacify the hard-liners in the military.

The political scenario seems to be in mayhem now. USDP is expected to run hard in the elections in view of the tough competition anticipated from NLD, mainly in the ethnically Bamar areas. NLD, on the other hand, though hopeful of its victory, suffers from leadership vacuum. Given the rising expectations of the people, one of the most significant challenges is to revitalize the party and introduce inner-party democracy, which has long been dominated by the aging political leaders of the 8888 generation. Ethnic based political parties may perhaps, play a greater role in this election in the regions inhabited by ethnic nationalities. This would significantly increase their bargaining power in the new legislature. This complex matrix between the three power-centres in post-election Myanmar would shape the formation of a new government in the country and guide the future road-map to Presidency in March 2016.

To conclude, it can be said that even after six decades of armed conflict, beginning from the Japanese invasion of British colonial Burma in 1942 and continuing through insurgency and counter-insurgency up until the present times, Myanmar is still lagging behind its neighbours on most socio-economic indicators. Poverty, health and education display significant suffering by the population, with ethnic minority populations experiencing the most badly, particularly as a result of decades of armed conflict in their regions (Steinberg 2005: 89-90). Decades of armed conflict, isolation and repression has led to the legacy of limited presence of social capital in society. Rigid adherence to hierarchy and patronage system leaves little room for genuine dialogue and leads to a feeling of threat and exclusion, often resulting in marginalisation and fragmentation (Tegenfeldt 2006: 219). Myanmar is a society that has been cut off from exposure to broad discourse on political or economic systems through rigid censorship of internally published or imported materials and an educational curriculum emphasizing in free inquiry into these subjects (Steinberg 2005: 97). This lack of cohesion in the society and the resultant psychological resistance to cooperation constitutes a fundamental obstacle to political and economic progress which transcends the nature of the political system. According to Pederson (2005: 167), "a democratic process could facilitate inclusion of presently excluded groups and interests and allow the healing to begin."

Democratisation, thus, augurs well for modernisation of Myanmar. Building up of a modern robust economy which is high on Human Development Index requires regime transition in the country. Eradication of poverty, disease and hunger, better educational facilities and human resource development necessitates a shift towards democracy and a more responsible social welfare state. Thus, underdeveloped socio-economic factors are crucial agents for regime transition. Unless the democratisation process becomes genuinely inclusive and credible, it will only serve the narrow interests of the military rulers of the erstwhile regime who drove Myanmar isolation since last five decades. In the absence of genuine political change, the situation in Myanmar is likely to continue to deteriorate.

References

1. Based on Presentation by Dr. Tint Swe, "Burmese Military's Constitution: Perpetual Military Authoritarianism".
2. Pyithu Hluttaw Election Law, SPDC Law No. 3/2010
3. For details see New light of Myanmar 17th March 2011, pp 12.
4. To quote President Thein Sein,

   "Regarding the health sector, we will improve quality of the hospitals opened over past two decades and skills of medical staff. In addition, we will improve the quality of rural health centres and medical staff. In the process, we will work together with international organizations including the UN, INGOs, and NGOs. We have a plan to promulgate necessary laws to standardize the health care services of private health centres. We also have a plan to set up a health care system covering the participation of the State, the people and altruistic organizations to beef up community health care. We will work more closely with international organizations in pursuit of the national projects on control and prevention of the three diseases: AIDS, tuberculosis and malaria".
5. To quote President Thein Sein,

   "Regarding the education sector, the 24 regions for special development have been established with universities and colleges so that local youths can pursue higher education in their regions or states. Rural areas have seen a massive number of basic education schools. In order to promote the nation's education standard to the international level, we will practise free compulsory primary education system, improve the standards of present universities, colleges, and high, middle and primary schools, provide more teaching aids, sharpen the abilities and improve the socio-economic status of educational staff, and increase the enrolment rates in middle and high schools. In that regard, we will work in cooperation with international organizations including the UN, INGOs, and NGOs. We will promulgate necessary laws for private education schools. Moreover, we will provide stipends for higher education abroad and stipends for outstanding students at home."
6. To quote President Thein Sein,

   "Another task we will have to implement is environmental conservation. In that regard, we will pay serious attention to conservation of forests and woodlands and take measures in various sectors to reduce air and water pollution, control dumping of industrial waste and conserve wildlife. We will lay down a new policy in which we will work for economic development in parallel with environmental conservation. We will mobilize participation of the people and social organizations in the tasks for environmental conservation and create renewable energy at low cost. We will review and amend laws and enact new laws on environmental conservation".

7. Notification No. 9/2013 dated 8 January, 2013.
8. President Thein Sein's address to the Parliament on the first anniversary of the Government's inauguration. NLM March 2, 2012.
9. All ceasefire groups were asked to form BGF by September 1, 2010.
10. For details see The Economist: 2015; Sun: 2015; Los Angeles Times: 2015; Bhaumik: 2015; Kipgen 2015; Clapp: 2015.
11. The military alliance was formed in January 2010 by Kachin Independence Army (KIA) the Karen National Liberation Army (armed wing of KNU) and the Chin National Army (armed wing of Chin National Front -CNF)
12. Based on the President Thein Sein's 1 March 2012 address to the Union Parliament.
13. Mrs Clinton is the first US Secretary of State to visit Myanmar in December 2011since John Foster Dulles visited in 1955. Barack Obama visited Myanmar on 19 November 2012 just for six hours on his way to attend the US-ASEAN and East Asia summit in Cambodia.
14. David Cameron arrived in Myanmar on 12 April 2012, just two weeks after the historic by-elections in which NLD got a landslide victory. William Hague visited the country in January 2012.
15. Groups usually positioned against each other across ethnic, religious or political lines on this issue appear united. "Burmese or Kachin; existing regime or opposition; religious or secular; Christian or Buddhist; pro-West, pro-military or pro-China political factions – almost all agree that the government was right to shelve the project at the source of the Irrawaddy River" (Hui 2012).
16. Based on Harn Yawnghwe's visit to Myanmar from 20-28 October, 2011. URL: http://www.shanland.org/index.php?option=com_content&view=article&id=4151:harn-yawnghwe-winds-up-fruitful-tour-of-home-country&catid=85:politics&Itemid=266
17. The National League for Democracy (NLD), the main opposition party to Myanmar's ruling military junta, was disbanded on 6 May, 2010 because it had refused to register for the upcoming elections in November 2010. The party's Central Executive Committee voted unanimously not to take part in the elections, to protest against elections rules, especially the one that requires it to expel its leader because of prior convictions (particularly Aung San Suu Kyi).
18. NLD won 43 seats, USDP secured only one seat, for which there was no NLD candidate. The Shan Nationalities Democratic Party also took one seat, defeating the NLD candidate in an upper house constituency in Shan State (Than 2012; ICG 2012: 9).
19. Based on interaction with Daw Aung San Suu Kyi at her residence in Naypyitaw on 7 March, 2013.

Chapter - 7

Conclusion

Almost from the day Burmese regained their independence from British rule in 1948, their nation has been torn by civil war, which persists till today. Renowned in the pre-colonial era as the 'hermit' kingdom of Southeast Asia, it has remained, until recently, isolated in a region of dynamic change (Carey 1997: 1). During the more than quarter century of General Ne Win's 'Burmese Road to Socialism' (1962-88), the country experienced steep economic decline, which left it by late 1980s as one of the ten 'Least Developed Countries' (LDCs), with a per capita income of less than US $250. Previously, at the forefront of regional and international politics—it had been one of the founders of the Non Aligned Movement in the mid 1950s—it became, under Ne Win, the great non-joiner, an introvert state dominated by xenophobic military and a dictator swayed more by 'numerology than normality' (Carey 1997: 1).

In 1988 a popular uprising occurred, which seemed likely to topple the Ne Win's regime. Ne Win in fact resigned from the presidency (though initially remaining as BSPP leader) and some liberalisation followed. Although, Ne Win stepped down, the army in Myanmar held firm and the country briefly had a civilian head of state, when the government promised multiparty elections and other reforms the military staged another coup. Since then, Myanmar has been ruled directly by the military through a State Law and Order Restoration Council (SLORC).[1] The people were sorely tested in 1988 when they demonstrated for freedom and change but the army ruthlessly suppressed their peaceful revolution. And even though they complied with martial law, and participated in the election of May 1990 to vote for members of a national assembly as a first step toward the restoration of democracy, their patience went unrewarded as the military found one excuse after another to delay change. All real hopes for peaceful change were dashed when military government refused to hand over power to the democratic forces.

In November 1997, Burma's ruling military junta announced it was changing its name from the State Law and Order Restoration Council (SLORC) to the "State Peace and Development Council" (SPDC). The change was meant to project a softer image, because the regime had been ridiculed for years for calling itself by such a hard-sounding name (Fink 2001: 94). The 1997 re-organised polity under the SPDC shows every indication of sustaining the myth of invincibility that has accompanied the regime from its birth in 1962.[2]

As a part of the attempt by the military regime to establish 'disciplined democracy' in Myanmar, SPDC announced the 'Seven point Roadmap' in 2002 and as per this roadmap a new Constitution was drafted by the National Convention. In spite of the devastating cyclone Nargis in 2008, the SPDC proceeded with a referendum on a new Constitution in May 2008, which it claimed was approved by overwhelming majority of votes. The elections in 2010 were also the culmination of the junta's seven point roadmap towards disciplined democracy. Less than a week after the elections, Myanmar's democracy icon and Nobel Peace Prize laureate, Aung San Suu Kyi, was released from house arrest.

The new national and regional parliaments are the centerpiece of the country's claimed return to civilian rule. Still, the new Constitution greatly inhibits the creation of a genuine civilian government in Myanmar. One reason is the reservation of 25 per cent of all seats in the national Parliament for military personnel (Turnell 2011: 139). It also assigns key ministerial portfolios such as Defense and Home Affairs exclusively to military representatives. Likewise, the Constitution grants extraordinary powers to an unelected "Commander in Chief of the Defense Services," who during a self-declared state of emergency may assume all legislative, executive, and judicial authority. Finally, constitutional amendments require the approval of over 75 per cent of parliamentary members, effectively giving the military a veto over constitutional change.

Although, the change is coming slowly to the isolated country, but still, it has a long way to go. Despite, the obvious limitations of the parliamentary process, the members are hopeful that the government would sometime listen. It would prepare a ground for the next general elections in 2015. Most of the opposition parties, though they were against military engineered elections, but still they participated in it, thinking that it is only through engagement and reconciliation with the junta that they would be able to move towards greater freedom and openness and democratic reforms.

Summary of the Central Arguments

The main objective of this book is to study the process of democratisation in general and its application in the case of Myanmar. The study seeks to explore the reasons for delayed democracy in Myanmar by looking into the institutional and the authority structure that has developed in the country in the post colonial period. Another empirical issue which the study outlines is the role of internal crises and contradictions in guiding the militarised transition and establishment of disciplined democracy in Myanmar. Finally, the purpose is also to study the reform agenda of the new regime and challenges of democratisation and political transition in Myanmar. With the aforesaid goal, the study has put forward following arguments. Firstly, the failure of the regime performance in the economic front has delayed democracy in Myanmar. Secondly, survival of the regime has rested on the Burmese military cohesion. Finally, the role of the political elites has significantly influenced the transition process in Myanmar.

As it has been pointed out in the hypothesis of the study, economic growth, stability and financial security are pre-conditions for regime transition in Myanmar. Revenues generated by the regime have been for long not used for constructive purpose. Although, being sufficiently adequate for its investment in health, education, social security and infrastructural development, but it has been grossly misappropriated. The government continued its long-standing practice of using the funds for arms and military infrastructure spending, while appropriating a major proportion of the revenues in overseas and local banks. Myanmar attracts little in the way of foreign direct investment (FDI) beyond that associated with resource extraction primarily in the construction of gas pipelines, mines, and hydroelectric dams.

The quasi-privatisation drive and liberalisation in the wake of the November 2010 elections ensured that power, wealth and patronage was concentrated in the hands of a military-linked establishment, as previously seen in Indonesia. Altogether, nearly 300 entities were sold off, including ports, rice mills, textile factories, cinemas, hotels, an airline, fish and agricultural processing plants, and precious stone and gold mines—as well as dozens of government buildings in Yangon. The buyers of these assets were largely devoid of public tenders or transparency, were mostly prominent regime connected conglomerates. The most likely motivation for the sell-off, given that it was unaccompanied by policies to increase competition or other liberal measures, was to create opportunities for economic rent-seeking by Myanmar's leadership while they possessed the indisputable coercive authority to do so.

Although, failure of regime performance in the economic front had delayed democracy in Myanmar but the new regime has taken all the possible steps for rebuilding the economy. President Thein Sein in his inaugural speech in the Parliament has focused on the 'economic might' for growth and development of the country. He has focused on agricultural development as well as industrialisation to transform country into a developed, rich one with a lot of employment opportunities and high per capita income. The new regime has invited a delegation from the different International financial institutions to visit the country and advise policymakers on how to tackle problems with the kyat currency, which has appreciated 20 percent in a year, hurting farmers and exporters and bankrupting businesses. After months of inaction and simmering anger, the government in July 2011 cut taxes for exporters and has promised agriculture loans and price guarantees for millions of farmers.

As per the second argument, regime's survival has rested on the military cohesion. A major split or schism in the military may likely have contributed to the break-up of the regime. If the ruling coalition in the military regime appears to be cohesive, they can perpetuate authoritarianism. Myanmar's experience exemplifies this. A study and analysis of the factional struggles and splits within the different regimes in Myanmar shows that schisms were visible during the breakdown of the Parliamentary model in 1958 and 1962 and the subsequent takeovers by the military. After the 1956 election the internal cohesion of the

AFPFL became weak. In April 1958, there was a major split in the party which subsequently broke up into major factions—AFPFL Clean and AFPFL Stable. The acquisition and counter acquisitions led to an unstable political situation which eventually ended by the military takeover and formation of a caretaker government under Ne Win. Further, after 1961 Election, factionalism continued to exist. The AFPFL Clean government was formed which was renamed as *Pyidaungsu.* Three different factions were created—Thakin group, U-group and the Bo group. The continued clash of interest between these groups had torn apart AFPFL and finally paved the way for military takeover in 1962. According to Tint Swe, "the success of the stability of the SPDC regime in Burma substantiates this fact." Although, there have been factional struggle and conflicts but it is not visible at the top level. The five military officers' at the apex appeared to be united and no major differences have surfaced since the removal of Khin Nyunt."[3] It has been observed that once the power struggle between Khin Nyunt and Than Swe ended with the detention of the former, the longstanding factional struggle between the intelligence and army units came to an end. However, if a factional struggle emerged among the remaining senior army officers, it was more likely to contribute to the break-up of the regime. In the wake of the 2007 uprising by the monks and the subsequent crackdown by the junta, brutality of the regime had exposed the veil of political legitimacy. It attracted vehement condemnation from all across the region and the world. With most of the soldiers practicing Buddhism, they seemed to be disillusioned. The government had a much harder time controlling security forces. So this could have provided as a potential spark. Major splits may likely appear in near future as frustration has also grown among the civil servants over the new administrative capital, Naypyitaw, which has been very hard on their families. There is also an apparent displeasure in the military in the lower ranks against their meager salary and short ration. But, all these have been suppressed with an iron grip.

Beliefs, actions and strategic choices of political elites are significant variables for democratic transition in Myanmar. An analysis of the post-colonial development in Myanmar and the role of the subsequent regimes bring to light that, in fact, elites in Myanmar were more concerned with amassing wealth and forging closer ties with the junta. This was done deliberately to get favours and fulfill their business and economic interests. In the context of many developing countries, state elites have promoted business elites forging a top-down managerial relation. The elites in Myanmar have also played a significant role in regime transition as is evident in the outcome of the 1961 elections. The business elite which suffered due to Ne Win's caretaker government regulatory measures and socialistic policies were dissatisfied and showed their opposition by supporting to AFPFL Clean faction as against the AFPFL-stable which was closely allied with the military in its economic reform measures. In this context, Myanmar political record clearly demonstrates how it is possible for the state elites to transform into business elite, thus, seizing the commanding heights of the economy themselves. Through a variety of joint ventures, the state elites have doubled as business elites. In this way, they have operated a backward economy, but a stable form of authoritarianism. It has been observed that military regime's incessant endurance has rested on the Burmese elite cohesion.

The military has learnt to patronize the economic class for its own benefits. The generals have made local entrepreneurs work for military rule through an evolving economic and political symbiosis. Liberalisation in the 1990s have given rise to crony capitalism where the state has acquired a patrimonial character and elites have failed to emerge as an independent force in Myanmar. Based on this study, it is apparent that the elites in Myanmar were a lose force united only on economic grounds and serving their selfish motives rather than representing a dynamic force as agents of regime transition. It is particularly, due to this passive role of the elites in the preparatory stage of regime transition that Myanmar's transformation towards democracy has been largely delayed. In this regard, the 2010 election was merely an attempt to liberalise the regime and free itself from the shackles of economic sanctions. Furthermore, the noble gesture shown by the release of the noble laureate was also made to project a softer and transformed image of the regime towards the global community. Though, in the recent 2015 elections, political elites in Myanmar have been significantly successful in mobilizing the public opinion, but their role in the Government appears to be limited given the representation of armed forces in the Regional and Union Parliament and important ministerial portfolios still under the control of the armed forces.

Concluding Remarks

Having undergone transition from authoritarianism to democracy in 2010, Myanmar's 'disciplined' democracy is on move since the first free and fair democratic elections in 2015 held after a gap of six decades. However in its current phase of transition, on the one hand it is facing the daunting task of re-building its institutions, while on the other, forces of the past remain powerful which demands a delicate balancing and thoughtful compromises both, from the wielders of past regime and the present leadership.

New Government in Myanmar remains deeply entangled amidst the tussle between the hardliners and soft-liners in the authority. This is visible both in the military as well as the democratic camp. The hardliners in the military are more concerned about securing their position and seats in the Parliament and the Cabinet whereas reformists are providing space for the democracy to blossom which is still in its nascent stage. However, what is more alarming is that the reform process in Myanmar is scared by reformists and the hardliners in the democratic camp as well. NLD suffers from lack of professionalism and centralised structure. There has been a strong discontentment amongst its members during the pre-election phase on the issue of selection of candidates and distribution of party tickets, which has further deepened in the post-election scenario owing to the distribution and allocation of ministerial portfolios.

The complicated and delicate relationship between the military and Aung San Suu Kyi has been the bedrock of the current reform process in Myanmar. Any strain in this relationship is going to adversely affect the transition process in the country. The changing political dynamics with the entry of Aung San Suu Kyi and her party in the Parliament is going to shape the future of political transformation in Myanmar. Her entry in the Parliament has been a means of legitimizing regime's mandate to govern and enhance its own reform credentials. The military needs her in the Parliament to bolster its authority in the Government. However, Aung San Suu Kyi needs the military perhaps more than anyone else if she is to advance politically and amend the Constitution, given that a quarter of seats are reserved for the military in the Parliament. Therefore, any effort to amend the Constitution cannot disregard the role and support of the military officers present in the Parliament.

Amidst the current state of affairs, choosing a 'proxy' candidate as the President (reasons for which are obvious); creating the post of 'State Counsellor' and assuming it and reserving the Cabinet berth of Minister in the President's Office for herself, in addition to the Foreign ministry explains the appeasement of the military to retain its influence as prescribed and specified within the letters of the Constitution. However, at this juncture, Aung San Suu Kyi also cannot afford a confrontationist strategy if she has to assume a 'pseudo' Presidential role outside the framework of the Constitution. This compromise between the 'letter of the law' versus the 'spirit of the law' echoes a unique 'love-hate' relationship and a 'marriage of convenience' by both—the military and the NLD to retain their control over authority in Myanmar respectively.

Demilitarising politics and sending military 'back to the barracks' is the foremost challenge for the new Government which requires consistent effort and perseverance. Notwithstanding the reform initiatives, army still wields enormous influence over Myanmar's institutions. The Ministry of Defence, Home and Border Affairs remain under armed forces (Article 232 (b) (ii) of the 2008 Constitution). Furthermore, Article 201 related with the formation of a National Defence and Security Council (NDSC) and its role during Emergency is a sign of military being sacrosanct. Failure of the democratic forces to bring about constitutional reforms and the amendment of the controversial article 59(f) of the Constitution has ruled out all the possibilities of Aung San Suu Kyi becoming the President, though being the leader of the largest ruling party in the Parliament. On top, Article 60 provides for the procedure of electing the President who is chosen from the candidates put forward by each of the two Houses of Parliament, in addition to a third nominee from the military. The winning candidate becomes the President while the succeeding two serve as first Vice-President and second Vice-President respectively. In the current Parliament U Htin Kyaw won with 360 of the 652 votes cast in the two Houses of Parliament who emerged as the President. He was followed by Myint Swe, who was nominated by the military and received 213 votes. Third place was taken over by an ethnic Chin candidate Henry Van Thio, nominated by the Upper House, who got 79 votes. In addition, the most infamous article 74 laying down the procedure for formation of the Union Parliament according to which one-third of the seats would be reserved for the Defence Forces in both the Houses and article 161 extends this modus operandi to the Regional Parliaments. In view of that, Myanmar's experience reflects its fragile experiment with democracy which still depends upon the relics of the previous regime.

In view of the growing centre-periphery contestations, the issue of ethnic reconciliation demands high priority of the government, which has signed the Nationwide Ceasefire Agreement (NCA) as a part of the three-stage process towards peace and ethnic reconciliation. Though, the Government had signed bilateral ceasefire agreements with 15 armed groups, but only 8 out of these were party to the NCA. However, some of the volatile groups such as the Kachin Independence Army, the United Wa State Army and the abrogation of the ceasefire agreement by the Kokang ethnic armed group have challenged the reconciliation process and hope for durable peace in Myanmar. Critics are apprehensive about the peace deal because of the ongoing skirmishes with some of the major armed groups and the deep seated mistrust that some of these ethnic groups share towards the military. Nevertheless, resolving the ethnic issue will be Myanmar's biggest challenge now. Overcoming of sixty years old ethnic conflict will not be easy and the Government will have to do a great deal to build the trust necessary to move beyond the ceasefires to resolve the underlying political issues and last but not the least, 'post-conflict reconstruction' and 'peace building' which remains crucial for post-conflict security and stability in Myanmar.

Economic reconstruction and recovery in a country where corruption is endemic is an Achilles' heel. Much of the dominance by the military which remains in Myanmar is also because of its "economic might" and control over resources. Extension of military control over the national economy under Ne Win's *Burmese Way of Socialism* and antagonism to private capital, liberalisation and xenophobia has led to the stagnation of the economic institutions in Myanmar. Adoption of the nationalistic policies in the modernisation of the country has led to the establishment of a state led 'developmental model' and absence of strong corporatist elites emerging separate from the military. Pacifying this growing internal urge for economic recovery in recent years, financial stability and security is going to be the single most significant challenge of change for Myanmar.

The newly inaugurated President U Htin Kyaw must focus on safeguarding the interest of the minorities, women, children and other marginalised communities, release of political prisoners and Child soldiers and cushion the pressures generated by the anchors of global political economy. The widening 'majority-minority' divide has been an unfortunate development in Myanmar. This historic conflict has flared up communal violence in recent past, thereby complicating the socio-religious fabric and aggravating tensions. On this particular front, the advocate of democracy—Aung San Suu Kyi appears to have failed to act, given the possibility of alienating voters during the elections, which otherwise would have been crucial in mainstreaming them. Her critics also appear to be at loggerheads for not having come out openly on this issue of worsening sectarian violence. Thus, consolidating her position amidst the waves of sectarian violence and widening rift between Buddhist majority and Muslim minority is another formidable challenge faced by the new President and Aung San Suu Kyi.

Given the manner it is spreading in the region, if remained uncontrolled, its spillover effect would have repercussion for the bordering regions as 'violence respects no borders'. The apprehension of transforming this sectarian violence from local to the regional issue has left many Myanmar watchers amused. Questions are also being raised against the confrontation and retaliation and it is beyond doubts that soon it would assume an international character. Even though, there are applauds for the reformist regime, but the approach adopted for getting to the bottom of the present crisis is certainly going to be a testing ground for the 'new regime' in Myanmar. Building up trust and winning the confidence of the people is the need of the hour. At this point of time, it would be interesting to know the strategy of the ruling party to bridge the trust deficit.

It is however, believed that recent surge in the nationalistic fervor is an outcome of the sudden opening up and surfacing of democracy in the country. We see a new political dynamics emerging in Myanmar. Nevertheless, only regime change in not enough, it has to be supplemented with the social and economic transformation. While procedural democracy has been established, but the stability and survival of the regime would rest on deepening of democracy and its consolidation. This requires the institutions of liberal democracy to take deep roots in the society. Transformation from procedural to substantive democracy has to be inclusive. It needs to be cautioned against the problems and challenges of majoritarianism which has widened the gulf and fostered hatred and mistrust between the majority Burmans and the ethnic minorities living in the frontier areas. As an advocate of democracy, Nobel laureate Aung San Suu Kyi must champion the cause of minority rights, empowerment and enfranchisement of all ethnic nationalities. According to her, "we require to have a national policy and a vision to move forward on the path of democracy ahead. The call of the hour should be identification of the 'need' of the people by the government of Myanmar." She further adds, "Best business practices, responsible investment and respect for human rights and dignity may help in building up our long term convictions."[4]

To conclude, it can be said that although Myanmar has ushered into a new age of democracy and civilian rule and the new civilian regime has made some promising changes but it has a long way to go towards democratic consolidation. Amidst the limited political role she is expected to play according to the Constitution (theoretically) and deep skepticism existing towards the political institutions which are still largely dominated by the military, she needs to take calculated steps in this democratic re-engineering and re-structuring.

References

1. SLORC was formed when the Burmese armed forces, commanded by General Saw Maung seized power on 18 September 1988 crushing the 'Four Eights' (8888) uprising.
2. For details on SPDC see Mathews (1997).
3. Based on interview with Tint Swe.
4. Based on interaction with Daw Aung San Suu Kyi at her residence in Nay Pyi Taw on 7 March, 2013.

References Cited

Primary Sources

1. BSPP (1964), *System of Correlation of Man and Environment*, third edition, Rangoon: Burma Socialist Programme Party. Online Edition. Accessed on October 19, 2008. URL: http://www.burmalibrary.org/docs/System-of-correlation.htm
2. Burmese Way to Socialism—BWS (1962), Published by the Information Department for the Revolutionary Council. Online Edition. Accessed on October 19, 2008. URL: http://www.burmalibrary.org/docs/The_Burmese_Way_to_Socialism.htm
3. Constitutional Principles Approved by the National Convention. Online edition. Accessed on October, 2008. URL: http://www.blc-burma.org/pdf/Constitution/bmic.pdf
4. Democratic Voice of Burma Documentation "The 1990 Multi-Party Democracy General Election." Accessed on October 31, 2008. URL: http://www.ibiblio.org/obl/docs4/1990_multi-party_elections.pdf
5. HLUTTAW SESSIONS OF 16 MARCH 2011, NLM, March 17, 2011, URL: http://www.burmalibrary.org/docs11/Hluttaws-NLM2011-03-17.pdf
6. Human Rights Watch (2008 a), "Vote to Nowhere: The May 2008 Constitutional Referendum in Burma", Accessed on October 31, 2008. URL: http://www.hrw.org/en/reports/2008/04/30/vote-nowhere
7. Human Rights Watch (2008 b), *Chronology of Burma's Constitutional Process*. Accessed on October 31, 2008. URL: http://www.hrw.org/reports/2008/burma0508/burma0508chronology.pdf

8. International Burmese Monks Organisation—IBMO (2008), Statement on the One-year Anniversary of the Saffron Revolution. Accessed on October 31, 2008. URL: http://www.burmesemonks.org
9. International IDEA (2001), *Challenges to Democratizaton in Burma Perspectives on Multilateral and Bilateral Responses*, Sweeden: International IDEA.
10. Interview with Burmese pro-democracy activists, ethnic nationalities, Buddhist monks, students and civil society members.
11. National Convention Procedural Code, January 1, 1993. Accessed on October, 2008. URL: http://www.blc-burma.org/pdf/Constitution/bmic.pdf
12. New light of Myanmar (2003), "Mass rally supports seven-point roadmap clarified by Prime Minister", Sunday 21 September. Online edition. Accessed on April 7, 2007. URL: http://mission.itu.ch/MISSIONS/Myanmar/03nlm/n030921.htm
13. Notification 7/2011, Self-Adminstered Divisions and Self-Administered Zones Announced, EBO, Election Monitor No. 12.
14. President Thein Sein Inaugural Speech in the Parliament, Online Edition. URL: http://democracyforburma.wordpress.com/2011/04/06/president-u-thein-sein-first-speech-engl/
15. Pyithu Hluttaw Election Law, SPDC Law No. 1/2010. Online edition. Accessed on May 21, 2010. URL: http://www.burmalibrary.org/docs08/Announcement_1-2010.pdf
16. Pyithu Hluttaw Election Law, SPDC Law No. 2/2010. Online edition. Accessed on May 21, 2010. URL: http://www.burmalibrary.org/docs08/Announcement_2-2010.pdf
17. Pyithu Hluttaw Election Law, SPDC Law No. 3/2010. Online edition. Accessed on May 21, 2010. URL: http://www.networkmyanmar.org/images/stories/PDF3/l3b.pdf
18. SLORC Declaration No. 1/90 of July 27, 1990. Accessed on October 14, 2008. URL: http://www.burmalibrary.org/docs/Declaration_1-90.htm
19. SPDC Constitution — Online edition. Accessed on October, 2008. URL: http://d.scribd.com/docs/1sa6nutywy63lve274w2.pdf

20. The Constitution of 'The Socialist Republic of the Union of Burma,' 1974. Online edition. Accessed on September 10, 2008. URL: http://www.thailawforum.com/database1/constmyanmar.html
21. The Constitution of BSPP for the transitional period of its Construction adopted by the Revolutionary Council, 1962. Online Edition. Accessed on October 19, 2008. URL: http://www.burmalibrary.org/docs/BSPP_CONSTITUTION.htm
22. The Constitution of the 'Union of Burma' 1947. Online edition. Accessed on September 10, 2008. URL: http://www.blc-burma.org/html/Constitution/1947.html
23. The Constitution of the Republic of Indonesia, 1945. Online edition. Accessed on September 10, 2008. URL: http://www.indonesia-ottawa.org/page.php?s=10001945constitution
24. The Manifesto of the National League for Democracy on Multi-Party Democracy General Election. Accessed on October 31, 2008. URL: http://burmalibrary.org/docs/NLDElectionManifesto1989.htm
25. The Panglong Agreement, 1947, Online edition. Accessed on September 10, 2008. URL: http://www.burmalibrary.org/docs/panglong_agreement.htm
26. UNCTAD (2006), UN list of LDCs after the 2006 triennial review, Accessed on September 3, 2008. URL: http://www.unctad.org/Templates/Page.asp?intItemID=3641&lang=1
27. Union of Myanmar Commission for Holding the Referendum. — *Announcement No 10/2008*, Nay Pyi Taw, 15 May 2008. Online at: http://mission.itu.ch/MISSIONS/Myanmar/statement&speech/No%2010_2008%20Announcement%20for%20refrendum.htm

Secondary Sources

1. Acharya, Amitav (2003), *Democratisation and the Prospects of Participatory Regionalism in Southeast Asia,* Third World Quarterly, Vol 24 (2), pp. 375-390.
2. Akkoyunlu K. (2007), "Military Reform and Democratisation: Turkish and Indonesian Experience at the turn of the Century", *Adelphi Paper* 392, London: IISS.

3. Alagappa, Muthiah (2001), "Asian Civil Military Relations: Key Developments, Explanations, and Trajectories" in Muthiah Alagappa (ed). *Coercion and Governance: The Declining Political Role of the Military in Asia*, Stanford, California: Stanford University Press, pp. 433-498.
4. Alagappa, Muthiah (2004), "Introduction" in Muthiah Alagappa (ed). *Civil Society and Political Change in Asia: Expanding and Contracting Democratic Space,* Stanford University Press, pp. 1-24.
5. Alamgir, Jalal (1997), "Against the Current: The Survival of Authoritarianism in Burma", *Pacific Affairs*, Vol. 70(3), pp. 333-350.
6. Altsean (2011 a), Burma 2011: Still a Military Dictatorship, No. 1078, March 24. URL: http://www.altsean.org/Reports/ Burma 2011.php
7. Altsean (2011 b), 100 Days Of Burma's Parliament: Strengthening The Status Quo, No. 1079, May 11. URL: http:// www.altsean.org/Reports/100days.php
8. Amnesty International (2010), *Myanmar's 2010 Elections: A Human Rights Perspective*, May 11. Online edition. Accessed on May 21, 2010. URL: http://www.amnesty.org/en/library/asset/ ASA16/007/2010/en/923dd424-81c1-4f04-9743-b74894b9bad7/ asa160072010en.pdf
9. Asian Development Bank (2005), *Key Indicators of Developing asian and African Countries*, Online Edition. Accessed on 5 July 2012. URL: http://www.adb.org/publications/key-indicators-developing-asian-and-pacific-countries-2005?ref=countries/ myanmar/publications
10. Aung, Htet (2010), "Party Registration Regulations Favour Wealthy", *Irrawady*, March 18. Accessed on May 29, 2010. URL: http://www.irrawaddy.org/election/electoral-laws/ 160-party-registration-regulations-favor-wealthy.html
11. Bangkok Post (2011), Burma military rule ends, but army retains grip, March 30. URL: http://www.bangkokpost.com/ breakingnews/229488/burma-military-rule-ends-but-army-retains-grip

12. Barr, Michael D. (2002), Cultural Politics and the Asian Values: The Tepid War, London, New York: Routledge.

13. BBC (2012), "William Hague welcomes end of 'long darkness' in Burma", January 6. http://www.bbc.co.uk/news/world-south-asia-16450519

14. BBC News (2007), "Burma Agrees UN Labour Provision", Tuesday, 27 February. Online Edition. Accessed on April 10, 2007. URL: http://news.bbc.co.uk/2/hi/business/6400391.stm

15. BBC News (2010), "Burma's Aung San Suu Kyi has foot soldier's support", November 17. Accessed on 15 June 2012. Online Edition. URL: http://www.bbc.co.uk/news/world-asia-pacific-11775469

16. Bissinger, Jared (2012), "Foreign Investment in Myanmar: A Resource Boom but a Development Bust?" Contemporary Southeast Asia, Vol. 34 (1), pp. 23-52.

17. Bowman, Vickey (2007), "The Political Situation in Myanmar", in Monique Skidmore and Trevor Wilson (eds), *Myanmar: The State Community and the Environment,* Asia Pacific Press, Australian National University, pp. 1-17. Online edition. Accessed on January 15, 2009. URL: http://epress.anu.edu.au/myanmar/pdf/whole_book.pdf

18. Brown, Gordon and Nicolas Sarkozy (2007), "Time for serious dialogue" International Herald Tribunal, November 30. Online Edition. Accessed on November 12, 2008. URL: http://www.iht.com/articles/2007/11/30/opinion/edbrown.php

19. Burma Centre for Ethnic Studies-BCES (2012), *Burma's By-elections: A Chance For Future Reconciliation?,* Briefing Paper No. 5, April. Online edition. Accessed on April 24, 2012. URL: http://www.burmaethnicstudies.net/pdf/BCES-BP-No.5.pdf

20. Burma Net News (2007), "Myanmar ends constitution convention, marking step one of junta's 'road map to democracy'", September 3 Online Edition. Accessed on September 7, 2007. URL: http://www.burmanet.org/news/2007/09/03/associated-press-myanmar-ends-constitution-convention-marking-step-one-of-juntas-road-map-to-democracy/

21. Burma News International (2011), "Hobson's choice: Burma's 2010 Elections." Online Edition Accessed on January 8, 2011.

URL: http://www.kaladanpress.org/v3/images/stories/document/HobsonsChoice-Burmas-2010-Elections.pdf

22. Callahan, P. Mary (2001), "Burma: Soldiers as State Builders" in Muthiah Alagappa (ed). *Coercion and Governance: The Declining Political Role of the Military in Asia*, Stanford, California: Stanford University Press, pp. 417-429.
23. Callahan, P. Mary (2003), *Making Enemies: War and State Building in Burma,* Ithaca: Cornell University Press.
24. Carey, Peter (1997), "From Burma to Myanmar: Military Rule and the Struggle for Democracy", *Conflict Studies*, No. 304: 1-27.
25. Carothers, Thomas (2002), "The End of the Transition Paradigm," *Journal of Democracy,* Vol. 13(1). pp 5-21.
26. Case, William (1996), 'Can the "Halfway House" Stand? Semi-democracy and Elite Theory in Three Southeast Asian Countries', *Comparative Politics* 28 (4): pp. 437-64.
27. Case, William (2005), "Southeast Asia's hybrid regimes: When do voters change them?" *Journal of East Asian Studies,* Vol. (5). May-August. pp 215-237.
28. Cheesman, Nick (2009/10), "Myanmar: Thin Rule of Law?", *Pacific Affairs,* Vol (82): 4, pp. 597-613.
29. Clapp, P. (2007), "Building Democracy in Burma", *Working Paper*, No. 2. United States Institute for Peace. Accessed on 9th August 2008. URL: http://www.usip.org/pubs/working_papers/wp2_democracy_burma.pdf
30. Davies, M (2012), 'The Perils of Incoherence: ASEAN, Myanmar and the Avoidable Failures of Human Rights Socialisation?', Contemporary Southeast Asia, Vol. 34(1), pp. 1-22.
31. Diamond Larry (2000), "The Global State of Democracy", *Current History*, Vol. 99 (641), December, pp. 413-418.
32. Diamond, Larry (2002), Thinking about hybrid regimes, *Journal of Democracy,* Vol. 13(2), (April): pp. 21-35.
33. Diller, Janelle M. (1993), "Constitutional Reform in a Repressive State: The Case of Burma" *Asian Survey*, Vol. 33, No. 4, pp. 393-407.

34. Dorning, Karl (2006), "Creating an Environment for participation: International NGOs and the growth of Civil Society in Burma/ Myanmar", in Trevor Wilson (ed), *Myanmar's Long Road to National Reconciliation*, ISEAS, pp. 188-217.
35. EBO (2011), "The Burma Army's Offensive Against the Shan State Army – North", Analysis Paper No. 3.
36. Economist (2011), "A long march", March 31, 2011, Online Edition, Accessed on 15 May 2012. URL: http:// www.economist.com/node/18486051
37. Fink, Christina (2001), *Living Silence: Burma Under Military Rule*, London, New York: Zed Books.
38. Ganesan, N. & Kyaw Yin Hlaing (2007), *Myanmar: State Society and Ethnicity*, ISEAS.
39. Gill, Graeme (2000), *The Dynamics of Democratisation: Elites, Civil Society and the Transition Process,* Macmillan.
40. Gravers, Mikael (1993), *Nationalism as Political Paranoia in Burma: An Essay on the Historical Practice of Power*, NIAS.
41. Guyot, James (1998), "Burma in 1997", *Asian Survey*, Vol. 32 (2), pp. 190-195.
42. Gyi, Maung Maung (1983), Burmese Political Values: The Socio-Political Roots of Authoritarianism, New York: Preager.
43. Hadiz, Vedi R. (2004), "The Rise of Neo-Third Worldism? The Indonesian Trajectory and the consolidation of Illiberal Democracy", *Third World Quarterly*, Vol. 25(1), pp. 55-71.
44. Hlaing, Kyaw Yin (2005), "Myanmar in 2004: Why Military Rule Continues", *Southeast Asian Affairs*, Singapore: Institute of Southeast Asian Studies. pp. 231-256.
45. Hlaing, Kyaw Yin (2008), "Power and factional struggles in post-independence Burmese Government", *Journal of Southeast Asian Studies*, Vol. 39 (1), pp. 149-177.
46. Horton, Guy (2005), *Dying Alive: A Legal Assessment of Human Rights Violation in Burma*, A Report funded by Netherlands Ministry for Development and Cooperation.
47. Houtman, Gustaaf (1999), *Mental Culture in Burmese Crisis Politics: Aung San Suu Kyi and the National League for Democrac,* Study of Languages and Cultures of Asia and Africa

Monograph Series No. 33, Tokyo University of Foreign Studies, Institute for the Study of Languages and Cultures of Asia and Africa. Online edition. Accessed on September 20, 2008. URL: http://homepages.tesco.net/~ghoutman/chapter_05.htm

48. HRW (2008), "Vote to Nowhere: The May 2008 Constitutional Referendum in Burma", Accessed on October 31, 2008. URL: http://www.hrw.org/en/reports/2008/04/30/vote-nowhere

49. HRW (2011), *Burma: Army Should Act to End Abuses*, March 24. URL: http://www.hrw.org/en/news/2011/03/24/burma-army-should-act-end-abuses

50. Huntington, Samuel P. (1991), *The Third Wave: Democratisation in the late Twentieth Century,* Norman: University of California Press.

51. IBAHRI (2012), *Rule of Law in Myanmar: Challenges and Prospects*. Online edition. URL:

52. IBMO (2008), *Statement on the One-year Anniversary of the Saffron Revolution*, September 26. Online Edition. Accessed on August 10, 2011. URL: http://burmesemonks.org/statements/1st-saffron-revolution-anniversary.pdf

53. ICG (2000), "Burma/Myanmar: How Strong is the Military Regime" Asia Report No. 11: Brussels.

54. ICG (2010), "Myanmar Elections" Asia Briefing No. 05: Brussels.

55. ICG (2011 a), "Myanmar's Post Election Landscape" Asia Briefing No. 118: Brussels.

56. ICG (2011 b), *Myanmar: Major Reform Underway*, Asia Briefing No.127, September. Online Edition. Accessed on December 28, 2011. URL: http://www.crisisgroup.org/~/media/Files/asia/south-east-asia/burma-myanmar/B127%20Myanmar%20-%20Major%20Reform%20Underway.pdf

57. ICG (2012), *Reforms in Myanmar: One Year On*, Asia Briefing No.136, April. Online Edition. Accessed on April 22, 2012. URL: http://www.crisisgroup.org/~/media/Files/asia/south-east-asia/burma-myanmar/b136-reform-in-myanmar-one-year-on.pdf

58. Indian Express (2007), "Deep in jungle, generals feel safe in new capital: No Cellphones, no Net", October 5.

59. International IDEA ed. (2001), *Challenges to Democratizaton in Burma Perspectives on Multilateral and Bilateral Responses*, Sweeden: International IDEA.

60. Irrawaddy (2012), "Hardliners will be left behind", May 14. Online Edition. URL: http://www.irrawaddy.org/archives/4147

61. Irrawady, (2011 c), "Than Shwe to Head Extra-Constitutional 'State Supreme Council", Feb 10. URL: http://www.irrawaddy .org/article.php?art_id=20730

62. Irrawady, (2011 d), "Burma's Disciplined Democracy", January 20. URL: http://irrawaddy.org/article.php?art_id=20572

63. Irrawady, (2011 e), "Than Shwe Grants Himself Power to Access 'Special Funds", March 4. URL: http://irrawaddy.org/ article.php?art_id=20878

64. Irrawady, (2011a), "Shan Vice President is a Window Dressing", February 7. URL: http://www.irrawaddy.org/article.php? art_id=20686

65. Irrawady, (2011b), "Thein Sein Urges Decentralisation", April 8. URL http://www.irrawaddy.org/article.php?art_id=21107

66. Islam, Syed Serajul (1996), "Myanmar's Road to Socialism and Indonesia's New Order: A Comparative Analysis", *Asian and African Studies*, Vol. 5(2), pp. 183-196.

67. Jaggan, Larry (2006), "Burma's Military: Purges and Coups Prevent Progress Towards Democracy", in Trevor Wilson (ed), *Myanmar's Long Road to National Reconciliation*, ISEAS, pp. 29-37.

68. Jakarta Post (2011), "ASEAN gives Myanmar nod for 2014 chairmanship", November 18. http://www.thejakartapost.com/ news/2011/11/18/asean-gives-myanmar-nod-2014-chairmanship. html

69. Jayasurya, Kanishka and Gary Rodan (2006), "Conflict and the New Political Participation in Southeast Asia", *Working Paper*, No. 129, Asia Research Centre.

70. Katanyuu, Ruukun (2006), "Beyond Non-Interference in ASEAN: The Association's Role in Myanmar's National Reconciliation and Democratisation" *Asian Survey,* November/December, Vol. 46(6): 825-845.

71. Kingston, Jeff (2008), "Burma's Despair", *Critical Asian Studies*, Vol. 40(1), pp. 3-43.

72. Kudo, T and Fumiharo Mieno (2007), Trade, Foreign Investment and Myanmar's Economic Development during the Transition to an Open Economy, *IDE Discussion Paper*, No. 116. Online edition. Accessed on 20 July, 2012. URL: http://www.ide.go.jp/English/Publish/Download/Dp/pdf/116.pdf

73. Kyaw Yin Hlaing, Robert H. Taylor and Tin Maung Maung Than eds. (2005), *Myanmar: Beyond Politics to Societal Imperatives*, ISEAS.

74. Lawson, Stephanie (2003), *International Relations*, Polity Press.

75. Leifer, Michael (2001), "National Unity Party" in *Dictionary of Modern Politics of Southeast Asia*, London, New York: Routledge.

76. Levenstein, Susan L. eds (2010), "Finding Dollars, Sense and Legitimacy in Burma", Woodrow Wilson International Centre. Online edition. Accessed on May 18, 2011. URL: http://www.wilsoncenter.org/topics/pubs/ASIA_092010_Burma_rpt_for%20web.pdf

77. Levesque, Julien (2007), "After years of fruitless sanction: Time for effective cooperation", *Mainstream*, Vol. XLV (43): pp 31-33.

78. Levitsky, Steven and Lucan A. Way (2002), "The Rise of Competitive Authoritarianism." *Journal of Democracy,* 13, No. 2 (April): pp. 51-65.

79. Linz Juan J. and Alfred Stepan (1996), "Toward Consolidated Democracies", *Journal of Democracy*, Vol 7 (2), p. 14-33.

80. Linz Juan J. and Alfred Stepan (1998), "Towards Consolidated Democracy" in Takashi Inoguchi (ed), *The Changing Nature of Democracy,* Tokyo: United Nations University Press. Pp. 48-68. Quoted in Abubakar E. Hara (2001), "The Difficult Journey of Democratisation in Indonesia", *Contemporary Southeast Asia*, Vol. 23 (2), August, pp.307-326.

81. Linz Juan J. and Alfred Stepan (2001), "Toward Consolidated Democracies", in Larry Diamond and Marc F. Plattner (eds) *The Global Divergence of Democracies*, John Hopkins University Press, p. 93-112.

82. Los Angeles Times (2013 a), "The repressed Rohingya of Myanmar", August 9. Online Edition. URL: http://www.latimes.com/news/opinion/editorials/la-ed-myanmar-rohingya-20130809,0,3167729.story

83. Los Angeles Times (2013 b), "Myanmar army releases child soldiers", August 7. Online Edition. URL: http://www.latimes.com/news/world/worldnow/la-fg-wn-myanmar-army-releases-child-soldiers-20130807,0,7398316.story

84. *Luwarso,* Lukas (2000), "The Paradox of freedom in Southeast Asia." *Jakarta Post*, 3 May. Online Edition. Accessed on 7th September 2008. URL: *www.inma.org/subscribers/papers/2003-Yin.doc*

85. Marshal, Monty G. *Authority, Opportunity, and Outbreaks of Violent Societal Conflicts 1955-1999.* Centre for Systemic Peace. Accessed on March 20, 2006. URL: http://members.aol.com/CSPmgm/cspframe.htm

86. Mathews, Bruce (1998), "The Present Fortune of Tradition-Bound Authoritarianism in Myanmar", *Pacific Affairs*, Vol. 71(1), pp. 7-23.

87. Mathews, Bruce (2001), "Ethnic and Religious Diversity: Myanmar's Unfolding Nemesis", Visiting Researchers Series No. 3, ISEAS.

88. Maung, Mya (1997), "Burma's Economic Performance under Military Rule: An Assessment", *Asian Survey,* Vol. 37(6), pp. 503-524.

89. Mc Coy, Cliffered (2011), "Man in the Mirror in Myanmar", *Asia Times Online*, Online Edition. Accessed on 12 June, 2012. URL: http://www.atimes.com/atimes/Southeast_Asia/ME04Ae01.html

90. Mc Grew, Anthony (2005), "Globalisation and Global Politics", in William Baylis and Steve Smith (eds), *Globalisation of World Politics*, Oxford University Press.

91. McCarthy, Stephen (2000), "Ten Years of Chaos in Burma: Foreign Investment and Economic Liberalisation under the SLORC-SPDC, 1988 to 1998", *Pacific Affairs*, Vol. 73(2), pp. 233-262.

92. McCarthy, Stephen (2008), "Overturning the alms bowl: the price of survival and the consequences for political legitimacy in Burma", *Australian Journal of International Affairs*, Vol. 62(3), pp. 298-314.

93. Mizzima (2010), "Election 2010." URL: http://www.mizzima.com/political-pro/new-parties/ndf.html

94. Mizzima (2012), "Thein Sein gives a 'state of the Union' address to Parliament", March 1, Online edition. Accessed on April 24, 2012. URL: http://www.mizzima.com/news/inside-burma/6685-thein-sein-gives-a-state-of-the-union-address-to-parliament.html

95. Mutebi, Alex (2005), "Muddling Through Past Legacies: Myanmar's Civil Bureaucracy and the need for Reform", in Kyaw Yin Hlaing, Robert H. Taylor and Tin Maung Maung Than (eds), *Myanmar: Beyond Politics to Societal Imperatives*, ISEAS, pp. 140-160.

96. Myanmar Times (2013), "Japan-Myanmar Centre opens in Yangon", *Myanmar Times*, August 2013.

97. Myay, Moe (2011), "Propaganda with New Media is required for Democratisation in Burma", PPP 184: New Media and Democracy, Online Edition. URL: http://www.assknetwork.org/knowledge-centre/research-paper/211-propaganda-with-new-media-is-required-for-democratisation-in-burma.html

98. Mydans, Seth (2011), Documentary Shows Rare Look at Dissent in Myanmar Military, January 21, New York Times, Online Edition, Accessed on 28 July, 2012. URL: http://www.nytimes.com/2011/01/22/world/asia/22myanmar.html?_r=0

99. Myo Khin Ma Ma (2007), "Get Out", Burma Digest, August 25. Accessed on September 4, 2007. URL: http://burmadigest.info/2007/08/25/get-out/

100. Myoe, Maung, Aung (2009), *Building the Tatmadaw: Myanmar Armed Forces Since 1948*, ISEAS.

101. NDI (2010), "Burma's 2010 Electoral Framework: Fundamentally Undemocratic: A Legal and Human Rights Analysis." Online Edition Accessed on January 8, 2011. URL: http://www.ndi.org/files/NDI_Burma_Elections_0810_1.pdf

102. New York Times (2000), "By Deals With Burmese Junta, Minorities Thrive" Online Edition. Accessed on 10 November 2008. URL: http://query.nytimes.com/gst/fullpage.html?res=9500E7DE123BF934A25752C1A9669C8B63&sec=&spon=&pagewanted=all

103. New York Times (2011), "In Myanmar, Government Reforms Win Over Some Skeptics", November 29. Online Edition. URL: http://www.nytimes.com/2011/11/30/world/asia/in-myanmar-government-reforms-win-over-countrys-skeptics.html?pagewanted=all&_r=0

104. Ng, May (2008), "Overturning the bowl", *Himal*, Vol.21 (3), pp. 56-59.

105. Nilsen & Tonnesson (2013), "Political Parties and Peace Building in Myanmar", *Policy Brief*. Peace Research Institute: Oslo. Online edition. URL: http://file.prio.no/publication_files/PRIO/Nilsen%20&%20T%C3%B8nnesson%20%282013%29%20Political%20Parties%20and%20Peacebuilding%20in%20Myanmar%20%28PRIO%20Policy%20Brief%205-2013%29.pdf

106. O'Donnell, Guillermo (1994), "Delegative Democracy," *Journal of Democracy,* 5 (January): pp. 55–69.

107. O'Donnell, Guillermo. (1996) "Illusions about Consolidation." *Journal of Democracy.* Vol. 7(2), pp. 34-51.

108. O'Donnell, Guillermo and Philippe C. Schmitter (1986), Transitions from authoritarian rule: Tentative conclusions about uncertain democracies, Baltimore, MD: Johns Hopkins University Foreign Policy Institute.

109. Ojendal, J (2005), "Democratisation amidst Globalisation in Southeast Asia: Emperical Findings and Theoretical Refelections", in Francis Loh Kok Wah and Joajin Ojendal (eds), *Southeastasian Response to Globalisation: Restructuring Governance and Deepening Democracy*, NIAS, pp. 345-372.

110. Oo, Zao and Kai Grieg (1999), "Carrots and Sticks for Democratisation in Burma: Policies of the EU and the ASEAN", in Stokke, H, and Tostensen, A. eds., *Human Rights in Development: Global Perspectives and Local Issues.* Kluwer Law International, The Hague, 1999: pp. 91-136. On line edition.

Accessed on April 10, 2007. URL: http://www.kus.uu.se/Burma/Burma_ZO.pdf

111. Ottaway, Marina. (2003). Democracy challenged: The Rise of Semi-Authoritarianism, Washington, DC: Carnegie Endowment for International Peace.
112. Pederson, Morten B. (2005), "The Chalenges of Transition in Myanmar", in Kyaw Yin Hlaing, Robert H. Taylor and Tin Maung Maung Than (eds), *Myanmar: Beyond Politics to Societal Imperatives*, ISEAS, pp. 161-184.
113. Pederson, Morten B. (2007), "Myanmar: The Future Takes Form, But Little Change in Sight", Southeast Asian Affairs, ISEAS, pp. 217-241.
114. Reuters (2012), "Suu Kyi's party claims landslide win in Myanmar vote", April 2, 2012. Online edition. URL: http://www.livemint.com/Politics/5DUgrtry1dlYHk8CHZNy3K/Suu-Kyi8217s-party-claims-landslide-win-in-Myanmar-vote.html?facet=print
115. *Rieffel, Lex (2010),* "*Myanmar/Burma: Inside Challenges, Outside Interest*", Brookings Institution Press.
116. Rober, Christopher (2009), *ASEAN's Myanmar Crisis: Challenges to the Pursuit of a Security Community*, ISEAS.
117. Rueters (2013), "Myanmar Could Quadruple Its Economy With Smart Reforms, But Only If The Government Acts Now", June 5, Online Edition. URL: http://www.ibtimes.com/myanmar-could-quadruple-its-economy-smart-reforms-only-if-government-acts-now-1291681
118. Rustow, D. A (1970), "Transitions to Democracy: Towards a Dynamic Model", *Comparative Politics,* Vol. 2 (3): pp. 337-363.
119. Sarkin, Jeremy J., Marek Pietschmann (2003), "Legitimate Humanitarian Intervention under International Law in the Context of the Current Human Rights and Humanitarian Crisis in Burma (Myanmar)" Hong Kong Law Journal, Vol. 33(2): p-371.
120. Schedler, Andreas (2002), "The Menu of Manipulation." *Journal of Democracy,* Vol. 13(2), pp. 36-50.
121. Schedler, Andreas (2006), *Electoral Authoritarianism: The Dynamics of Unfree Competition.* Boulder and London: Lynne Rienner Publishers.

122. Schedler, Andreas (2010), "Authoritarianism's Last Line of Defense" *Journal of Democracy, Vol.* 21(1), pp. 69-80.
123. Schmitter, Philippe C. (1994), "Dogmas and Dilemmas of Democracy" *Journal of Democracy,* 5:2, pp. 57-67.
124. Seekins, Donald M. (2009), "Myanmar in 2008: Hardship Coumpounded", *Asian Survey,* Vol. 49(1), pp. 166-173.
125. Shin, Doh Chull (1994), "On the Third Wave of Democratisation: A Synthesis and Evaluation of Recent Theory and Research," *World Politics,* 47 (October), pp 135-170. URL http://links.jstor.org/sici?sici=0043-8871%28199410%2947%3A1%3C135%3AOTTWOD%3E2.0.CO%3B2-M
126. Silverstein, Josef (1977), *Burma: Military Rule and the Politics of Stagnation,* Ithaca and London: Cornell University Press.
127. Silverstein, Josef (2004), "Burma's Struggle for Democracy: The Army Against the People", in R.J May and Viberto Selochan (eds), *The Military and democracy in Asia and the Pacific*, Melbourne: ANU Press Publication, Electronic versions, URL: http://epress.anu.edu.au/mdap/mobile_devices/index.html
128. Singh, Udai Bhanu (2012), "An assessment of Manmohan Singh's Visit to Myanmar", IDSA Issue Brief, June 1. Online edition. URL: http://www.idsa.in/issuebrief/AnAssessmentofManmohanSinghsVisittoMyanmar
129. Sleth, Andrew (2001), "Burma's Armed Forces Under Civilian Rule: A Return to the Past", Technical Advisory Network of Burma, *Working Paper*, No. 02.
130. Sleth, Andrew (2008), "Burma's 'Saffron Revolution' and the Limits of International Influence", *Australian Journal of International Affairs*, Vol. 62(3), pp. 281-297.
131. Sleth, Andrew (2010), "Modern *Burma Study*" *Modern Asian Studies,* Vol. 44(2), pp. 401–440.
132. Smith, Martin (1999), *Burma: Insurgency and the Politics of Ethnicity*, London, New York, Dhaka: Zed Books.
133. Smith, Steve and William Baylis (2005), "Introduction", in William Baylis and Steve Smith (eds), *Globalisation of World Politics*, Oxford University Press.

134. Sorenson George (1998), *Democracy and Democratisation: Process and Prospects in a Changing World*, Boulder, Colorado: Westview Press.

135. South, Ashley (2004), "Political Transition in Myanmar", *Contemporary Southeast Asia*, Vol. 26 (2), pp. 233-255.

136. South, Ashley (2007), "Conflict and Displacement in Burma/ Myanmar", in Monique Skidmore and Trevor Wilson (eds), *Myanmar: The State Community and the Environment,* Asia Pacific Press, Australian National University, pp. 54-81. Online edition. Accessed on January 15, 2009. URL: http://epress.anu.edu.au/myanmar/pdf/whole_book.pdf

137. Steinberg David I. (1981), Burma's Road Toward Development: Growth and Ideology under Military Rule, Boulder, Colorado: Westview Press.

138. Steinberg David I. (1982), Burma, a Socialist Nation of Southeast Asia, Boulder, Colorado: Westview Press.

139. Steinberg, David (2005), "Myanmar: The roots of Economic Malaise", in Kyaw Yin Hlaing, Robert H. Taylor and Tin Maung Maung Than (eds), *Myanmar: Beyond Politics to Societal Imperatives*, ISEAS, pp. 86-116.

140. Steinberg, David I. (2001), *Burma: The State of Myanmar,* Washington DC: Georgetown University Press.

141. Steinberg, I. David (2009), *Burma/Myanmar: What Everyone Needs to Know*, Oxford University Press.

142. Stepan, Alfred (1978), *The State and Society: Peru in Comparative* Perspective, Princeton, New Jersey: Princeton University Press. Quoted in Porter Donald J, (2002), *Managing Politics and Islam in Indonesia*, London and New York: Routledge Curzon.

143. Sundhaussen, Ulf (1995), "Indonesia's New Order: A model for Myanmar, Asian Survey, Vol. 35(8), pp. 768-780.

144. Taylor, Robert H. (1998), "Myanmar: Military Politics and Prospects for Democratisation", *Asian Affairs*, Vol. 29, pp-3-12.

145. Taylor, Robert H. (2005), "Pathways to the Present", in Kyaw Yin Hlaing, Robert H. Taylor and Tin Maung Maung Than (eds), *Myanmar: Beyond Politics to Societal Imperatives*, ISEAS, pp. 1-29.

146. Taylor, Robert H. (2006), "One Day, One Fathom, Bagan won't Move: On the Myanmar Road to Constitution", in Trevor Wilson (ed), *Myanmar's Long Road to National Reconciliation*, ISEAS, pp. 3-28.

147. Tegenfeltd, David (2006), "More Than Saving Lives: The Role of International Development Agencies in Supporting Change Processes in Myanmar", in Trevor Wilson (ed), *Myanmar's Long Road to National Reconciliation*, ISEAS, pp. 218-230.

148. Than, Tin Maung Maung (2007), *State Dominance in Myanmar: The Political economy of Industrialisation*, ISEAS.

149. Than, Tin Maung Maung (2010), "Political Parties in Myanmar: Hard Choices Ahead", Opinion Asia, March 12. Online edition. Accessed on May 21, 2010. URL: http://opinionasia.com/MyanmarHardChoices

150. Than, Tin Maung Maung (2012), Burma/Myanmar's By-Elections: Will Personalities Trump Institutions? , Asia Pacific Bulletin, No. 161, Washington, D.C.: East-West Center in Washington. Online Edition. Accessed on April 22, 2012. URL: http://www.eastwestcenter.org/publications/burmamyanmar%E2%80%99s-elections-will-personalities-trump-institutions

151. Thant, Myint U (2007), "What to do About Burma", *London Review of Books*, Vol. 29 (3). Accessed on March 27, 2012. URL: http://www.lrb.co.uk/v29/n03/-thantmyint-u/what-to-do-about-burma.

152. Thawnghmung, Ardeth Mung (2003), "Pre-conditions and Prospects for Democratic Transition in Myanmar", *Asian Survey*, Vol. XLIII (3), May/June, pp. 443-460.

153. The Hindu (2012), "Myanmar's historic vote", April 7.

154. The New Light of Myanmar (2003), "Mass rally supports seven-point roadmap clarified by Prime Minister", Accessed on November 14, 2008. Online edition. URL: http://www.myanmar.gov.mm/NLM-2003/enlm/Sep21_h1.html

155. The New Light of Myanmar (2010), "Putting a small boat in a larger one", Wednesday, 8 December, 2010, URL: http://www.burmalibrary.org/docs09/NLM2010-12-08.pdf

156. The New Light of Myanmar (2011), "President U Thein Sein addresses second regular session of first *Pyidaungsu Hluttaw*", August 23.

157. The New Light of Myanmar (2011), "President U Thein Sein delivers Inaugural Addresses to Pyidaungsu Hluttaw", March 30. http://www.burmalibrary.org/docs11/NLM2011-03-31.pdf

158. Thompson, Mark R. (2004), "Pacific Asia after 'Asian values': authoritarianism, democracy, and 'good governance'", *Third World Quarterly*, Vol. 25(6), pp. 1079–1095.

159. Thomson, Curtis N. (1995), "Political Stability and Minority Groups in Burma" *Geographical Review,* Vol. 85(3), pp. 269-285.

160. TNI (2011), "Burma's New Government: Prospects for Governance and Peace in Ethnic States", Policy Brief No. 6.

161. Tomsa, Dirk (2007),"Party Politics and the Media in Indonesia: Creating a New Dual Identity for Golkar", *Contemporary Southeast Asia*, Volume 29(1), pp. 77-96.

162. Trevor Wilson ed. (2006), *Myanmar's Long Road to National Reconciliation*, ISEAS.

163. Turnell, Sean (2011), "Myanmar in 2010: Doors open Doors Close", *Asian Survey,* Vol. 51(1) pp. 148-154. http://www.jstor.org/pss/10.1525/as.2011.51.1.148.

164. Turnell, Sean (2012), "Myanmar in 2011: Confounding Expectations", *Asian Survey,* Vol. 52, No. 1 (January/February 2012), pp. 157-164.

165. Vatikiotis, Michael R. J. (1996), *Political Change in Southeast Asia: Trimming the Banyan Tree*, London: Routledge.

166. Voice of America (2012), "French Foreign Minister meets Burmese opposition figure", January 15. http://www.voanews.com/tibetan-english/news/French-Foreign-Minister-Meets-Burmese-Opposition-Figure-137426608.html

167. Wah, Francics Loh Kok (2005), "Globalisation, Development and Democratisation in Souheast Asia" in Francis Loh Kok Wah and Joajin Ojendal (eds), *Southeastasian Response to Globalisation: Restructuring Governance and Deepening Democracy*, NIAS.

168. Wall Street Journal (2012), "Myanmar Reforms Challenge Military's Holdings", Online Edition. Accessed on December 1, 2012. URL: http://online.wsj.com/article/SB10001424127887324705104578151061996230172.html?mod=googlenews_wsj

169. Wilson, Trevor (2010), "Significance of Myanmar's 2010 Elections", *New Mandala*, December 15 URL: http://asiapacific.anu.edu.au/newmandala/2010/12/15/the-significance-of-myanmar%E2%80%99s-2010-election/

170. Win, Khin Zaw (2007), "The Perspective on Prospects for Progress", in Monique Skidmore and Trevor Wilson (eds), *Myanmar: The State Community and the Environment,* Asia Pacific Press, Australian National University, pp. 18-35.

171. Yamashita, Shinji (2003), "Introduction: Glocalising Southeast Asia" in Shinji Yamashita and J. S. Eades (eds), *Globalisation in Southeast Asia*, Berghahn Books, pp. 1-20.

172. Yhome, K. (2008), Myanmar: Can the Generals Resist Change, Rupa: New Delhi.

173. Zakaria, Fareed (1997), "The Rise of Illiberal Democracy", *Foreign Affair,* 76 (November-December): pp 22–41.

174. Zan, Myint (2000), "Judicial Independence in Burma: No March Backwards towards the Past", *Asian Pacific Law and Policy Journal*, Online edition. URL: http://blog.hawaii.edu/aplpj/files/2011/11/APLPJ_01.1_zan.pdf

175. Zarni, Maung Maung (2010), "Why Soldier's don't Rebel in Than Shwe's Burma", *Irrawaddy Magazine*. October 17. Online Edition. Accessed on September 2, 2012. URL: http://www2.irrawaddy.org/opinion_story.php?art_id=19625

Index

V

W

Y

Z